SPACE LAW IN THE UNITED NATIONS

SPACE LAW IN THE UNITED NATIONS

by
Marietta Benkö, Willem de Graaff and Gijsbertha C.M. Reijnen

1985 **MARTINUS NIJHOFF PUBLISHERS**
a member of the KLUWER ACADEMIC PUBLISHERS GROUP
DORDRECHT / BOSTON / LANCASTER

Distributors

for the United States and Canada: Kluwer Academic Publishers, 190 Old Der
Street, Hingham, MA 02043, USA
for the UK and Ireland: Kluwer Academic Publishers, MTP Press Limite
Falcon House, Queen Square, Lancaster LA1 1RN, UK
for all other countries: Kluwer Academic Publishers Group, Distribution Cente
P.O. Box 322, 3300 AH Dordrecht, The Netherlands

Library of Congress Cataloging in Publication Data

```
Benkö, Marietta, 1948-
    Space Law in the United Nations.

    Includes bibliographies.
    1. Space law.  2. United Nations.  I. Graaff, W.
de, Dr.  II. Reijnen, Gijsbertha Cornelia Maria.
III. Title.
JX5810.B43  1985      341.4'7      85-7290
ISBN 90-247-3157-7
```

ISBN 90-247-3157-7

PRINTED IN THE NETHERLANDS

'Vivons en paix, exterminons discort;
Ieunes et vieulx, soyons tous d'ung accort'
    'Le Lais',
    Francois Villon, 1456

Acknowledgements

A number of close friends and colleagues have encouraged and supported us in the writing of the present book. We wish to thank them cordially for everything they did to help us to attain our end. Simply to name them all would fail to indicate the degree to which we feel ourselves in their debt. We would, however, like to single out a few names:

Prof. *C. Voûte* and his staff, of ITC Enschede (Netherlands), who, as an initiator of many important international undertakings, never failed to supply us with latest information on a wide range of subjects covered by the present book, and who gave us meticulous comments on chapters 1 and 4.

M. Benkö owes appreciation to the Federal Ministry for Research and Technology in Bonn, Section for Multilateral Co-operation, and in particular to Dr. *Ch. Patermann* and Dr. *K. Damian*. She has been co-operating with this Section in space law matters since 1979. She expresses her thanks to Mrs. *S. Roser*, Federal Foreign Office in Bonn, for her unfailing friendship, help and collaboration during the sessions of the UNCOPUOS Legal Sub-Committee and Main Committee between 1980 and 1983. Her warmest thanks go to Prof. Dr. *K.-H. Böckstiegel*, Director of the Institute of Air and Space Law at Cologne University, where her parts of chapters 2 and 3 were written. She expresses her gratitude to Ms. *A. Ritter*, who for more than two years acted as her 'test reader', and proved her linguistic proficiency in checking and revising the manuscripts of chapters 2 and 3.

W. de Graaff is grateful to Dr. *J. Bunnik*, of the Dutch National Aerospace Laboratory at Amsterdam for his valuable technical comments on a draft version of chapter 1.

G.C.M. Reijnen is much indebted to Mr. *B. Khabirov*, of the United Nations Legal Affairs Division who, over the years, continuously sent her legal documentation otherwise difficult to obtain, and to Dr. *K. van Kesteren*, of the Dutch Ministry of Foreign Affairs for several important improvements which he proposed for chapter 1.

Introduction

The aim of this book is to reflect the current state of discussions about problems relating to space law within the United Nations. Primarily, we shall deal with problems referring to agenda items of the United Nations Committee on the Peaceful Uses of Outer Space. These are:

1. Remote sensing of the Earth from outer space.
2. Problems relating to the use of nuclear power sources in outer space.
3. Questions relating to the definition/delimitation of outer space and outer space activities and the character and utilization of the geostationary orbit.
4. The prevention of an arms race in outer space.

We shall discuss these issues from two angles. First, we shall give a survey of the state of technology, *i.e.* the technological background, otherwise we would face the old problem of lawyers talking at cross-purposes with technicians. Evidently, technology has developed to such a complex and advanced stage that lawyers have no choice but to acquire at least a basic knowledge in this field. Only then shall we deal with the legal aspects of the issues at stake. In doing this, we shall restrict the presentation of the legal debate in chapters 1 and 3 to the present state of affairs, since their discussion has been going on for more than a decade already. In chapter 2, however, we shall present the legal debate as a whole, as well as the debate in the UNCOPUOS Scientific and Technical Sub-Committee. Chapter 4 likewise considers the whole history of militarization since the beginning of the debates. The reason is to be seen in the importance of these issues and in the fact that they became part of the basic discussion in the United Nations only a few years ago. Each chapter is followed by Notes and Annexes.

The authors are well aware of the fact that there are quite a number of problems which are not represented in the agenda and which are only marginally touched in the course of the debates, *e.g.* the exploration and exploitation of outer space by private enterprise, the establishment and use of space stations, and the protection of the environment. We have deliberately restricted our presentation to discussions current in the United Nations primarily in order to inform the reader which problems are being debated at present and what solutions are being offered. Consequently, we shall not go into details of the earlier work of the Outer Space Committee, for example, the six international legal instruments that have been elaborated. These instruments have already been extensively discussed by other authors and we would like to refer in this connection to some excellent and outstanding works in space literature.

VIII   That the chapter on militarization is a particularly sad one will not escape the attention of the reader. The tendencies described in it as well as the history of space technology apparently relativize and question to a large degree the discussion put forward in the first three chapters, relating essentially to the peaceful uses of outer space. Still, by no means do we want to be rated as pessimists. Facts will have to be faced and analysed if anything is to be changed in the current tendencies.

This book is the work of a team of three authors who have been sharing scientific work for years. The different chapters, however, were not written by all of the three together, but by any one or two, in varying combinations. Therefore, since the authors' personalities differ, the several chapters also differ, and we hope that the reader will find this inspiring rather than troublesome. It goes without saying that the opinions stated only reflect the personal views of the responsible authors; they do not reflect those of the organizations or institutions the individual authors are attached to or work for.

The law is stated as at September 1, 1984
Cologne and Utrecht   M. Benkö

                                             W. de Graaff

                                             G.C.M. Reijnen.

Contents

CHAPTER ONE
REMOTE SENSING BY SATELLITES

by W. de Graaff and G.C.M. Reijnen

CHAPTER TWO
THE USE OF NUCLEAR POWER SOURCES IN OUTER SPACE

by M. Benkö and W. de Graaff

CHAPTER THREE
QUESTIONS RELATING TO THE DEFINITION/
DELIMITATION OF OUTER SPACE AND OUTER SPACE
ACTIVITIES AND THE CHARACTER AND UTILIZATION OF
THE GEOSTATIONARY ORBIT

by M. Benkö and W. de Graaff

CHAPTER FOUR
THE PREVENTION OF AN ARMS RACE IN OUTER SPACE

by G.C.M. Reijnen

UN Charter

Charter of the United NationsEntered into force on October 24, 1945(United Nations Conference on International Organization Documents Vol. XV p. 335; as to the amendments of the Charter in Arts. 23, 27, and 61 as well as in Art. 109 and Art. 61 see UNTS Vol. 557 p. 143; 638 p. 308; 892 p. 119)

Outer Space Treaty

Treaty on Principles Governing the Activities of States in the Exploration and Use of Outer Space, including the Moon and other Celestial Bodies
Entered into force on October 10, 1967
(UNTS Vol. 610 p. 205; ILM Vol. VI p. 386)

Rescue Agreement

Agreement on the Rescue of Astronauts, the Return of Astronauts and the Return of Objects launched into Outer Space
Entered into force on December 3, 1968
(UNTS Vol. 672 p. 119; ILM Vol. VII p. 149)

Liability Convention

Convention on International Liability for Damage caused by Space Objects
Entered into force on September 1, 1972
(UNGA Res. 2777 (XXVI) Annex, of November 29, 1971)

Registration Convention

Convention on Registration of Objects launched into Outer Space
Entered into force on September 15, 1976
(UNGA Res. 3235 (XIXX) Annex, of November 12, 1974; ILM Vol. XIV p. 43)

Moon Agreement

Agreement Governing the Activities of States on the Moon and Other Celestial Bodies Entered into force on July 12, 1984
(UNGA Res. 34/68 Annex, of December 5, 1979; ILM Vol. XVIII p. 1434)

List of Acronyms

ABMT	Anti-Ballistic Missiles Treaty
APT	Automatic Picture Transmission
ASAT	Anti-Satellite Programmes
ATS	Applications Technology Satellite (USA)
BMD	Ballistic Missile Defence (system) (USA)
CNES	Centre National d'Etudes Spatiales (France)
COMSAT	Communications Satellite Corporation (USA)
COSPAR	Committee on Space Research (of ICSU)
DARPA	Defense Advanced Research Project Agency (USA)
DBS	Direct (television) Broadcast Satellites
DOD	Department Of Defense (USA)
ECA	Economic Council of Africa
ECWA	Economic Council of Western Asia
ELINT	Electronic Intelligence
ENMOD	Environmental Modification (techniques)
EROS	Earth Resources Observation System (USA)
ERS	1. ESA Remote-Sensing Satellite
	2. Earth Resources Satellite (Japan)
ERTS	Earth Resources Technology Satellite (USA)
	(later renamed into Landsat)
ESA	European Space Agency
ESSA	Environmental Science Service Administration (TOS)
GAO	General Accounting Office (USA)
GARP	Global Atmospheric Research Programme
GMS	Geostationary Meteorological Satellite
	(also called Himawari; Japan)
GOES	Geostationary Operational Environmental Satellite
GPS	Global Positioning System
GSO	Geo-Stationary Orbit
IAEA	International Atomic Energy Agency
IAF	International Astronautical Federation
ICAO	International Civil Aviation Organization
ICRP	International Commission for Radiological Protection
ICSU	International Council of Scientific Unions
IISL	International Institute of Space Law

ILA	International Law Association
ILM	International Legal Materials
INMARSAT	International Maritime Satellite Organization
INTELSAT	International Telecommunication Satellite Organization
IRS	Indian Remote-Sensing Satellite
ISIS	International Space Information System (of the UN)
ISMA	International Satellite Monitoring Agency
ISRO	Indian Space Research Organization
ITOS	Improved TOS
ITU	International Telecommunication Union (WARC)
LASER	Light Amplification by Stimulated Emission of Radar
LIDAR	Light Detection And Ranging
LODE	Large Optics Demonstration Experiment (USA)
MIDAS	Missile Defence Alarm System (USA)
MIT	Massachusetts Institute of Technology (USA)
MKF	Mnogozonal'ny Kosmicheski Fotoapparat (Russian abbreviation)
MSS	Multi-Spectral Scanner
NASA	National Aeronautical and Space Administration (USA)
NASDA	National Space Development Agency (Japan)
NATO	North Atlantic Treaty Organization
NOAA	National Oceanographic and Atmospheric Administration (USA)
NPS	Nuclear Power Source
OTRAG	Orbital Transport und Raketen Aktien-Gesellschaft (FRG)
RADAR	Radio Detection and Ranging
RBV	Return-Beam Vidicon
RES	Resolution (United Nations)
RSS	Remote Sensing Satellites
RTG	Radio-isotope Thermo-electric Generator
SALT	Strategic Arms Limitation Talks
SAMOS	Satellite And Missile Observation System (USA)
SAR	Synthetic Aperture Radar
SDS	Satellite Data System (USA)
SEO	Satellite for Earth Observation (India)
SIG	Senior Interagency Group (USA)
SIPRI	Stockholm International Peace Research Institute
SIR	Shuttle Imaging Radar (USA)
SLR	Side-Looking Radar
SMS	Synchronous Meteorological Satellite
SNAP	System for Nuclear Auxiliary Power
SPOT	Système Probatoire d'Observation de la Terre (France)
STS	Space Transportation System

List of Organizations within the United Nations System dealing with Space Activities*

A. United Nations

1. Outer Space Affairs Division
2. Natural Resources and Energy Division
3. Regional commissions
4. Office of the United Nations Disaster Relief Co-ordinator (UNDRO)
5. United Nations Environment Programme (UNEP)
6. United Nations Development Programme (UNDP)
7. United Nations Industrial Development Organization (UNIDO)

B. Specialized agencies and other organizations

1. International Telecommunication Union (ITU)
2. World Meteorological Organization (WMO)
3. United Nations Educational, Scientific and Cultural Organization (UNESCO)
4. Food and Agricultural Organization of the United Nations (FAO)
5. World Health Organization (WHO)
6. International Civil Aviation Organization (ICAO)
7. Inter-Governmental Maritime Consultative Organization (IMCO)
8. International Labour Organization (ILO)
9. World Intellectual Property Organization (WIPO)
10. International Atomic Energy Agency (IAEA)
11. World Bank / International Bank for Reconstruction and Development (IBRD) /

* Reprinted from UN Doc. A/Conf.101/BP/11, of February 12, 1981

REMOTE SENSING BY SATELLITES

by W. de Graaff and G.C.M. Reijnen

Introduction

The item of remote sensing by satellites has been on the agenda of the United Nations Outer Space Committee since 1971, when the United Nations General Assembly requested the Committee to establish a Working Group, by Resolution 2778 (XXVI) during the 1998th Plenary Meeting of the General Assembly in its 26th session. This being the first time that remote sensing by satellites was dealt with in the United Nations, it was, however, by no means the first time that remote sensing by satellites had been practised. History has it that already in 1958 (Sänger[1], p. 91) examples could be given of satellites observing the Earth with a view to the control of earthly warfare.

Actually, the technique of remote sensing by satellites started to be developed and applied in an organized and regular way shortly after the launching of the first man-made spacecraft, Sputnik 1.
Until in the late seventies of this century the *civilian* use and benefits of remote sensing by satellites were heavily emphasized, notwithstanding the fact that the history of the development of the remote sensing technique points in the direction of an excellent means to secure a reliable armament control system. In 1981, it was even stated in a United Nations Document (A/AC.206/14, of August 6, 1981, p. 17, item 32) that remote sensing of land resources, so the civilian use of remote sensing satellites, at least partly, is a *by-product* of the development of military observation satellites.

Though the emphasis in the use of remote sensing satellites is, basically, of a barely hidden military nature, this chapter endeavours to do credit to both sides of the use of these satellites, *i.e.* both the civilian and military uses.

In order to elucidate the consequences and the many complications, including the legal ones, of remote sensing by satellites, we first offer a technical overview of the instrumental aspects, which will be followed by a survey of the main existing remote sensing satellite systems as per 1984.

The second part of the chapter will be devoted to the legal implications of the use of remote sensing satellites.

The crucial point in the matter of a legal regulation of remote sensing by satellites is basically a conflict between the principle of the freedom of outer space for *all* States, as worded in the Outer Space Treaty, and the principle of complete and exclusive sovereignty of States over their territories, as guaranteed by general international law.

The principle of State sovereignty is one of the oldest principles in general international law. It dates back to about 3000 B.C., when seafaring nations in the Mediterranean area started to discover foreign territories and, consequently, the need for a clear delimitation of these territories arose. First, only land areas and the adjacent coastal seas were involved, but later also natural resources intimately connected with the territory, such as crop harvests and mineral resources, were included in the sovereignty concept.

In the past, natural resources had to be discovered by prospecting on the spot, and thus with the approval of the State whose territory the area belonged to. However, with the advent of the space era it has become possible and common practice to carry out a significant part of this prospecting from outer space, with instruments mounted in spacecraft. In this way, vital information about the nature and distribution of natural resources within the territory of a State can be obtained without the consent or even the knowledge of that State. Such a situation might, under certain circumstances, lead to serious economic disadvantages for the State under consideration.

The Outer Space Treaty stipulates in Art. I that 'Outer space ... shall be free for exploration and use by all States ... on a basis of equality and in accordance with international law ...', and that 'The exploration and use of outer space ... shall be carried out for the benefit and in the interests of all countries, irrespective of their degree of economic or scientific development ...'. Art. II reads: 'Outer space, including the Moon and other celestial bodies, is not subject to national appropriation by claim of sovereignty, by means of use or occupation, or by any other means.' The Treaty does not contain any provisions regarding the acquisition of information from outer space by certain States about the territory of other States.

In the debate on remote sensing a number of States, in particular the technologically developing ones, take the position that the concept of sovereignty includes the images and other types of information obtained about their natural resources by other States from outer space. They feel that their national interests are not well served by the existing rules of space law. Although these rules, as we have seen, do guarantee them the freedom of exploration and use of outer space '... on a basis of equality ...', they do not in any way indicate their right on information regarding their own territory obtained by other States with the aid of, *e.g.*, remote sensing satellites. As, for the time being, most of the developing countries do not possess the technological and organizational facilities to launch and operate their own remote sensing satellites, they are at a disadvantage as compared to States which do have such facilities. Understandably, these States fear that their national security as well as their capability to direct their own economic development will be jeopardized by the existence of vital information regarding their territory which is available to other States, but not, or only at second-hand, to themselves.

As we see, the conflict between the two principles, *i.e.* the freedom of outer space and the national sovereignty of States, leads to two opposing views in the debate: on the one hand a number of States maintain that not only the natural resources of a State, but also any information concerning them obtained from outer space, should be considered as subject to the sovereignty of the State under consideration; on the other hand States consider that the present rules of outer space do not permit such an appropriation.

Before, however, entering into the investigation of these positions, we first explain what remote sensing by satellites is, how it operates, and how it is organized.

1.1 The Technique of Remote Sensing by Satellites

In the strict sense of the word, remote sensing simply means to obtain information about something from a distance. Thus, when we see with our eyes, or hear a sound with our ears, or smell a scent with our nose, or feel the heat radiated by something with our body, such an observation could be called 'remote sensing'. In present-day practice, however, this term is mainly used to describe ways by which information on objects or phenomena located or occurring on or near the Earth's surface is being obtained from somewhere up in the air, or above it, *i.e.* from outer space. As far as the techniques used for the collection of the information are concerned, there is no fundamental difference between remote sensing from the air and from outer space. In the present work, however, we restrict ourselves to space applications.

The first remote sensing instrument ever used in outer space was a US photographic camera placed on board a modified V-2 rocket which was launched to an altitude of about a hundred km from New Mexico in 1947. After the successful recovery of the payload capsule, photographs were obtained showing the California Peninsula as seen from outer space.

More than ten years later, when the first artificial satellites were launched from Earth, some of these, too, were equipped with photographic and other sensing instruments. In some cases where photographic film was used it was necessary to recover the film cassettes intact on the ground; in other cases systems were developed capable of transmitting images or other information via radio communication links to ground stations on Earth.

The first observations of the Earth from space were carried out mainly for meteorological purposes. In the United States, the first dedicated meteorological satellite TIROS (Television and Infra-Red Observations Satellite) was launched in April, 1960. It transmitted nearly 23,000 television images of cloud patterns from all over the world, which marked the beginning of a new era in meteorological forecasting. Some later satellites of this series were also equipped with scanning infra-red radiometers, and with instruments to monitor the radiation which is re-emitted by the Earth after having been received from the Sun.

4   A number of different, ever more sophisticated instruments were developed to register various properties of the Earth's surface and atmosphere. These include passive instruments such as cameras, line scanners and radiometers, and active instruments such as side-looking radar, scatterometers and lasers. A description of a number of these instruments is given below[2,3].

1.1.1 Passive Sensors

The *cameras* used in remote sensing by satellites are in general modified television cameras. Only when recovery of film capsules is foreseen (as is, *e.g.*, often the case with manned space missions) it is practicable to use a photographic camera. In all cases, however, a complete image of a selected target area is produced on the focal plane of the camera optics system during one single exposure period. When no photographic film can be used, this image is recorded and stored on the photosensitive surface of an image (vidicon) tube. After the exposure, this surface is scanned by a beam of electrons which are reflected by the surface with an intensity which depends upon the exposure and which are recorded afterwards. Because of this scanning process the instrument is called a Return-Beam Vidicon (RBV) camera. The recorded picture information can then either be transmitted directly, *i.e.* in real time, to a ground station, or it can be stored on tape on board the satellite and transmitted afterwards on command, or both.

It should be recalled here that normally the spacecraft is moving in its orbit around the Earth at a speed of approximately 8 km per second. Unless corrections are envisaged to compensate for this forward motion of the camera this implies that, in order to achieve a ground resolution of, *e.g.*, 80 m in the flight direction, the exposure time has to be 10 msec or less. With the modern Metric Camera and the Large Format Camera a ground resolution of 10 m is achieved.

With such a camera system images of target areas on the ground can be obtained not only in the visible region, but also in the adjacent ultraviolet and infrared wavelength regions. These latter images, which show features not visible to the naked eye in nature, can be made visible by printing them in black and white or in a suitably chosen, so-called 'false' colour (*i.e.* a colour not corresponding to the actual colour seen in nature). They can be extremely useful in obtaining different types of information about the surface of the Earth shown in the images.

With *line scanning instruments* the radiation flux in a selected wavelength band emitted by a certain spot on the surface of the Earth into the direction of the instrument is recorded. Pictures of a larger part of the surface can be obtained by means of a scanning process. The easiest way to do this is to provide the optical system with a rotating mirror directing the instrument's field of view to scan the surface perpendicularly to the flight path of the satellite. When this scanning process is rapidly repeated the orbital motion of the satellite itself ensures that each subsequent scan covers a strip of spots adjacent to that of the previous scan. Thus, an endless image band winding itself all around the Earth is continuously built up. For convenience sake, this band can be split up in separate images consisting of a suitably selected set of strips similar in appearance to, *e.g.*, the vidicon or film images obtained with a camera system. A typical ground resolution obtained with such a scanning instrument at satellite altitudes between 500 and 1000 km is about 30 to 100 m. The width of the scanned ground track band is usually between 100 and 200 km.

By combining the optical imaging system necessary for the production of the spot recordings with a spectrometer it is possible to obtain simultaneously images in different wavelength bands in the visible, ultraviolet and infrared regions. Such an instrument is called a Multi-Spectral Scanner (MSS).

A *radiometer* is an instrument which measures radiation emitted by an object, usually in the microwave region (wavelengths between about 1 and 500 mm, frequencies between 300 and 0.6 Gc/s). The incoming radiation is focused by some kind of antenna system (*e.g.*, a simple array of a parabolic reflector) onto the sensor area, so only radiation from a certain area is recorded. The dimensions of this area may well be fairly large, of the order of a few to a few tens of kilometers, as for these wavelengths the resolution obtained with antenna dimensions of a few to a few tens of meters is rather poor. Although the information thus obtained is necessarily rather crude, it can still be extremely useful for the study of, *e.g.*, global thermal and humidity properties of the Earth, such as the monitoring of ocean temperatures, and the distribution of ocean ice and of water vapour in the atmosphere.

1.1.2 Active Sensors

In the examples of the previous sub-section the radiation recorded by the sensor is either spontaneously emitted by the object under investigation, or reflected by it from another source, such as the Sun. The 'active' sensors record radiation which is reflected by the object after previously having been transmitted to it for this purpose. In the case of microwave radiation radar-type instruments are used; in the visible and infrared wavelength regions the emitted radiation is provided by a laser.

A *Side-Looking Radar (SLR)* is a special type of radar placed on board a moving object such as a satellite (or an aircraft). It is provided with an antenna with a narrow field of view in a direction perpendicular to the flight direction of the object. At regular intervals very sharp, short-duration pulses are directed along the field of view. By carefully analysing the recorded back-scattered pulses according to frequency (yielding direction with respect to the flight direction) and echo delay time (yielding distance from the instrument) the echos from a small spot in the target area can be distinguished and recorded separately, and combined with other echos from the same spot recorded at different times. Thus, it is possible to construct an infinite series of line images which together form an image band not unlike those obtained with the optical line-scanning instruments discussed above. The ground resolution of these images is theoretically equal to half the length in the flight direction of the radar antenna, but in actual practice a ground resolution of about 25 m has been achieved. Because in this system pulses received at different times and therefore at different positions along the satellite's orbit are combined analytically to produce high-resolution images, this system is also called Synthetic Aperture Radar (SAR). As the intensity of the back-scattered pulse depends critically upon the roughness of the target surface, very valuable information can be obtained from such images.

A *scatterometer* is a modification of the SLR system described above. Here, a few narrow-beam antennae are used to illuminate target areas on the ground of, *e.g.*, some 50 km wide and 1000 km long, pointing away from the instrument, at an acute angle to the flight path. In this case a ground resolution of some 50 km is possible by distinguishing positions along the length of the target area according to their frequency shift. Such instruments are very useful for the determination of surface roughness and wave patterns of the oceans and for wind speed determinations in the lower atmosphere.

Lasers (acronym for Light Amplification by Stimulated Emission of Radiation) are used for a number of purposes, such as precision altimetry of the satellite (necessary for the derivation of the precise gravity field of the Earth from accurate determinations of the satellite's orbit), analysis of a number of properties of the Earth's surface and atmosphere, etc. As the operation of the laser is analogous to that of the radar (acronym for RAdio Detection And Ranging), the acronym lidar (from LIght Detection And Ranging) is often used for this type of instrument.

Radar altimeters are used for the determination of, *e.g.*, the height amplitude of ocean waves, the general topography of the oceans, and the borders between water and ice masses.

1.1.3 Military Instrumentation

Instruments of the types described above are currently in use for a number of civilian Earth observation missions, details of which can easily be found in the relevant literature. Less profusely publicized are the more sophisticated instruments used for a variety of military reconnaissance purposes. Although no official data are available about these projects, it is assumed that, *e.g.*, some military reconnaissance satellite camera systems can provide a ground resolution of least a few tens of centimeters, rather than a few tens of meters as is the case with the best comparable civilian systems. Other projects are capable of observing, *e.g.*, the launching of missiles and spacecraft, or the motions of ships and submarines across the oceans, and of fulfilling similar military objectives.

A ground resolution of a few tens of centimeters would imply that even minor details of objects on the ground, such as buildings, roads, vehicles, ships, and even people could be recognized. A resolution of a few tens of meters allows

merely to establish the existence of buildings, roads and larger vehicles and
ships, but not their detailed structure.

1.1.4 Ground Support Facilities

Particularly when image information obtained with the aid of remote sensing satellites is transmitted to Earth via telemetry, special ground receiving stations equipped with suitable decoding facilities are needed. In the case of general-purpose meteorological satellites these facilities may be relatively simple and inexpensive, but in the case of, *e.g.*, the US Landsat missions the cost of a ground station with equipment is in the order of 5 million US $, with annual exploitation expenses running at a level between 1 and 2 million US $. Moreover, for the proper use of these facilities fairly advanced technical and scientific knowledge is required.

In some cases, when direct transmission of data to a certain ground station is not possible, indirect transmission via other ground stations or via suitably positioned national or international communications satellites can be arranged for.

The acquisition of a fully equipped ground station will permit any State to receive images and other information regarding its territory and its surroundings transmitted by the satellites as it passes over the station. In actual practice, already a number of States have availed themselves of these facilities.

A distinction is sometimes made between 'primary data' (*i.e.* the coded information as it is received and recorded at a ground station) and 'analysed information' (*i.e.* information concerning for example the crop condition of a certain agricultural area, or the possible occurrence of certain minerals). It is clear that the user is mainly interested in the latter category of data, although on occasion he might wish to improve the methods used to transform the primary data into analysed information. In any case, primary data are only useful if the proper methods to analyse them are available.

1.2 Remote Sensing Satellite Systems in Existence

The Introduction to this chapter already indicated the heavy emphasis on the military potential of remote sensing by satellites, though remote sensing satellites are also being used for civilian purposes.

In this part of our chapter the main existing remote sensing satellite systems will be described in a general way. These systems can be distinguished in civilian and military systems, although it must be emphasized that this distinction itself is not always an easy one to make. In many respects the distinction refers to the use that is made of the system, rather than to its technical characteristics. Therefore it is quite possible that a certain system might serve both civilian and military purposes, and such situations do indeed occur in actual practice. Here we shall list all systems which are not explicitly military in designation as civilian, and indicate their actual or potential military use as appropriate.

The objectives of civilian missions include, *e.g.*, the continuous supervision of crops and other vegetation; the inventory of natural resources such as mineral and fuel deposits; the monitoring of the icecaps and the drift courses of large icebergs after they have broken away from these caps; the observation of the changing global cloud patterns, in particular the birth and development of typhoons, hurricanes and similar hazardous weather phenomena; the search for potential brooding places of locust swarms, to mention but a few.

Military objectives of Earth observation satellites include, *e.g.*, area survey missions, close look missions with high ground resolution, early warning missions based on infrared sensing of ground events such as the launching of rockets and missiles, electronic reconnaissance ('ferret') missions to record and radar transmissions from the ground and from aircraft, and ocean surveillance missions to monitor the movements of ships with the aid of radar.

The construction and launching of remote sensing satellites can be either national or international. However, the data acquired through such satellites are always 'international' in nature because, due to the orbital motion of the spacecraft around the Earth and the rotation of the Earth underneath the orbit, it will repeatedly pass over most of the Earth's surface. This is an important fact since it implies that a State's territory can be, and actually very often is, sensed by such a satellite, even without the State's prior knowledge or consent.

Leaving the legal consequences of the above for sec. 1.3 of this chapter, we concentrate here on a description of existing and planned systems, national and international.

1.2.1 Remote Sensing Satellites for Civilian Use

1.2.1.1 Meteorological Missions

The first satellite ever designed to observe the global cloud distribution of the Earth was Vanguard 2, which was launched in February 1959 after five unsuccessful attempts during the previous year. Because of orientation problems (the spacecraft was tumbling irregularly instead of spinning around a well-defined axis) the first satellite images of clouds were, unfortunately, difficult to interpret.

The first real, dedicated meteorological satellite, however, was TIROS 1 (Television and Infra-Red Observation Satellite), successfully launched on April 1, 1960. Since that day some 80 weather satellites have been launched in the United States, some 50 to 60 in the Soviet Union, and a few by the European Space Agency and Japan.

The US meteorological space programme comprises satellites of the types TI-
ROS, Nimbus, ESSA (Environmental Science Service Administration, also
named TOS = Tiros Operational Satellite), ITOS (Improved TOS), NOAA
(National Oceanographic and Atmospheric Administration), SMS (Synchro-
nous Meteorological Satellite), GOES (Geostationary Operational Environmental Satellite), and, partly, also the more general purpose geostationary
ATS (Applications Technology Satellite). Some of these satellites were used
to support the Global Atmospheric Research Programme (GARP) of the
World Meteorological Organization (WMO).

In the USSR some 40 dedicated weather satellites of the types Meteor 1 and
Meteor 2 were launched, starting in March 1969. In addition, some 30 satellites of the Cosmos series were, in some cases very probably, either experimental civilian or military weather satellites, starting with Cosmos 14 in April
1963.

Both ESA and Japan have so far launched two geostationary weather satellites
each. The ESA satellites are called Meteosat 1 and 2; the Japanese satellites
are GMS (Geostationary Meteorological Satellite or Himawari) 1 and 2.

In some cases these weather satellites are equipped with Automatic Picture
Transmission (APT) systems. These pictures can be received in real time with
relatively inexpensive ground stations anywhere on Earth when the satellite is
passing overhead.

Basically, weather research is a civilian activity. However, it is clear that military operations may also be influenced by weather conditions, so it is not sur-
prising that the military, too, show a deep interest in this topic. In some cases
they make use of the information obtained from civilian satellites, in other
cases they launch their own, dedicated meteorological satellites.

1.2.1.2 Earth Resources Missions

After the first weather satellites had transmitted their cloud pictures, it took
only a few years before it was realized that with better and more diverse images
much more information could be obtained from space about the Earth's surface than cloud distributions alone. Later, more sophisticated weather satellites were actually used for the investigation of ground surface conditions. In
addition, particularly the manned space programmes such as the Mercury,
Gemini, Apollo and Skylab projects in the USA and the Vostok, Voskhod and
Soyuz-Salyut flights in the USSR provided beautiful, detailed pictures of our
planet, full of valuable information. However, it was not before July 1972
when a satellite was launched in the USA which was dedicated especially to
Earth observations. This was the ERTS (Earth Resources Technology Satellite, or Landsat 1 as it was later called[3]). Its construction was based upon the
earlier meteorological Nimbus satellites, but its sensors were different: Landsat 1 contained two imaging systems, a Return Beam Vidicon camera and a
Multi-Spectral Scanner. The RBV could produce images in three colour

10   bands: blue-green, yellow-orange and red-infrared; the MSS comprised sensors for four colours: yellow-orange, red, and two infrared bands. Both systems worked satisfactorily till they were switched off in January 1978; more than 300,000 pictures of the Earth were obtained, each covering an area of 185 times 185 km with a resolution of some 80 m.

Landsat 2, 3, 4 and 5 were launched in January 1975, March 1978, July 1982 and March 1984, respectively. Although some of them were suffering from technological problems they, too, provided a wealth of information about our planet.

Landsat images are, in principle, available to anybody wishing to buy them from the EROS (Earth Resources Observation Systems) Data Center in Sioux Falls, South Dakota, USA, or from regional facilities located in a number of countries.
More than a hundred countries have made use of these facilities. In addition, more than ten countries have, so far, established their own ground stations where they can receive their own pictures. The European Space Agency (ESA), through Earthnet (its network for the acquisition, processing and distribution of remote sensing data) makes use of ground stations in Italy and Sweden to obtain Landsat (and other) images.

The military importance of such pictures is demonstrated by Landsat photographs of rocket and missile launching facilities in, *e.g.*, the USSR and China, which have been published[4].

Another satellite mission, called Seasat, is mainly devoted to detailed investigations of the ocean surface, although it is also very useful to obtain land images[3]. This satellite, which was launched in June 1978, carried five different types of sensors: a scanning multichannel microwave radiometer to measure surface temperatures and wind speeds, a radar scatterometer to measure the fine-scale roughness of the sea and to convert these data into wind speed and direction information, a synthetic aperture radar (SAR) providing pictures of coastal, wave and ice phenomena, a radio altimeter to monitor wave heights and the satellite's altitude with a precision of about 10 cm, and a visual and infrared radiometer producing images of coastal regions and cloud distributions.

During several flights of the US Space Shuttle, various Earth observation instruments were flown. Thus, the SAR, in this case called Shuttle Imaging Radar (SIR) first flew on STS 2 (Space Transportation System) in November 1981. A remote sensing radar with a 2 m parabolic antenna providing a ground resolution of 30 m, and a metric camera with a ground resolution of 20 m were first flown with Spacelab 1 on STS 9 in November-December, 1983. The more than 1000 Earth pictures obtained with this camera were released by NASA's Defense Department liaison office after having been screened for scenes important from a military viewpoint[5].

In the USSR, the Meteor 2 series of satellites are equipped with instruments suitable for Earth observations in a number of spectral bands, with a ground resolution of about 80 m. A first experimental flight in this field seems to have been carried out with Cosmos 149 in 1967, whereas later observations were obtained from Cosmos 1076 and 1151 in 1979 and 1980[6].

Also, during several manned Soyuz and Salyut missions a number of Earth observation programmes have been carried out. In a combined publication of the USSR and GDR Academies of Sciences[7] an extensive description is given of Earth observations made with a sophisticated Multispectral Cosmic Photographic camera (MKF) during the flight of the Soyuz 22 spaceship in September 1976. Observations of a number of surface features on the territories of the USSR and the GDR are described in considerable detail. Reference is made, with some illustrations, to earlier observations obtained with Soyuz 11 (whose crew died during the return to Earth of the spacecraft) in June 1971, with Soyuz 12, 13, 16 and 19 and with the space stations Salyut 3 and 4. The pictures obtained with Soyuz 22 have a ground resolution of about 20 m. It is evident that such a camera system, too, is quite suitable for a variety of military investigations as well.

In June 1979, the first Indian Satellite for Earth Observations (SEO), also called Bhaskara 1, was launched from Kapustin Yar with a Soviet Intercosmos rocket. It was a relatively simple satellite, spinning about its axis at 6 to 10 revolutions per minute, with two slow-scan TV cameras operating in the visible and near-infrared wavelength bands, and a passive microwave radiometer. The pictures obtained with the TV camera have a ground resolution of about 1 km. Unfortunately, after launch it turned out to be impossible to switch on the camera system. Meteorological data could be obtained, however, from the other instruments.

A second satellite of this type was launched in November 1981, again with a Soviet rocket. The camera system of this satellite provided TV pictures of the Earth for several months. At present, India is preparing a new space mission, the Indian Remote sensing Satellite (IRS) with more sophisticated instrumentation and with a ground resolution of 70 and 40 m in the visible and near-infrared (with assistance from the Federal Republic of Germany) regions. The first of these satellites will be launched in 1985-86[6,8].

In 1977, France decided to build its own remote sensing satellite, called SPOT (Système Probatoire d'Observation de la Terre). It will contain two identical high-resolution camera systems operating in the visible and near-infrared wavelength regions. It will circle the Earth at an altitude of about 830 km in a near-polar, sun-synchronous orbit which will permit the satellite to operate under the same conditions of solar illumination during each pass over a certain area on Earth. The two instruments can operate in two modes: the multi-spectral mode with three separate wavelength bands and a ground resolution of 20 m, and the panchromatic mode with one broad wavelength band and a ground resolution of 10 m.

The two instruments each have a field of view corresponding to a width of 60 km on the ground at vertical viewing. These fields of view will have an overlap

12   of 3 km, so that together they will scan a 117 km wide strip on the ground. As adjacent ground tracks are to be observed at five days' intervals, complete coverage of the Earth can be obtained under conditions of vertical viewing. In addition, both cameras can point up to 27 degrees away from the vertical, permitting the observation of selected regions up to 475 km on either side of the ground track. Thus, stereoscopic images can be obtained. The first SPOT will be launched in 1985 with an Ariane rocket[9].

After some earlier tentative discussions a workshop was held in Indonesia in 1979 to consider the possibility of launching a special remote sensing satellite in an equatorial orbit, in order to serve particularly the needs of Indonesia and other equatorial countries. Negotiations are continuing between Indonesia and the Netherlands to build up a Tropical Earth Resources Satellite (TERS) system which could provide a ground resolution of 20 m or better. The advantage of an equatorial orbit over a polar one for the countries involved would be that such a satellite would pass over them once every orbit, *i.e.* for the selected orbit 11 times a day, instead of only once or twice a day [6].

In Japan, studies have been going on since 1980 aiming at the development of an Earth Resources Satellite (ERS), capable of studying geological features, agriculture, forestry and other forms of land use, and environmental preservation with the aid of a SAR system and a visible and near-infrared radiometer. Both systems will have a ground resolution of about 25 m. A near-polar, sun-synchronous orbit at an altitude of about 570 km is being considered[6].

In 1982 the ESA Council authorized a detailed design study for the first ESA Remote sensing Satellite, ERS 1. According to the present planning schedule it will be launched in 1989 in a near-polar, sun-synchronous orbit at an altitude of nearly 780 km. Among the instruments envisaged are a wind scatterometer to measure wind direction and speed, a SAR system to observe the ocean surface and its wave patterns with a ground resolution of 30 m, a radar altimeter and a laser retroreflector to measure wave heights as well as distances from the spacecraft[10].

Most civilian remote sensing programmes have been so far administered by national and international governmental institutions such as NASA (National Aeronautics and Space Administration) in the USA, ESA (European Space Agency) in Western Europe, Interkosmos, an organization of the USSR and a number of other socialist countries, CNES (Centre National d'Etudes Spatiales) in France, NASDA (National Space Development Agency) in Japan, ISRO (Indian Space Research Organization) in India, to name but a few of the most important ones. In recent years, however, a tendency towards commercialization of remote sensing from space becomes apparent in the Western world. One may wonder why this commercialization and privatization of remote sensing by satellites did not start before the eighties. One reason is that private enterprise, both national and multi-national, did see the benefits to be derived from them, but not so clearly the profits. The problem is that designing, building, launching, and even using a sufficiently sophisticated satellite-borne remote sensing system is a very costly enterprise. Furthermore, the de-

mands of the user community are highly diverse, different sections of it pre-
ferring different types of specialized instrumentation. Another problem is that private enterprise requires unrestricted and exclusive rights to the data produced by their space-based remote sensing systems, whereas, *e.g.*, the US Government insists on maintaining a strict supervision on all commercial activities in space, including the dissemination of remote sensing data. Thus, even in the USA, where the entrepreneurial spirit is said to be a national characteristic, private industry hesitates to take over such systems completely, although progress in this direction is certainly being made. For the time being, however, the supervision of not only military, but also civilian use of remote sensing from space will remain in the same, governmental, hands.

In 1980 it was still stated that a fully operational land remote sensing satellite system with state-of-the-art advances in sensor technique to meet customers' needs could not be expected to be in service until 1989 at the earliest[10]. In 1983, however, it was announced[11] that COMSAT (COMmunication SATellite corporation) was likely to take over Landsat and weather satellite operations, with the US government providing a guaranteed market for land and weather data for 15 years. This would mean that the US government would have to pay for its own data, as a form of subsidizing.
Subsidizing, however, is not the general policy of the US government. The ultimate economic value of land remote sensing by Landsats to the USA might approach US $ 10 billion per year.

On January 31, 1983, management responsibility for the Landsat system was transferred from NASA to NOAA (National Oceanographic and Atmospheric Administration), which now has primary responsibility for all civilian remote sensing activities in the USA. Under the present operational regime, NOAA would continue to provide ground receiving stations to other countries, and to make data available on a public, non-discriminatory basis[12].

In the non-governmental sector it was announced by a group of American aerospace companies in September 1983[13] that plans existed to offer the world a private remote sensing satellite service capable of providing detailed photographs of the Earth from space at prices lower than those asked by the Landsat picture distributors. A consortium called Space America has been established which will launch a remote sensing satellite into a polar orbit at an altitude of 900 km in 1986, aiming especially at the foreign market which is interested in images of the Earth with a ground resolution of about 80 m and is lacking an adequate supply of data. It should be mentioned here that it was also an American private enterprise, Space Services Inc., which successfully launched, in September 1983, the first entirely private orbital launch vehicle.

As the Administration proceeded with its Landsat exercise, the US Congress was preparing the necessary legislative support to provide the framework for phased commercialization of land remote sensing. This ultimately emerged as the Land Remote Sensing Commercialization Act of 1984. Among the key international and foreign policy aspects of this legislation, which took effect on July 17, 1984, are the following:

14   — a finding that land remote sensing by the government or private parties involves international commitments which must be observed and a requirement that a private operator observe and implement US international obligations;

— a provision that the Department of State provide guidance on all matters which affect international obligations and in particular determine those conditions for non-government remote sensing activities which are necessary to meet international obligations and foreign policy requirements of the United States;

— a legislative requirement that a private operator of the existing Landsat system continue to provide foreign ground stations with unenhanced data, in accordance with the terms of existing governmental agreements, but only for so long as the US government continues as the actual owner of the remote sensing system;

— a finding that the private sector, and in particular the 'value-added' industry is best suited to develop land remote sensing data markets in the United States and abroad;

— an authorization to NASA to conduct remote sensing research with foreign governments and international organizations.

Together then, the Landsat commercialization initiative, begun by the Administration and the Congressional action, provides the governmental framework to permit private commercial activity and innovation in taking over, developing and operating a US remote sensing system consistent with international obligations. Most importantly from the international perspective, the legislation provides the Secretary of State with the requisite authority for ensuring that private commercial earth remote sensing activities are conducted in strict accordance with the obligations of the United States under recognized international space law (Harry P. Marshall Jr. in: Outer Space Commercialization in the United States; Effects on Space Law and Domestic Law; paper for the 35th Congress of the IAF/ISSL, October 1984, Lausanne, Switzerland).

Other initiatives in the direction of privatization and commercialization of remote sensing satellite systems are the early 1980 plans of the British Government to return the British aerospace industry from its government-controlled position to that of its former private-sector status. In this respect it is interesting to note that on May 3, 1983, the British Minister of State, Mr. Kenneth Baker, announced the establishment of a National Remote Sensing Programme Board, to provide a forum for the co-ordination of remote sensing activities and for the development of a national strategy in this area.

In France, the Arianespace consortium intends to sell satellite space on board the European launching rocket Ariane, both to relieve the financial burden and to maximize benefits derived from its operation. The SPOT remote sensing satellite mentioned earlier in this paragraph is managed by SPOT Image in Toulouse (France) as a commercial operation. It is estimated that in 1988 UK £ 25 million worth of information obtained from the two SPOT satellites will be sold. A computer tape with all the information contained in such a SPOT image will cost about UK £ 500.

As a result of these developments it may be expected that in the nineties a large fraction of civilian remote sensing systems in the Western part of the world will be in private hands. In view of the military importance of at least part of the information obtained with the aid of civilian remote sensing systems, it may be expected that in this way private industry will be in a position to gather data of a military nature. If that would indeed be the case, this situation presents, in our view, an indication of an urgent need for international legal regulations of the launching and exploitation of remote sensing satellite systems. We shall return to this question in sec. 1.3 of this chapter.

1.2.2 Remote Sensing Satellites for Military Use

It is a general practice in all countries the world over that no details of military space missions are made public. Therefore, no accurate description can be presented here of the military remote sensing systems in existence.
However, some review papers have appeared in some Western journals and books in which the scanty data available concerning military satellite missions have been very carefully analysed[3,14,15,16,17,18].
Estimates are given about the existing categories of reconnaissance and other Earth observation satellites, and of the number of satellites flown in each category. In view of the unofficial character of this information only general trends will be quoted from these documents.

In this chapter only military missions in the field of remote sensing are considered. For a more general discussion of the impact of military use of outer space the reader is referred to chapter four of this book. The military importance of remote sensing from space can be derived from the fact that the first military satellites launched by the USA, the USSR and China, were remote sensing missions[3].

In the United States of America a total of 1036 satellites have been launched till the end of 1980[16]. Of these, 590 were primarily civilian in nature, and 446, or 43 percent, were primarily military in nature. Of the latter category, 363 had mission objectives in the general field of remote sensing, such as photographic and tv reconnaissance (231 satellites), electronic reconnaissance (ELINT, from ELectronic INTelligence) or 'ferret' (81), early warning systems (39), and ocean surveillance (12 satellites). The first military US satellite was launched in February 1959, less than one and a half year after Sputnik 1, and just over one year after the first US satellite Explorer 1.

The US photoreconnaissance programme[14] started with the Discoverer project. These satellites carried a photographic film camera, and a re-entry capsule to enable intact recovery of the exposed film on the ground. The first satellite in this series was orbited in February 1959, and the first successful recovery took place with Discoverer 13 in August 1960. In the following years two different types of reconnaissance missions were developed: area survey satellites to obtain pictures of relatively large surface areas with moderat resolution, and close-look satellites to investigate suspected areas in great detail with high ground resolution, possibly a few tens of centimeters. The first US area survey satellite, called SAMOS (Satellite And Missile Observation System) was launched in January 1961, the first close-look satellite in March 1962. Later, the need became apparent to be able to react immediately to the discovery of suspected features on the area survey images without having to wait for the launch of a suitable close-look satellite. The solution to this problem was the incorporation of both types of mission into one big satellite which was unofficially called 'Big Bird'. The first satellite in this category was launched in June 1971.

The electronic reconnaissance or ferret satellites are designed to monitor radio and radar transmissions when flying over foreign States in order to locate aircraft, defence radar systems and similar military objects, and to monitor foreign military and other official communication systems. These satellites are considered to be very sensitive by the military authorities, so very little is known about them. However, careful analysis of types of orbits permits the estimate of about 80 such missions launched by the USA between early 1960 and the end of 1980.

The early warning programme was initiated to supplement ground-based radar warning systems, which are capable of detecting foreign missiles and rockets only after they have risen above the horizon at the station's site. The satellite system was called MIDAS (MIssile Defence Alarm System), and its satellites carried microwave sensors which could detect the exhaust plumes of hot gases produced by missiles and rockets from the very beginning of their launch phase. The first US successful launch in this programme took place in May 1960.

The task of ocean surveillance systems is to monitor the movements of foreign naval vessels with the aid of radar. In the USA much of this monitoring could be accomplished from ground-based or aircraft systems, so the need for space-based systems did not arise until the seventies. The first full-scale satellite in this category was launched in April 1976. Three daughter satellites were released after orbit had been achieved, each carrying their own sensors. Data from these three satellites was first transmitted to the parent satellite for preliminary analysis, and from there relayed to the ground receiving stations.

The USSR has launched a total of 1946 satellites till the end of 1980 [15,16,17]. Of these, 758 were primarily civilian in character, and 1088, or 60 percent, were primarily military. An estimated 614 of these operated in the field of remote sensing: 501 were reconnaissance missions, 67 were ferret missions, 20 were early warning satellites, and 26 were ocean surveillance satellites. The first Soviet military satellite was launched in April 1962, four and a half years after Sputnik 1, and more than three years later than its US counterpart.

As in the USA, the first Soviet military satellite was a photoreconnaissance mission, designated Cosmos 4. A number of categories of reconnaissance missions can be distinguished, although some minor discrepancies occur between different authors in the designation of these categories. A first generation of reconnaissance satellites was based upon the original manned Vostok capsule, and carried low-resolution photographic equipment. Some 40 of these satellites were launched between April 1962 and May 1967, most of them with a lifetime of about 8 days. The second generation contained both high and low resolution systems, first (between November 1963 and August 1970) with lifetimes of 8 days, later (between March 1968 and May 1978) with lifetimes of 12 days. These satellites were based upon a heavier version of the Vostok spaceship. Later generations were probably based on the Soyuz spaceship, and had in general a lifetime of two weeks or more (since September 1975). In recent years reconnaissance satellites have been launched in the USSR at a rate of over 30 per year, as compared with between 1 and 6 per year in the USA. The reason for this is that the US satellites remain in orbit for many months, whereas the Soviet satellites have a much shorter lifetime, as indicated before.

Soviet ferret satellites are currently being launched at a rate of between 4 and 7 per year, probably starting with Cosmos 189 in October 1967, *i.e.* some 7 years after the first US ferret satellite.

Early warning missions in the USSR, too, started some 7 years after their US counterparts, very probably with Cosmos 159 in May 1967. Currently, between 1 and 5 of these satellites are being launched.

In ocean surveillance missions the USSR clearly has a lead over the USA. The first satellite in this category very probably was Cosmos 198, launched in December 1967. These spacecraft carry powerful radar systems to locate ships in both good and bad weather conditions. In order to provide the energy needed for such a radar, nuclear power sources are used, both of the radio-isotope thermo-electric generator and of the reactor type. Out of the 26 of these satellites launched till the end of 1980, Cosmos 954 re-entered the Earth's atmosphere inadvertently, and radio-active fragments of it fell on Canadian territory in January 1978, necessitating an expensive recovery operation. In early 1983, the radio-active core of Cosmos 1402 burned up completely during re-entry. The problems connected with the use of such nuclear power sources in outer space are extensively discussed in chapter two of this book.

Of the other countries taking part in space programmes only the People's Republic of China is supposed to have launched a few military photoreconnaissance satellites, such as, very probably, China 4 in November 1975, and China 7 in December 1976[15].

A special case of interest in this field is the German private company OTRAG (Orbital Transport und Raketen Aktien-Gesellschaft)[3]. This company is developing a very simple and inexpensive family of launching rockets. In December 1975 it concluded an agreement with Zaire for the building and operation of a launching facility in that country. In return, OTRAG promised to launch a reconnaissance satellite for the exclusive use of Zaire. After some test flights in 1977 and 1978, Zaire decided in 1979 to terminate this agreement. Since that time, OTRAG operates in other developing countries such as Libya, where test flights were conducted in 1980 and 1981, as well as in Northern Sweden[19].

1.3.1 General Survey of Legal Problems Involved

In the years that remote sensing by satellites has taken place, much was said on the legality of the remote sensing by satellites practice. As long as remote sensing by satellites was applied on a small scale, it was not much discussed in international law. This became different when in the early sixties the major space powers gathered in the newly established United Nations Committee on the Peaceful Uses of Outer Space (UNCOPUOS) and started negotiations on the formulation of the legal principles as regards the use of outer space.

The three major legal instruments preceding these negotiations were, significantly, called

1. 'Declaration of Legal Principles Governing Activities of States in the Exploration and Use of Outer Space' (UN Resolution 1962 (XVIII), of December 13, 1963)
2. 'International Co-operation in the Peaceful Uses of Outer Space' (UN Resolution 1963 (XVIII), also of December 13, 1963)
3. 'Question of General and Complete Disarmament' (UN Resolution 1884 (XVIII), of October 17, 1963).

These three legal instruments, as well as the five subsequent ones which were formulated in UNCOPUOS (Rescue Agreement 1968; Liability Convention 1972; Registration Convention 1976; Moon Agreement 1979; Principles on DBS 1982) all reaffirmed the idea that 'outer space, including the moon and other celestial bodies, is not subject to national appropriation by claim of sovereignty, by means of use or occupation, or by any other means' (Art. II, 1967 Outer Space Treaty). This text was and still is interpreted as indicating that no claims of national sovereignty can be derived from any activity in outer space. The text of all space treaties has been based on the concept of outer space being an international region, under international law. Two other regions of this kind are the High Seas and the Polar regions.

With the advent of the technological possibilities to *exploit* outer space, also by means of remote sensing by satellites, the principle of State sovereignty received new impetus in that those sovereign States capable of financially and technologically investing in space, desired benefits for their huge *national* investments in space technology.

At this point international law in general and - since the early sixties - its newly-formed branch space law, came on a tense footing in so far as the principle of State sovereignty is concerned.

The said antithesis is intensified by the opinion of those States which lack space technology that - on a basis of equality with the technologically developed States - they have a right of sharing the benefits derived from the use of outer space.

The above legal antithesis is preceded, however, by a financial one. We think it is not put too strongly if we state that the legal principle of *freedom* in the use of outer space might be hampered by the financial striving of sovereign States to gather benefits from the exploitation of outer space. These benefits are enormous, as can be seen in sec. 1.2.1 of this chapter.

The above legal antithesis is, also, in fact, the crux in the matter of regulating the access to and dissemination of space imagery of foreign territories. The legal regulation of remote sensing by satellites started in the UNCOPUOS Legal Sub-Committee in 1972. By 1984, the item has been a priority item on the annual agenda of UNCOPUOS, entitled: 'Legal implications of remote sensing of the Earth from space, with the aim of formulating draft principles'.

During the twelve years that have elapsed since 1972, many proposals for draft principles have been tabled, the majority of which were not accepted. We shall discuss the negotiations in some detail here below.

1.3.2 Background Problems Preventing a Legal Regulation

The struggle for the formulation of a set of principles regarding remote sensing of the Earth by satellites and data gathered with these satellites, essentially centres around the interpretation of the term 'sovereignty', as has been explained in the Introduction to this chapter.
As a consequence of the divergence between these two interpretations of the term 'sovereignty' it has been tried in many discussions in the UNCOPUOS Legal Sub-Committee to redefine the sovereignty interpretation problem as that of *information gathering*. But this sidestep was also unsuccessful, as it was, in fact, a means to introduce the principle of state sovereignty in space law - which is explicitly forbidden in Article II of the 1967 Outer Space Treaty. Moreover, under international law the legality of information gathering depends on the legal regime applicable to the *place* from which it is conducted and not on the *nature* or location of the data collected. Remote sensing satellites gather data of the Earth from outer space. The remote sensing satellite operates *in* outer space, and outer space is, under international law, an international region where no sovereign rights of States are applicable. In our view (but we acknowledge that others do not share this view) this implies that information collected in outer space about another State's territory cannot be the exclusive property of the sensing State.

It is precisely on the basis of the above rule of international law that the majority of the technologically developing countries formulate their opinion that if other States are gathering data about their territory, they should at least be asked for *prior consent* to do so.
The two problems just mentioned: 1/ the antithesis in interpretation of the term national *sovereignty* under international law and 2/ as a consequence, the necessity of the inclusion of the *prior consent* principle in any set of legal principles claimed by the technologically developing countries - are at the basis of the struggle for a legal regulation of remote sensing by satellites. They have prevented the formulation of a set of legal rules for over twelve years by now. From the point of view of the technologically advanced States it is understandable that they wish to retrieve their huge investments in space, if possible

20 without being hindered by undesired rules of international law. Unfortunately, however, part of the expected financial benefits are to be found in the exploitation of natural resources of technologically developing countries. If that is the case, the developing countries are of the opinion that any benefits to be derived from the exploitation of their territory are subject to their own sovereign jurisdiction.

A complication arises from the fact that some of the technologically developed States do possess the facilities necessary to acquire data through remote sensing satellites, whereas others do not. These latter States favour a free distribution of such data also about foreign territory to all interested parties, without being hindered by any rules of prior consent, either from the sensed or from the sensing States.

It is interesting to quote, by way of example, a few of the contributions to the discussions by the technologically developing States in this respect. According to *Uruguay* (UN Doc. A/AC.105/C.2/SR.389, of April 4, 1983), the set of principles 'must include advance notification to the State that was to be sensed, access to primary remote sensing data before it was made available to third parties, prior consent of the sensed State for the dissemination of any data to third parties, compatibility between the primary and analysed remote sensing data and the legitimate rights and interests of other States, continuous access to remote sensing data on a non-discriminatory basis and the holding of consultations between the sensing and the sensed States'.

A more conciliatory point of view is worded by the delegation of *India* (UN Doc. A/AC.105/C.2/SR.389, of April 4, 1983), which drew attention to the 'working paper submitted by the Soviet Union in 1979, in which it was proposed that the freedom to disseminate primary data and analysed information should be limited if the sensed State declared that certain types of data could be disseminated only with its express consent. Such a declaration might relate to the sensitive data with a spatial resolution of 50 metres or less. If a State did not make such a declaration, the sensing State would be free to disseminate the data in question'.

An interesting though at present futuristic suggestion was tabled by *Chile* when it said that 'a world authority should be set up in the near future to manage the resources of outer space for the benefit of mankind, to ensure that the transfer of technology was effected with due regard for the preferential interests of developing countries ...'.
Item 4 of our chapter gives further information on this interesting and important remark.

1.3.3 Endeavours to Formulate a Legal Regulation - 1972 through 1984

From 1972 onward the UNCOPUOS has been trying to come to the formulation of draft principles on remote sensing by satellites. Many States, especially the technologically developing countries, tabled draft texts in a continuous

flow, none of which were found to be acceptable to all members of the UN-
COPUOS.
UN Document A/AC.105/133, of June 6, 1975, gives a survey of these early contributions to a draft agreement on remote sensing by satellites.

Over the years, between 1976 and 1981, many principles have been formulated or re-formulated, without much change in the outcome: that the major legal problems regarding the principle of State *sovereignty* and *prior consent* could not be solved and thus prevented the drafting of the said agreement or set of principles.

In 1981, again an inventory was given, in Annex I to UN Document A/AC.105/288, of April 10, 1981, on the basis of which the Legal Sub-Committee proceeded in the following years.
This 1981 document is of special importance in so far as *Mexico*, one of the technologically developing countries, was successful in invigorating the discussions through its working paper (WG/RS(1981)/WP2, of 19.3.81) as regards
1. the responsibility of the sensing State(s) under international law for remote sensing activities of (a) sensed State(s) (principle XI)
2. the conditions under which data are made available as well as the matter of the necessity for notification and consultation between sensing and sensed States (principle XIII)
3. the dissemination of data (principle XV).
With a view to the importance of this working paper we give its full text as Annex I to this chapter.

In order to interpret the above three items correctly, it seems necessary to add
— that principle XI of the Mexico working paper refers to Article VI of the Outer Space Treaty 1967, which says that a State is responsible under international law for remote sensing activities irrespective of the fact whether these activities are realized by international, governmental or non-governmental entities.
The State is also held responsible for these activities in the context of the specific regulation in this field[20].
In actual practice it seems extremely difficult to define damage done to a State caused by remote sensing activities concerning its territory. No claims for indemnification in this connection have been tabled so far.
On the other hand, in those cases where remote sensing data are being used for the prevention of natural disasters (an example of such a case is the timely location of sites favourable for an explosive development of locust swarms, permitting their destruction), to withhold such information could well lead to catatrophes
— that principle XII refers to the discussion regarding the question whether sensed States should have a right to first and free access to the data gathered by remote sensing satellites from their territories. Technically speaking, the sensing State or any other State capable of directly receiving the data about the sensed State's territory with its own ground-stations necessarily have first access to these data.

In the opinion of the technologically developed countries the access should not be free and first. These States argue that, if the sensed States should have first and free access to data concerning their national territory, they might delay the access to these data by any other State than the sensed State, or even prevent such an access completely.

In the opinion of the technologically developing countries (like Mexico) the access should both be first and free, as these countries insist on the inclusion of the prior consent principle in a draft agreement on remote sensing by satellites
— that principle XV refers to the differences in view regarding the question whether or not data gathered with a high resolution, *i.e.* from 50 m to (perhaps less than) 10 cm (for military purposes), should be disseminated.

In this context we refer to note 4. of this chapter, where it is noted that early 1984 NASA's Defense Department Liaison Office released only *part* of the more than 1000 Earth pictures obtained with the STS 2 SAR camera after having screened those pictures to gain information important from a military point of view. The images of importance from the military point of view are *not* released. The technologically developing countries hold that the same may apply to even non-military data regarding their territories.

In 1982 the UNCOPUOS Legal Sub-Committee took the 1981 text as a basis for its future work (UN Doc. A/AC.105/305, of February 24, 1982).

Though no consensus could be attained on the greater part of the 17 principles, especially the principles XII (access to data) and XV (dissemination of data) presented major difficulties, as to the definition of the term 'third State'. These difficulties centred, as of old, around the matters of State sovereignty and prior consent. The majority of States held that 'sensing State' not only encompasses (the) launching State(s) but also all States capable of receiving remote sensing data with their own stations (see note[20]).

From the Report of the Working Group (A/AC.105/305, Annex I, 24.2.82) we quote here the comments as to the said principles.

14. *Principle XII* (access to data). Considerable efforts were undertaken in the Working Group and in an informal group to identify whether there were certain areas for compromise on the issues covered by this principle. In the course of discussions, reference was made to the proposals contained in: the Mexican working paper (WG/RS(1981)/WP.2, principle XIV); the working paper of the USSR (WG/RS(1982)/WP.10), which was later amended by the USSR in light of discussions; the working paper of Brazil (WG/RS(1982)/WP.11); and the working paper of China (WG/RS(1982)/WP.12). There was agreement that in principle sensing States should provide a sensed State with timely and non-discriminatory access to primary data concerning its territory obtained by remote sensing. Although the discussions on principle XII focused mainly on the same questions that had arisen at previous sessions of the Working Group, some delegations felt that some elements of the discussions at the present session could be viewed as a somewhat new approach. These delegations therefore welcomed a drafting effort made by the delegation of Greece, which submitted a new compromise proposal on principle XII (WG/RS(1982)/WP.13). In the view of some delegations, this proposal might present a wording susceptible to a compromise solution. Other delegations, however, expressed reservations with respect to the proposal of Greece and drew attention to the approach to principle XII reflected in the Working Group's text, and a reference was also made in this connexion to the Mexican proposal.

17. *Principle XV* (dissemination of data). A broad spectrum of views, still divergent in essence, characterized the discussions on this principle. Some delegations found this principle necessary and spoke in favour of its retention, while other delegations favoured the deletion of this principle. Some delegations, reaffirming views expressed at previous sessions of the Working Group, stated that the dissemination of data obtained by remote sensing and analysed information derived therefrom should not be subject to any restriction. They were of the view that unrestricted dissemination of data and information is fully consistent with international law, and that the application of restrictions on dissemination was not practical and would impair further development of remote sensing programmes. Some delegations which favoured the unrestricted dissemination of data and information also pointed out that no complaints had so far been raised about such dissemination and they pointed out that such dissemination was beneficial to all States. Some delegations were of the view that a restrictive system for dissemination would be an obstacle to international co-operation regarding, and participation in, remote sensing activities. These delegations also expressed concern that a restrictive system for dissemination would lead to a more dominant position of sensing States which had, or could acquire, data relating to all States with their satellites. Some delegations expressed the view that such wide dissemination of data and analysed information was acceptable only if the correlative obligation was established for sensing States to provide, on an equal footing, data and analysed information to all those so requiring.

In its 1983 session the Legal Sub-Committee returned to those draft principles which appeared to be of special interest, namely principles XI to XVII, and especially principles XI to XV (UN Document A/AC.105/320, 13.4.83). The text of the latter principles was intended to replace the text of the former. With a view to the importance of this text, we reprint the complete set of the 1983 draft principles as an Annex II to this chapter. The said draft principles were not changed in 1984 either. An extract will here be given of the official comment made by the Working Group on Remote Sensing by Satellites on the principles as formulated in the Legal Sub-Committee. Beforehand, a remark must be made as to the discussion of the square brackets mentioned. Square brackets around the words of (part of) the principles indicate that no consensus has been reached on those particular words and their alternatives contained in such a proposal.

Principle XI. The question of the deletion of the square brackets around the words "[or non-governmental]" was examined by the Working Group. Some delegations were of the view that the square brackets should be deleted because they felt that a State should be responsible for the activities of non-governmental entities within its jurisdiction and that that responsibility was in accordance with the provisions of article VI of the outer space Treaty. Other delegations, however, were of the view that the square brackets around the words "[or non-governmental]" should be retained. They pointed out that draft principle III contained a reference to the outer space Treaty and that therefore a reference to non-governmental entities, or to State responsibility with respect to remote sensing, in the present principle was superfluous.

Some delegations were of the view that deletion of the square brackets around principle XI as a whole should be considered. Other delegations, however, were of the view that they should be retained.

Reference was also made, in the course of the discussion of principle XI, to the working paper submitted to the Working Group at the twenty-first session of the Sub-Committee by the delegation of Greece concerning principle XI (WG/RS(1982)/WP.1).

Principle XII. The Working Group considered the question whether it could agree on the elimination of one of the alternatives in the square-bracketed words "[no later than] [before]". Some delegations were of the view that the word "before" should be retained in order that the sensed State be accorded access before any third State and that such prior access would be in accordance with the sovereignty of a sensed State.

Some delegations were of the opinion that the words "[no later than]" should be retained because it would not be feasible in practice for a sensed State to be accorded prior access to data concerning its territory and because the concept of non-discriminatory access would in fact ensure that no State, including the sensing State, would alone have exclusive access to data.

The question was raised as to what was meant by "a third State", having regard to the possibility that in remote sensing activities more than one State could participate in the sensing, namely, the State operating the space object, the State on whose territory a receiving ground station is located, and other States participating in the remote sensing programme.

The view was also expressed that a sensed State should be accorded access to analysed information on moderate terms, but as the developing countries did not have the technology necessary for the processing of primary data, special consideration should be given to them for acquiring analysed information on favourable terms. Reference was made in this connection to the working paper submitted to the twenty-first session of the Sub-Committee by the delegation of China with respect to the question of access and dissemination (WG/RS(1982)/WP.12) and its relevant amendment at the present session as well as to the working paper of Greece appearing in document A/AC.105/305, annex I, page 21.

Some delegations expressed the view that principle XII was closely related to principle XV and that the two principles should therefore be considered together. Other delegations, however, were of the view that principles XII and XV dealt with different matters, principle XII dealing with "access" and principle XV with "dissemination".

The Working Group considered in some detail the proposal made at the twenty-first session of the Sub-Committee by the delegation of Brazil with respect to principles XII and XV, which proposal was also of relevance to principle XI (WG/RS(1982)/WP.11). Some delegations were of the view that the provisions of that working paper might provide a basis for a solution of matters referred to at present in principles XII, XV and also principle XI. Other delegations were of the view that the Brazilian working paper provided a very useful initiative but that it would require further examination and amendments. Some delegations considered that the concept of damage in the second paragraph of the Brazilian working paper should be further qualified. The view was expressed in this connection that damage to the rights and interests of a State is caused by unauthorized dissemination of remote sensing data and information, relating to its territory, with spatial resolutions finer than 50 metres since such data and information would make it possible to acquire detailed knowledge of its natural resources, economic and defence potential. Reference was made in this connection to the working paper submitted at the twenty-first session of the Sub-Committee by the delegation of the Union of Soviet Socialist Republics with respect to dissemination of data and information (WG/RS(1982)/WP.4). The view was also expressed that the dissemination of data should be unrestricted. It was also stated, without expressed reference to spatial resolution, that below a certain threshold the dissemination of data concerning the territory of a State should only be carried out with the agreement of that State.

Principle XIII. The Working Group examined the provisions of the present text of the principle together with a working paper submitted at the current session of the Working Group by the delegation of Greece (WG/RS(1983)/WP.1). Following a substantial discussion and informal consultations, the Working Group agreed on an amended version of that working paper (WG/RS(1983)/WP.1/Rev.1) which would replace the present text of draft principle XIII, on the understanding that a footnote should be included with reference to the words "or conducting" in the first line of the new text and that the footnote would refer to the relevant paragraph, namely, the present paragraph 21, of the Chairman's report.

However, the new text of principle XIII together with the footnote referred to above with respect to the words "or conducting" in the first line of the text, appears in the draft principles set out in the appendix to this report in square brackets, since at a later stage some delegations while agreeing with the general concept of the text, felt that a number of its elements needed further reflection.

However, it was understood that the words "or conducting" in the first line of the new text of principle XIII refer to manned space flights or to remote sensing programmes already being conducted at the moment of adoption of these principles.

Some delegations expressed the view that the words "or conducting" could refer to both manned and unmanned space flights. The view was also expressed that a principle should be drafted referring to the obligation of a sensing State to periodically inform the Secretary-General of the United Nations as to the countries from which actual data has been gathered in a given remote sensing programme.

The view was expressed that the terms "programmes" and "activities" should be used in all principles where appropriate.

Principle XIV. The Working Group examined the question whether the square brackets around the whole principle could be removed. Some delegations believed that these brackets could be removed, while others were of the view that examination of principle XIV should be postponed until other questions of importance in the set of principles had been resolved. The view was also expressed that the problems in this context should be resolved in connection with other principles. In view of those divergencies the Working Group did not reach agreement on the removal of the brackets. The view was expressed that the Working Group was in fact close to consensus on that question. The matter of the removal of the square brackets around the words "[in particular dissemination of data and information]" was also briefly considered but agreement was not possible.

Principle XV. Some delegations were of the view that the square brackets around principle XV as a whole should be removed. Other delegations did not agree. A reference was made to the working paper submitted at the twenty-first session of the Legal Sub-Committee by the delegation of Brazil (WG/RS(1982)/WP.11). That working paper, which proposed a new text for principle XII and the deletion of principle XV, was discussed at the present session of the Working Group in connection with principle XII, as noted above in paragraph 18 of this report.

Principles XVI and XVII. These principles were not specifically reviewed at the present session.

The 1983 draft principles text, compared with the 1982 version, has come one step forward in that principle XII (access to data) is new. Principle XIII, the notification principle, now reads as follows:

[A State intending to conduct or conducting activities and/or programmes for remote sensing of the earth from outer space shall notify promptly the Secretary-General of the United Nations of the nature, estimated duration of the programme, and the geographic area covered as well as any major modification of the programme. The Secretary-General shall immediately disseminate the information thus received to the States concerned and shall publish it accordingly. A State conducting activities and/or programmes for remote sensing of the earth from outer space should also furnish such information to the extent practicable directly to any State which so requests.]

In consequence, according to this 1983 text which is, however, still entirely in square brackets, a compromise has been reached in that the sensing State no longer needs notifying the sensed State. The sensing State must, however, notify, on its request, the sensed State, as well as, in any case, the Secretary-General of the United Nations.
The above text of principle XIII did not, however, receive consensus in the Remote Sensing Working Group of the Legal Sub-Committee.
Therefore, in 1983, too, no agreement on a set of draft principles regarding remote sensing by satellites could be obtained.

So far we have dealt with activities within the UNCOPUOS Legal Sub-Committee. The matter of remote sensing by satellites and legality was also discussed during the *UNISPACE 1982* Conference. An important outcome in respect to our subject was that the Conference recommended that States should have guaranteed access to data about their territories that such spacecraft collect. Some technologically developing countries, however, wanted more than that; they insisted on the right to veto the distribution of this information to other parties, *e.g.*, companies that could use the data in lucrative land deals [21].

These opposing views were only partly taken into account in the 1983 session of the UNCOPUOS Legal Sub-Committee, as may be inferred from the above.

In 1984, the main part of the spring session of the UNCOPUOS Legal Sub-Committee (see Report in UN Doc. A/AC.105/C.2/L.148, of April 2, 1984) was devoted to discussing the 1982 *Brazilian* working paper (WG/RS(1982)/WP.11). This discussion is, in the above document, recorded as follows: 'The Brazilian working paper contained a text which was to be in substitution for the present text of draft principle XII and proposed that draft principle XV [see Annex II to this chapter] should be deleted. The text contained in the working paper provided, in the first paragraph, 'that a sensed State shall have timely and non-discriminatory access to primary data obtained by remote sensing of the Earth from outer space concerning territory under its jurisdiction before access is granted to any third party and that this principle shall also apply to analysed information; and, in its second paragraph, that a State conducting remote sensing activities of the Earth shall be held internationally responsible for the dissemination of any primary data or analysed information that adversely affects the interests of a sensed State'.

The major outcome of the discussion on the above 1982 Brazilian working paper was the suggestion that a possible avenue for compromise might be to grant a sensed State access on a preferential basis to primary data and analysed information obtained by remote sensing with respect to its territory.

After thorough deliberations it was suggested that the Brazilian working paper represented a constructive avenue for further consideration and might prove useful in finding a compromise solution of the central issues involved, although no clear understanding was reached as to the implications of the proposed international responsibility of a sensing State for the dissemination of data.

Apart from the Brazilian proposal of 1982 as discussed hereabove, also texts by *France*(A/AC.105/C.2/L.144, of March 16, 1984, and A/AC.105/337, p. 33, June 1984) and *Chile* (WG/RS/(1984)/WP.1., also of March 16, 1984) were proposed and discussed.
Also, *Romania* (same document 337, p. 36) made an interesting proposal namely that of unlimited access to all available data by all States. The proposal entails a point of view which essentially differs from that of most developing countries as regards the request for prior consent. In fact, the prior consent

principle would, in this view, become superfluous. It is of importance to note
that *Brazil*, one of the major technologically developing countries, seems also
to become less strict in its view as regards the prior consent principle. The
above proposals can be found in Annex II to this chapter.

In the course of the discussions in the Working Group on Remote Sensing a
text was considered, in a preliminary manner, with a view to facilitating further
deliberations, though it was apparent that for some delegations this text involved difficulties. This text provided, in three paragraphs, that a sensed State
shall have timely and non-discriminatory access on reasonable terms to all primary data obtained by remote sensing of the Earth from outer space concerning territory under its jurisdiction on the basis of preferential treatment and
that this principle shall also apply to analysed information; that a State granting access to any data and information obtained by remote sensing of the Earth
from outer space that relates to the territory of other States to any third party
should take the necessary measures to ensure that through the granting of access it does not prejudice the legitimate rights and interests of those States; and
that a State granting access to data and information prejudicial to the legitimate rights and interests of the States referred to above, shall be held internationally responsible in accordance with international law.

While the discussions in the Working Group were not conclusive, the Working
Group recommended that work on the draft principles should continue on a
priority basis at the next session.
The text of the draft principles as discussed in the 1984 Legal Sub-Committee
session remained unchanged in comparison to that of the 1983 session. They
are to be found in Annex II to this chapter.

1.4 Internationalization of Remote Sensing by Satellites

In view of the fact that it mainly is the concept of State sovereignty that has prevented and still prevents the establishment of a legal instrument relating to remote sensing by satellites, many endeavours have been undertaken to interna-
tionalize remote sensing by satellites. The idea is to create an international remote sensing centre whose task it would be to conduct remote sensing programmes on a regional, not necessarily national, scale. From the legal point of
view such a centre would, when under UN auspices, be entirely in accordance
with existing space legal rules. It would also increase the efficiency of the various functions of remote sensing by satellites systems on a global scale.
On the other hand, it is argued that centralization will increase the dependence
of technologically developing countries on the technology of technologically
developed countries, in particular in regard to scientific and intellectual atti-
tudes[22].
Nevertheless, plans have been formulated - and have been temporized meanwhile - to create a *United Nations Remote Sensing Center*, the foremost task of
which would be to recapitulate the extensive activities already going on in remote sensing of the Earth from space. One reason of the initiative is that remote sensing may become available to nations worldwide solely on a commer-

cial basis which may leave important benefits to poorer technologically developing countries unmet; or remote sensing on a world-wide scale may become unavailable outright if the current practice of free flow of such information is not given an institutional basis.

Secondly, such a Center might serve as a framework within which the availability of information can be assured on existing and new remote sensing information sources to *all* nations.

Also, many commercial activities already provide numerous user services in co-operation with and parallel to governmental efforts.

Lastly, an international network of informal and formal co-operation between scientists, technologists and users has been developed on a variety of applications of remote sensing data.

All these efforts should be taken into account in the Center just mentioned. Any United Nations initiative should, however, be *complementary* to these already ongoing efforts, with a view to meet the needs of technologically developing countries.

It should be the final aim of the United Nations to build up an organizational structure which communicates through permanent national focal points, has access to a system of commercial and government relay satellites for data transmission and plans future remote sensing from space activities jointly with the satellite operating nations and supranational agencies[23].

Another step in the direction of internationalization of remote sensing by satellites is the decision of the United Nations General Assembly (UN Doc. A/Res/37/90, of February 4, 1983) to establish an *International Space Information Service (ISIS)*. The service would, initially, consist of a directory of sources of information and data services to provide directions - upon request - to accessible data banks and information sources. The ISIS would be a new function of the UN Outer Space Affairs Division.

Meanwhile, in May 1984, a United Nations International Meeting of Experts on Remote Sensing Information Systems was held in Feldafing and Oberpfaffenhofen/FRG.

The meeting devoted its attention to:
— a thorough review of existing remote sensing information systems and services
— identifying the mechanisms for establishing a viable clearing house on remote sensing information systems, and
— recommending appropriate programmes for achieving this goal, with emphasis on specific proposals and corresponding steps for their implementation in a given time scale.

One of the results of this meeting was to hold a review meeting 4 - 5 years from 1984 to assess programme accomplishment. In order to achieve the objectives of this meeting, the United Nations had requested that participants be representatives of national, regional and international organizations that have established some type of information system and could provide input into the clearing house on remote sensing information systems.

Both initiatives just mentioned are still in a preliminary state. They seem to be, however, a natural sequel to a technique of international scope as regards its political and legal consequences.

1.5 Conclusion

In the previous sections of this chapter it has been demonstrated that space based remote sensing continues to expand both in scope and in detail:
— more sophisticated observational systems are being developed with better spectral and ground resolution, leading to an expansion of existing application areas and to the development of new ones
— the number of countries capable to carry out their own space-based remote sensing programme is slowly increasing, encompassing not only the technologically advanced countries but also such technologically developing countries as India and, perhaps soon, Indonesia
— the military authorities in the countries with operational remote sensing satellite systems increasingly tend to assume control of all output of information produced by these systems, withholding any such information they consider sensitive from a military viewpoint
— although until now no independent commercial remote sensing satellite system(s) have become operational, a clear tendency exists in some parts of the Western world to increase the role of private industry in this field of space applications.

In spite of many endeavours over the long period of twelve years an international legal instrument regarding remote sensing by satellites has not yet been formulated in such a way that it was acceptable to the negotiating parties, *i.e.* sovereign States assembled in the United Nations Outer Space Committee. One of the main drawbacks preventing the establishment of a treaty, or a set of principles on remote sensing by satellites is that States cannot agree on the interpretation and subsequent implications of the term 'State sovereignty', which is a basic principle in international law. Another drawback is the difficulty for a great many States to accept a treaty, or a set of principles, without the express formulation of the prior consent principle.
Especially at present when both data of natural resources and data with a military connotation are representing huge economic values as well as a means to control the balance of power on Earth, the principle of State sovereignty has received new impetus.
These problems can be summarized as those referring to the disagreement on the principles of the access to and the dissemination of data.

Apart from the above difficulties in reaching an agreement there also is the matter of the internationalization of remote sensing by satellites. Many regional endeavours as to remote sensing activities on a global scale are reported as being undertaken.
In order to recapitulate and to stimulate these activities the establishment of a United Nations Remote Sensing Center is under consideration.

30   Already established - but not yet functioning - is an International Space Infor-
      mation Service (ISIS), also under the auspices of the United Nations, a service
      consisting of a directory of sources of information and data services.
      The advantages as well as the disadvantages of these intitiatives still have to be
      investigated.
      For a technique like remote sensing by satellites, which virtually covers the en-
      tire Earth, services like those mentioned here seem to us to be a prerequisite of
      any truly international co-operation.

1. Sänger, E.: *Raumfahrt - technische Ueberwindung des Krieges*, Rowohlt, Hamburg (FRG), 1958
2. Plevin, J.: *Remote sensing of Earth resources, a European point of view, ESRO/ELDO Bulletin* No. 27, April, 1975, p. 8;
   Hammond, M.J.: *A Survey of Earth-surface observation satellites and the interface between remote sensor and attitude control system, ESA Journal* Vol. 1, No. 4, 1977, p. 327;
   Kriegel, W.A.: *Remote sensing missions for the next decade, Journal of the British Interplanetary Society*, Vol. 37, No.2, 1984, p. 75
3. Gatland, K.W.: *The illustrated encyclopedia of space technology*, Harmony Books, New York, 1981
4. *Soviets construct new space facilities, Aviation Week and Space Technology* Vol. 118, No. 12, March 21, 1984, p.21
5. *Washington Roundup, Aviation Week and Space Technology* Vol. 120, No. 8, February 20, 1984, p. 15
6. Sheremetyevsky, N.N. & Ju. V. Trifonov: *Soviet Earth and atmosphere remote sensing space vehicles*, Paper IAF-83-115, 34th Congress of the IAF, Budapest, 10-15 October 1983, Abstracts of Papers, p. 108-109;
   Korotaev, G.K. et al.: *Results of space experiments on ocean study*, Paper IAF-83-103, idem, p. 94-95;
   Sagdeev, R.Z. et al.: *Remote sensing in the USSR Academy of Sciences, studies, experiments, main results, current objectives*, ESA-SP-134: *Proceedings of an International Conference on Earth Observations from Space*, Toulouse, 6-11 March, 1978, p. 203-216
7. *Soyuz-22 issleduyet zyemlyu/Sojus-22 erforscht die Erde, Izdatyelstvo Nauka*, Moscow, 1980/ *Akademie-Verlag*, Berlin, 1980;
   Uspyekhi Sovyetskogo Soyuza v issledovanii kosmicheskogo prostranstva 1967-1977, Izdatyelstvo Nauka, Moscow, 1978
8. Mama, H.P.: *India's Earth Resources Satellite, Spaceflight* Vol. 21, No. 7, July 1979, p. 300
9. *SPOT, satellite-based remote sensing system*, CNES, Centre Spatial de Toulouse, Toulouse (France)
10. Haskell, A.: *The ERS-1 programme of the European Space Agency, ESA Journal*, Vol. 7, No. 1, 1983, p. 1;
    Gillet, P.R.C.: *ERS-1, an ice and ocean monitoring mission, Journal of the British Interplanetary Society* Vol. 36, 1983, p. 387;
    Gregory, W.H.: *Free enterprise and Landsat, Aviation Week and Space Technology* Vol. 113, No. 2, July 14, 1980, p. 13
11. Waldrop, M.M.: *What price privatizing Landsat?, Science* Vol. 219, No. 4585, February 11, 1983, p. 752
12. U.N. Doc. A/AC.105/C.2/SR.287, of April 4, 1983
13. *New Scientist*, Vol. 99, No. 1375, September 15, 1983, p. 751
14. Kenden, A.: *U.S. reconnaissance satellite programmes, Spaceflight* Vol. 20, No. 7, July 1978, p. 243
15. *Outer space - battlefield of the future?*, Stockholm International Peace Research Institute (SIPRI), London, 1978
16. *Soviet space programs 1976-1980*, United States Senate Committee on Commerce, Science and Transportation, Washington / USA, December 1982
17. Clark, P.S.: *Aspects of the Soviet photoreconnaissance programme, Journal of the British Interplanetary Society* Vol. 36, No. 4, 1983, p. 169
18. Wolf, D.O.A., H.M. Hoose & M.A. Dauses: *Gefahr aus dem Weltraum*, Bonn (FRG), 1979
19. Lenorovitz, J.M.: *OTRAG prepares for full launch service, Aviation Week and Space Technology* Vol. 119, No. 11, September 12, 1983, p. 77-79;
    G.P.: *Die OTRAG startet wieder Raketen, Frankfurter Allgemeine Zeitung*, 5. Oktober 1983
20. for this remark and the next two see: Benkö M. and K. Damian, in: *Zeitschrift für Luft- und Weltraumrecht* 31, 1982, 4, pp. 336/337
21. *New Scientist*, August 26, 1982, p. 543
22. see also: Voûte, C., p. 2 of: *'Essential elements of educational programmes on space science and technology and their related applications including those that could be developed at/for local institutions in the developing countries'* - contribution for the UN Interregional (ECA/ECWA) Seminar on Space Applications focusing on the implementation of the recommendations of UNISPACE 1982, Addis Ababa/Ethiopia, July 4 - 8, 1983
23. UN Doc. A/Conf.101/NP/44, of September 23, 1981.

UN Doc. A/AC.105/
288
English
Annex I
Page 13
20.4.1981

MEXICO: WORKING PAPER

(WG/RS(1981)/WP.2 of 19 March 1981)

Principles relating to remote sensing of the earth, its
natural resources and its environment

Principle I

For the purpose of these principles, the term "remote sensing of the
earth" means remote sensing of the earth, its natural resources and its environment from outer space.

Principle II

Remote sensing of the earth and international co-operation in that field
shall be carried out for the benefit and in the interests of all States, irrespective
of their degree of economic or scientific development and taking into consideration the needs of the developing countries.

Principle III

International law, including the Charter of the United Nations, the Treaty on Principles Governing the Activities of States in the Exploration and Use
of Outer Space, including the Moon and Other Celestial Bodies, and the present principles shall be applicable to remote sensing of the earth.

Principle IV

1.   States carrying out programmes for remote sensing of the earth shall promote international co-operation in these programmes.

2.   States carrying out programmes for remote sensing of the earth shall
make available to sensed States opportunities for participation in these programmes.

3.   In order to maximize the availability of benefits from remote sensing of
the earth, States are urged to consider agreements for the establishment of
shared regional facilities.

Remote sensing of the earth shall promote the protection of the environment. To this end States participating in remote sensing of the earth shall identify and make available to the competent United Nations authorities any information useful for the prevention and control of phenomena detrimental to the environment of the earth.

Principle VI

States participating in remote sensing of the earth shall make available technical assistance to other interested States on mutually agreed terms. This principle is without prejudice to the rights of sensed States, as set forth in the present principles.

Principle VII

1. The United Nations and the relevant agencies within the United Nations system should promote international co-operation, including technical assistance, and play a role of co-ordination in the area of remote sensing of the earth.

2. States carrying out programmes for remote sensing of the earth shall, prior to the execution of these programmes, give notification thereof to the Secretary-General of the United Nations, who shall publish such notification.

Principle VIII

1. States carrying out programmes for remote sensing which have knowledge of the threat of a natural disaster shall immediately inform all States which might be affected and the United Nations authorities competent for natural disasters.

2. Likewise, States carrying out programmes for remote sensing shall communicate to States which have been affected by a natural disaster and to the competent United Nations authorities all information which would be useful in assisting the States affected to take measures to remedy the situation.

Principle IX

The results of remote sensing of the earth shall be used by States with strict respect for sovereign rights and in a manner compatible with the legitimate interests of other States.

Principle X

States participating in remote sensing of the earth either directly or through the relevant international organizations shall make available to the Secretary-General of the United Nations and other interested States, particularly the developing countries, upon their request, any technical information involving possible operational systems.

Principle XI

States conducting remote sensing of the earth shall bear international responsibility for national activities carried on by governmental agencies or by non-governmental entities, and for ensuring that national activities are carried out in conformity with the present principles. The activities of non-governmental entities shall require authorization and continuing supervision by the State which has jurisdiction or control over those non-governmental entities. In the case of activities carried on by an international organization, responsibility shall be borne both by the international organization and by the States members of such organization (text taken from article VI of the 1967 Treaty on Principles Governing the Activities of States in the Exploration and Use of Outer Space, including the Moon and Other Celestial Bodies).

Principle XII

A State which intends to carry out or authorize programmes for remote sensing of the earth shall give advance notification to the States whose territory, territorial sea or maritime areas under their jurisdiction will be sensed.

Principle XIII

Upon request of the sensed State, the State carrying out remote sensing shall consult with the said State in regard to such activity in order to comply with principle XIV and thus to promote international co-operation and friendly relations among States and to enhance the mutual benefits to be derived from this activity.

Principle XIV

States carrying out programmes for remote sensing of the earth shall provide States which are subject to remote sensing with the preliminary information and final results and conclusions relating to the natural resources of the territory, territorial sea and maritime areas under the jurisdiction of the sensed State.

Principle XV

States carrying out remote sensing of the earth shall not, without the approval of the sensed State, disseminate information or results and conclusions regarding the natural resources of that State.

Principle XVI

1. Without prejudice to the principle of the freedom of exploration and use of outer space, as recognized in article I of the Treaty on Principles Governing the Activities of States in the Exploration and Use of Outer Space, including the Moon and Other Celestial Bodies, remote sensing of the earth, which also constitutes exploration and use of the earth, including the territories and re-

sources of sovereign States, shall be conducted with strict respect for the full and permanent sovereignty which every State has and freely exercises over its wealth, natural resources and economic activity.

Principle XVII

1.   The Charter of the United Nations and the Declaration on Principles of International Law concerning Friendly Relations and Co-operation among States in accordance with the Charter of the United Nations shall be applicable to any dispute that may arise with respect to remote sensing of the earth.

2.   In the event that a dispute related to remote sensing of the earth arises, the States which are parties to that dispute shall hold consultations with a view to arriving at a peaceful solution.

3.   In the event that such consultations are not successful, the States shall have recourse to other means until a peaceful solution to the dispute is found.

ANNEX II

UN Doc.
A/AC.105/320
English
Page 16
13.4.83

APPENDIX

Section A.

TEXTS OF DRAFT PRINCIPLES AS CONTAINED IN THE REPORT OF THE LEGAL SUB-COMMITTEE ON THE WORK OF ITS TWENTIETH SESSION (A/AC.105/288, ANNEX I, APPENDIX), WITH CHANGES MADE AT THE PRESENT SESSION

Principle I [1]

For the purpose of these principles with respect to remote sensing of the

---

[1] The question of the application of these principles to international intergovernmental organizations will be considered later.

36 natural resources of the earth and its environment: [2]

(a) The term "remote sensing of the earth" means "remote sensing of the natural resources of the earth and its environment";[3]

(b) The term "primary data" means those primary data which are acquired by satellite-borne remote sensors and transmitted from a satellite either by telemetry in the form of electromagnetic signals or physically in any form such as photographic film or magnetic tape, as well as preprocessed products derived from those data which may be used for later analysis;

(c) The term "analysed information"* means the end-product resulting from the analytical process performed on the primary data as defined in paragraph (b) above combined with data and/or knowledge obtained from sources other than satellite-borne remote sensors.

Principle II

Remote sensing of the earth from outer space and international co-operation in that field [shall] [should] be carried out for the benefit and in the interests of all countries, irrespective of their degree of economic or scientific development, and taking into consideration, in international co-operation, the particular needs of the developing countries.

Principle III

Remote sensing of the earth from outer space [shall] [should] be conducted in accordance with international law, including the Charter of the United Nations and the Treaty on Principles Governing the Activities of States in the Exploration and Use of Outer Space, including the Moon and Other Celestial Bodies, and the relevant instruments of ITU.

Principle IV

1. States carrying out programmes for remote sensing of the earth from outer space [should] [shall] promote international co-operation in these programmes. To this end, sensing States [should] [shall] make available to other States opportunities for participation in these programmes. Such participation should be based in each case on equitable and mutually acceptable terms due regard being paid to principles ...

---

[2] The formulation "with respect to remote sensing of the natural resources of the earth and its environment" will be reviewed in light of the title to be given to the principles.

[3] This term is still subject to futher discussion. In the view of some delegations, it would be necessary in the future work to further define the meaning of the words "remote sensing of the earth and its environment".

*   The content, definition and necessity of the term "analysed information" is still to be clarified.

2.   In order to maximize the availability of benefits from such remote sensing data, States are encouraged to consider agreements for the establishment of shared regional facilities.

Principle V

Remote sensing of the earth from outer space [should] [shall] promote the protection of the natural environment of the earth. To this end States participating in remote sensing [should] [shall] identify and make available information useful for the prevention of phenomena detrimental to the natural environment of the earth.

Principle VI

States participating in remote sensing of the earth from outer space [should] [shall] make available technical assistance to other interested States on mutually agreed terms.

Principle VII

1.   The United Nations and the relevant agencies within the United Nations system should promote international co-operation, including technical assistance, and play a role of co-ordination in the area of remote sensing of the earth.

2.   States conducting activities in the field of remote sensing of the earth [shall] [should] notify the Secretary-General thereof, in compliance with article XI of the Treaty on Principles Governing the Activities of States in the Exploration and Use of Outer Space, including the Moon and Other Celestial Bodies.

Principle VIII

Remote sensing of the earth from outer space should promote the protection of mankind from natural disaster***. To this end, States which have identified primary data from remote sensing of the earth and/or analysed information in their possession which would be useful in helping to alert States to impending natural disasters, or in assisting States to deal with natural disasters should as promptly as possible, notify those States affected or likely to be affected of the existence and availability of such data and/or information. Such data and/or information should, upon request, be disseminated as promptly as possible.

Principle IX[1]

Taking into account the principles II and III above, remote sensing data

***   The meaning of this term is subject to further discussion.

[1] Should be considered in connection with the formulation of a principle on dissemination of data or information and subject to later discussion of the terms "information" and "data".

38   or information derived therefrom [shall] [should] be used by States in a manner compatible with the legitimate rights and interests of other States* **.

Principle X

States participating in remote sensing of the earth either directly or through relevant international organizations [shall] [should] be prepared to make available to the United Nations and other interested States, particularly the developing countries, upon their request, any relevant technical information involving possible operational systems which they are free to disclose.

Principle XI

[States [shall] [should] bear international responsibility for [national] activities of remote sensing of the earth [irrespective of whether]]where] such activities are carried out by governmental [or non-governmental] entities, and [shall] [should] [guarantee that such activities will] comply with the provisions of these principles.]

Principle XII

[A sensed State [shall] [should] have timely and non-discriminating access to primary data obtained by remote sensing of the earth from outer space, concerning its territory, on [agreed] reasonable terms and [no later than] [before] access is granted to any third State[1,2]. [To the greatest extent feasible and practicable,] this principle shall also apply to analysedinformation.]

Principle XIII

[A State intending to conduct or conducting* activities and/or programmes for remote sensing of the earth from outer space shall notify promptly the Secretary-General of the United Nations of the nature, estimated duration of the programme, and the geographic area covered as well as any major modification of the programme. The Secretary-General shall immediately disseminate the information thus received to the States concerned and shall pu-

---

*   Some delegations were of the view that, for the sake of consistency it was necessary to consider this principle in the light of draft principle II and III.

**   A delegation reserved its position on removing the square brackets around the words "in a manner compatible with" and on the deletion of the words "not" and "to the detriment of".

[1] The question of from which States access to and provision of data should be obtained, needs further consideration.

[2] Subject to review in the light of the discussion on access by third States.

*   With respect to the words 'or conducting', reference should be made to paragraph 21 of the Working Group Chairman's report at the twenty-second (1983) session of the Sub-Committee.

blish it accordingly. A State conducting activities and/or programmes for remote sensing of the earth from outer space should also furnish such information to the extent practicable directly to any State which so requests.]

Principle XIV

[A State carrying out remote sensing of the earth [shall] [should] without delay consult with a State whose territory is sensed upon request of the latter in regard to such activity, (in particular dissemination of data and information,) in order to promote international co-operation, friendly relations among States and to enhance the mutual benefits to be derived from this activity.]

Principle XV

[States carrying out remote sensing of the earth shall not, without the approval of the States whose territories are affected by these activities, disseminate or dispose of any data or information on the natural resources of these States to third States, international organizations, public or private entities.]

Principle XVI

[Without prejudice to the principle of the freedom of exploration and use of outer space, as set forth in article I of the Treaty on Principles Governing the Activities of States in the Exploration and Use of Outer Space, including the Moon and Other Celestial Bodies, remote sensing of the earth [should] [shall] be conducted with respect for the principle of full and permanent sovereignty of all States and peoples over their own wealth and natural resources [with due regard to the rights and interests of other States and their natural and juridical persons in accordance with international law] [as well as their inalienable right to dispose of their natural resources] [and of information concerning those resources].]

Principle XVII

[Any dispute that may arise with respect to the application of [(Activities covered by] these principles [shall] [should] be resolved by prompt consultations among the parties to the dispute. Where a mutually acceptable solution cannot be found by such consultations it [shall] [should] be sought through other [established] [existing] procedures for the peaceful means of settlement of disputes mutually agreed upon by the parties concerned.]*

---

* Subject to review in the light of the full set of agreed principles and a decision on the legal nature of the principles.

Section B

WORKING PAPERS SUBMITTED TO THE WORKING GROUP AT THE TWENTY-SECOND SESSION OF THE SUB-COMMITTEE

Greece: working paper

(WG/RS(1983)/WP.1 of 24 March 1983)

Principle XIII

A State intending to conduct remote sensing activities of the earth from outer space shall notify promptly the Secretary-General of the United Nations of the nature and duration of the programme as well as of the geographic area covered. The Secretary-General shall immediately disseminate the information thus received to the States concerned and shall publish it accordingly.

Greece: working paper

(WG/RS(1983)/WP.1/Rev.1 of 28 March 1983)

Principle XIII

A State intending to conduct or conducting activities and/or programmes for remote sensing of the earth from outer space shall notify promptly the Secretary-General of the United Nations of the nature, estimated duration of the programme and the geographic area covered as well as any major modification of the programme. The Secretary-General shall immediately disseminate the information thus received to the States concerned and shall publish it accordingly. A State conducting activities and/or programmes for remote sensing of the earth from outer space should also furnish such information to the extent practicable directly to any State which so requests.

UNITED NATIONS

GENERAL ASSEMBLY

Distr.
LIMITED

41

A/AC.105/C.2/L.144
16 March 1984

ENGLISH
Original: FRENCH

FRENCH PROPOSAL

COMMITTEE ON THE PEACEFUL
USES OF OUTER SPACE
Legal Sub-Committee
Twenty-third session
Geneva, 19 March-6 April 1984
Agenda item 3

DRAFT PRINCIPLES WITH RESPECT TO THE ACTIVITIES OF STATES CONCERNING REMOTE SENSING FROM OUTER SPACE

Principle I

For the purposes of these principles with respect to remote sensing activities:

(a) The term "remote sensing" means the sensing of the earth's surface from space by making use of the properties of electromagnetic waves emitted, reflected or diffracted by the sensed objects, for the purpose of improving natural resources management, land use and protection of the environment;

(b) The term "primary data" means those crude data which are acquired by remote sensors borne by a space object and which are transmitted to the ground from space by telemetry in the form of electromagnetic signals, by photographic film, magnetic tape or any other support;

(c) The term "processed data" means:

The products resulting from the preprocessing of the primary data, needed in order to made such data usable;

The products derived from the products of preprocessing and resulting from further processing or inputs of data and knowledge obtained from other sources.

(d) The term "analysed information" means the information resulting from the interpretation of processed data;

(e) The term "remote sensing activities" means activities with respect to the operation of remote sensing satellites, primary data collection and storage stations, and activities in processing and interpreting the processed data.

Principle II

Remote sensing activities shall be carried out for the benefit and in the interests of all countries, irrespective of their degree of economic or scientific development, and taking into consideration the particular needs of the developing countries.

Principle III

Remote sensing activities shall be conducted in accordance with international law, including the Charter of the United Nations, the Treaty on Principles Governing the Activities of States in the Exploration and Use of Outer Space, including the Moon and Other Celestial Bodies, and the relevant instruments of the International Telecommunication Union.

Principle IV

States carrying out remote sensing activities shall promote international co-operation in these activities.

To this end, they should make available to other States opportunities for participation therein. Such participation should be based in each case on equitable and mutually acceptable terms.

Principle V

In order to maximize the availability of benefits from remote sensing, States are encouraged to conclude agreements for the establishment and operation of data collection, storage, processing and interpretation facilities, in particular within the framework of regional agreements.

Principle VI

States participating in remote sensing activities should make technical assistance available to other interested States on mutually agreed terms.

Principle VII

The United Nations and the relevant agencies within the United Nations system should promote international co-operation, including technical assistance, and play a role of co-ordination in the area of remote sensing.

Principle VIII

State carrying out a programme of remote sensing by satellite shall notify the Secretary-General of the United Nations accordingly, in compliance with article IV of the Convention on Registration of Objects Launched into Outer Space. It shall, moreover, make available any other relevant information it is free to disclose to any other State, particularly any developing country, which is affected by the programme, at its request.

Remote sensing shall promote the protection of the earth's natural environment.

To this end, States participating in remote sensing activities shall disclose all information in their possession capable of averting any phenomenon harmful to the earth's natural environment.

Principle X

Remote sensing shall promote the protection of mankind from natural disasters.

To this end, States participating in remote sensing activities which have identified processed data and analysed information that may be useful to States affected by natural disasters, or likely to be affected by impending natural disaster, shall transmit them to the latter as promptly as possible.

Principle XI

Without prejudice to the principle of the freedom of exploration and use of outer space, as set forth in article I of the Treaty on Principles Governing the Activities of States in the Exploration and Use of Outer Space, including the Moon and Other Celestial Bodies, remote sensing activities shall be conducted in a manner compatible with the legitimate rights and interests of other States and in particular on the basis of respect for the principle of full and permanent sovereignty of all States and peoples over their own wealth and natural resources, with due regard to the rights and interests in accordance with international law, of other States and their natural and juridical persons.

Principles XII

Any sensed State shall have non-discriminating access on timely and reasonable cost terms to primary data, processed data and analysed information concerning the territory under its jurisdiction.

Principle XIII

A State carrying out a remote sensing programme by satellite shall consult a State whose territory is sensed, without delay and upon request by the latter State, in order to promote international co-operation and friendly relations among States and to enhance the mutual benefits to be derived from this activity.

Principle XIV

In compliance with article VI of the Treaty on Principles Governing the Activities of States in the Exploration and Use of Outer Space, including the Moon and Other Celestial Bodies, States operating remote sensing satellites shall bear international responsibility for their activities, irrespective of wheth-

44 er such activities are carried out by governmental or non-governmental entities or through international organizations to wich such States are parties. They shall guarantee that such activities comply with these principles.

Principle XV

Any dispute resulting from the application of these principles shall be resolved by prompt consultations among the parties to the dispute. Where a mutually acceptable solution cannot be found by such consultations, it shall be sought through other established procedures for the peacful means of settlement of disputes mutually agreed upon by the parties concerned.

WG/RS(1984)/WP.2
20 March 1984

DRAFT PRINCIPLES WITH RESPECT TO THE ACTIVITIES OF STATES CONCERNING REMOTE SENSING FROM OUTER SPACE

French proposal

Table indicating the correlation with the text of the draft principles, as emerging from the twenty-second session of the Legal Sub-Committee
(document A/AC.105/320, pp. 16-20)

FRENCH PROPOSAL	Doc.A/AC.105/320
PRINCIPLE I	PRINCIPLE I
PRINCIPLE II	PRINCIPLE II
PRINCIPLE III	PRINCIPLE III
PRINCIPLE IV	PRINCIPLE IV
PRINCIPLE V	PRINCIPLE V
PRINCIPLE VI	PRINCIPLE VI
PRINCIPLE VII	PRINCIPLE VII
PRINCIPLE VIII	PRINCIPLES VII, X, XIII
PRINCIPLE IX	PRINCIPLE V
PRINCIPLE X	PRINCIPLE VIII
PRINCIPLE XI	PRINCIPLES IX, XVI
PRINCIPLE XII	PRINCIPLE XII
PRINCIPLE XIII	PRINCIPLE XIV
PRINCIPLE XIV	PRINCIPLE XI
PRINCIPLE XV	PRINCIPLE XVII

GE.84-61037

UNITED NATIONS

GENERAL ASSEMBLY

Distr.
LIMITED

A/AC.105/C.2/L.145
26 March 1984

ENGLISH
Original: FRENCH

45

COMMITTEE ON THE PEACEFUL
USES OF OUTER SPACE
Legal Sub-Committee
Twenty-third session
Geneva, 19 March-6 April 1984
Agenda item 3

ROMANIA: WORKING PAPER

Principle I

(d) These principles shall apply to data obtained from outer space by means of operational remote sensing satellites of the Landsat D (United States), SPOT (France) and MOS (Japan) types and others with similar performances.

Principle XV

States and international or national organizations conducting remote sensing activities by satellite under the conditions set forth in these principles should give other States the possibility of access to all remote sensing primary data obtained, including those on seas, oceans and free territories, without any discrimination and on agreed reasonable terms.

WG/RS(1984)/WP.12
20 March 1984

WORKING PAPER: CHILE

Draft principles on remote sensing

Preamble
Bearing in mind that the exploration and exploitation of outer space by States must be conducted for the benefit of mankind,
Recalling that one of the cardinal principles of space activities is that they should be carried out for exclusively peaceful purposes,
Recalling General Assembly resolutions 1803 (XVII) concerning perm-

anent sovereignty over natural resources and 2131 (XX) on the inadmissibility of intervention in the domestic affairs of States and the protection of their independence and sovereignty,

Principle II

Remote sensing of the Earth shall be carried out for the benefit of peoples, regardless of their degree of economic, scientific or technical development and in strict observance of the rights of peoples to permanent sovereignty over their natural resources.

Principle III

Notwithstanding the provisions of the present principles, the legal bases of remote sensing shall be the Charter of the United Nations, the Treaty on Principles Governing the Activities of States in the Exploration and Use of Outer Space, including the Moon and other Celestial Bodies, the Declaration on Principles of International Law concerning Friendly Relations and Co-operation among States in accordance with the Charter of the United Nations, and the relevant instruments of ITU.

Principle XI

States, through their governmental and non-governmental agencies and through international agencies, shall bear international responsibility for improper or discriminatory use of analysed information resulting from remote sensing, in accordance with the provisions of these principles and of international law.

Principle XV

1. A sensed State shall have timely and non-discriminating access to primary data obtained by remote sensing from outer space and concerning its territory, natural resources, territorial sea and maritime areas under its jurisdiction.
2. A sensed State shall have access, on a priority basis, to data concerning its territory which are considered crucial for its development. The sensing State may not divulge such data to third parties without the prior consent of the sensed State.

LIST OF ORGANIZATIONS PARTICIPATING IN SPACE-BASED RE-
MOTE SENSING ACTIVITIES

A. United Nations

Outer Space Affairs Division (space applications programme)
Department of Technical Co-operation for Development (TCD)
Natural Resources and Energy Division (NRED)
Economic and Social Commission for Asia and the Pacific (ESCAP)
Economic Commission for Latin America (ECLA)
Economic Commission for Africa (ECA)
Economic Commission for Western Asia (ECWA)
United Nations Environment Programme (UNEP)
United Nations Industrial Development Organization (UNIDO)
Office of the United Nations Disaster Relief Co-ordinator (UNDRO)
United Nations Development Programme (UNDP)

B. Specialized agencies and IAEA

Food and Agricultural Organization of the United Nations (FAO)
United Nations Educational, Scientific and Cultural Organization (UNES-
CO)
International Civil Aviation Organization (ICAO)
World Bank
International Telecommunication Union (ITU)
World Meteorological Organization (WMO)
Inter-Governmental Maritime Consultative Organization (IMCO)
International Atomic Energy Agency (IAEA)

Source: United Nations Document A/CONF.101/BP/11/Add.1, 21 October 1981

THE USE OF NUCLEAR POWER SOURCES IN OUTER SPACE

by M. Benkö and W. de Graaff

Introduction

The present discussion of legal problems concerning the use of nuclear power sources (NPS) in outer space was opened in 1978. It was induced by the crash of the Soviet NPS satellite Cosmos 954 on January 24, 1978 over Canada[1]. Although this was not the first accident in which a nuclear power source was involved[2], the crash of Cosmos 954 was the first event to demonstrate quite clearly the hazards[3] connected with the use of NPS in outer space.

The re-entry of another NPS satellite, *i.e.* Cosmos 1402 in 1982/83, confirmed once again that this problem had to be dealt with on an international basis from the legal as well as from the scientific and technical point of view.

In order to outline the problems arising from the use of NPS in outer space, a short account will be given of the accidents which happened since 1961, when the first NPS satellite (SNAP 3) was launched by the United States. Subsequently, some background information will be provided on problems relating to the different orbits of satellites which are about to re-enter the atmosphere, and also on the construction and operation of diverse types of NPS in general.

2.1 Accidents in the History of the Use of NPS

2.1.1 Accidents in the USSR Space Programme

2.1.1.1 The Crash of Cosmos 954 in 1978

The most spectacular NPS accident which caused considerable damage to a foreign State was that of the above-mentioned Cosmos 954[1].

Cosmos 954 was launched on September 18, 1977. According to the official Soviet announcement it carried 'scientific apparatus, radio-system for precise measurements of orbital elements and radio-telemetry system'[4], but according to unofficial Western sources it was an ocean surveillance satellite[5] weighing several tons. It was equipped with a small nuclear reactor containing approx. 55 kg of 90% enriched uranium-235. This reactor served as a 10-20 kW thermal power plant to the satellite[6].

Cosmos 954 was placed into a nearly circular near Earth orbit at about 270 km altitude, circling the Earth once within about 90 minutes[7]. Due to the fact that the orbital plane is nearly stable in space, whereas the Earth underneath it rotates around its polar axis once within 24 hours, every country (except those near the polar regions) was overflown by the satellite at least twice a day.

A few weeks after the launching of the satellite it could be observed that Cosmos 954 was malfunctioning. The reason for this is still unknown. According to Academician Leonid Sedov, who presented his country's official view of the accident, it was due to a sudden depressurization which occurred beyond the range of Soviet tracking facilities. Since the satellite's depressurization was so rapid, it was assumed that Cosmos 954 collided with 'some other object of natural or artificial origin'[8].

The re-entry of Cosmos 954 into the dense layers of the atmosphere was anticipated by Western scientists for within a few months after the incident. The exact date and site of the satellite's re-entry, however, were uncertain. Nevertheless, in early January 1978 it could be estimated with sufficient certainty that it would occur within that month[9].

On January 24, 1978 Cosmos 954 finally entered the Earth's atmosphere over the sparsely inhabited section of Canada's Northwest Territories - without notice or warning from the launching State[10]. To explain this lack of information the Soviet Union later claimed that the satellite's re-entry had not been expected over Canadian territory but over the Aleutian Islands. In addition, competent authorities had excluded the possibility of any sizable hazard resulting from the satellite's re-entry - especially as the construction of the nuclear reactor on board the satellite aimed at its complete destruction upon re-entry[10]. Indeed, most of Cosmos 954 - initially weighing several tons - burned up in the dense layers of the atmosphere. But about 65 kg of debris were scattered along a wide stretch of 600 km in length. All fragments (except two) and some 3,500 particles were radio-active[11]. On the one hand, the radio-active level of some debris varied from a few thousandths to millionths of 1 roentgen/hour, which implies only a negligible intensity of radiation to human organism and natural environment. On the other hand, some parts of the satellite were of considerable, even lethal radio-activity; e.g. one small fragment (ML-3(10)) which had the size of 25 mm x 15 mm x 10 mm had a radiation level of 500 roentgen/hour. This is sufficient to kill a person or a number of persons remaining in continuous contact with that part for a few hours.

In order to be able to organize the clean-up and recovery operations promptly and effectively, Canada transmitted a number of questions about the satellite's design and its nuclear reactor to the Soviet Union and requested that precise responses be provided urgently. The USSR, however, offered to render immediate assistance to Canada by sending a group of specialists for the recovery of the satellite's remnants. Complete and prompt answers to the questions were not given. Not until March 21 did Canada receive the general information that the satellite carried on board 'an ordinary nuclear reactor working on uranium enriched with the isotope uranium-235'[10].

The clean-up and recovery operations of Cosmos 954 were finally carried out by Canadian and US experts, and it took almost eight months until all parts were found and further radiological risks could be excluded[12]. The search operations were extremely difficult and strenuous, as the Cosmos 954 accident had happened during a typical subarctic winter 'when lakes were frozen, landmarks were masked or covered by ice and snow'[13]. Temperatures under these conditions usually reach -40°C or less, and the wind chill factor included are at times as low as -100°C[13].

For the search and clean-up operations the Canadian Government had to afford approx. Can $ 14,000,000[14]. On January 23, 1979 Canada raised a claim against the Soviet Union for compensation for at that time only less than half of its expenses, *i.e.* Can $ 6,041,174.70[15]. Not before April 2, 1981 could the negotiations be brought to an end, and the Soviet Union agreed to pay the modest sum of three million dollars 'in full and final settlement of all matters connected with the disintegration of the Soviet satellite 'Cosmos 954' in January 1978'[15].

2.1.1.2 The Accident of Cosmos 1402 in 1982/83

Another accident in the Cosmos series happened in 1982/83. Fortunately, this time the satellite's NPS re-entered the Earth's atmosphere over the High Seas and was disintegrated during the process, so that no nuclear damage was caused on foreign territory. Therefore, as far as its consequences are concerned, this accident cannot be compared with the crash of Cosmos 954. Nevertheless, the Cosmos 1402 incident gave a very clear demonstration of problems which may i.a. arise from communication difficulties between the launching State and those States whose territories might be polluted by radioactive debris from the re-entering NPS.

The history of the events connected with the incident can be summarized as follows. Cosmos 1402 had a mission and construction similar to that of Cosmos 954. It was placed into a near-Earth orbit on August 30, 1982 at an altitude of about 270 km and with a revolution period of about 90 minutes. Experts estimated that the Cosmos 1402 reactor generated approx. 100 kW thermal energy, with an electrical power output in the range of 10-20 kW[16]. During the following months the satellite showed abnormal behaviour, according to observers in the Western world[17]. At this stage no notification was given by the USSR about the character of the malfunctioning in general and the ways in which it could affect the behaviour of the NPS on board the satellite in particular (*i.e.* especially whether or not a re-entry of the NPS into the dense layers of the atmosphere had to be expected and under what circumstances).

On December 28, 1982 it was observed by Western specialists that the satellite had split into three fragments. This led to the assumption that the satellite's reactor had been separated by remote control from the other, less or probably non-radio-active parts of the satellite[18]. Normally, with a satellite of this kind, the fragment containing the reactor core would be boosted up into a new orbit

52 at an altitude of about 900 km, where it could continue circling around the Earth for hundreds or thousands of years before reaching the dense layers of the atmosphere and burning up, and by that time the radio-active material on board would have largely decayed[19]. In this case, however, no such orbital change of any of the fragments was observed, which led to the assumption that the boosting procedure probably had failed[20]. The first fragment of Cosmos 1402 re-entered the atmosphere on December 30, 1982, burning up in the process.

More than a week after this event, *i.e.* on January 8, 1983 the Soviet newspaper 'Pravda' published, on page 2, information according to which the Cosmos 1402 satellite had ended its active life as planned on December 28, 1982. It had been split into fragments in order to separate the nuclear reactor core from the rest of the satellite. Thereby it had been ensured - according to the above-mentioned article - that the satellite would disintegrate during its re-entry into the atmosphere in such a way that any radio-active fallout which could reach the Earth would stay well within the internationally accepted safety limits. A similar statement was made by a leading Soviet specialist, Academician Oleg M. Byelotserkovskij, on Moscow television a week later and published in 'Pravda' on January 16, 1983.

The first *official* Soviet reaction, however, was given on January 18, 1983 by means of a formal notification from the Permanent Mission of the USSR to the Secretary-General of the United Nations[21]. It stated:

> 'Cosmos 1402, carrying on board a small nuclear energy unit of the reactor type, completed its programme of work and, on command from earth, ended its active existence on 28 December 1982. The safety system with which the satellite was equipped then split it into three fragments, one of which burnt up on entry into the dense layers of the atmosphere on 30 December 1982. The two remaining fragments consist of the main part of the satellite structure and the reactor core, which has been separated from it. Before the satellite was split into fragments, the reactor was shut off on command from earth'.

Re-entry of the structure was predicted for the end of January, and of the reactor core for mid February 1983.

Only this notification finally clarified which of the remaining satellite fragments, that were expected to re-enter at different times and in different places, contained the reactor core and could theoretically cause nuclear hazard - provided it survived re-entry into the Earth's atmosphere[22]. The notification, however, ended with the following assurance:

> 'Radiation after the fragments of Cosmos 1402 enter the dense layers of the atmosphere will be within the limits recommended by the International Commission on Radiological Protection'.

In three further notifications, dated January 21[23] and 25[24], and February 7, 1983[25], the Soviet authorities confirmed the re-entry and decay of both of the remaining fragments. In particular, the reactor core re-entered the atmosphere on February 7, 1983 at 10:56 hours UT and burned up. From that time, it was stated, Cosmos 1402 'completely ceased to exist'. The radio-activity contained in the reactor was transformed into a radio-active cloud, and it was expected that this cloud would be dispersed in such a way that the respective amounts of radio-activity descending to the Earth would not be harmful to its population and environment.

However, a number of countries recalling the Cosmos 954 accident over Canada in 1978 felt seriously concerned about the risks this new incident might involve for their population. They had the impression that the splitting up of an NPS satellite into three parts without boosting up the part containing the NPS into a higher, safe orbit in order to prevent its re-entry could not be considered a routine treatment of a malfunctioning NPS satellite. So they felt to have the obligation towards their citizens to take every necessary step to ensure their safety, in case that any dispersal of radio-active material over their territory should occur[26]. Although to some extent reassured by the press reports of the first half of January 1983, some of these countries felt that due to the unofficial character of these press reports they could not yet relax their safety measures. Even after the official Soviet notifications had been rendered to the United Nations the situation did not change, since, in the opinion of the potentially affected States, the notifications did not contain a sufficient amount of detailed information to permit independent verification of the reassuring statements given in the notifications. Therefore, as they felt unable to exclude potential damage to their territories on the basis of their *own* calculations and predictions - although the probability of such an emergency situation was admittedly very small - precautionary measures were taken by a number of States (*e.g.* the USA, Canada, the Netherlands, and the Federal Republic of Germany). Since, in the worst case, a nuclear hazard could be involved, the measures had to provide for the location and de-activation of radio-active fragments and perhaps even the evacuation of the accident area. It should be considered in this context that theoretically all countries whose territories are located between 65° northern latitude and 65° southern latitude, as determined by the orbital inclination of the Cosmos 1402 satellite, might have been affected in case of an accident[22] (*cf.* sec. 2.2 below).

2.1.1.3 Frequency of Accidents in the Cosmos Series

According to Western estimates approx. 20-30 nuclear powered satellites have so far been launched by the Soviet Union since the mid-sixties. After the Cosmos 954 incident in 1978 the Soviet Union had stopped launching this type of satellite for the time being. But already two years later another NPS satellite was launched. There were three more launches in 1981 and four during 1982 - one of which was Cosmos 1402[27].

Subsequent to the Cosmos 1402 incident in 1983/84 the Soviet Union once again stopped using NPS spacecraft in near Earth orbits. On June 29, 1984 however, she launched Cosmos 1579 which according to Western sources is a reactor powered spacecraft[27a].

As to the frequency of accidents this shows that the accident rate in this series is quite considerable (between 1980 and 1983 2 accidents on 8 launches, *i.e.* 25%). It is, though, actually as high as it used to be in the US space programme (sec. 2.1.2 below).

The two accidents described above were not the only ones in the history of NPS. But, in the first place, they happened to be the most recent ones drawing world-wide attention to the risks involved in the use of NPS. In the second place, the Cosmos 954 accident gave rise to the first case in the history of space law in which a claim was raised by one sovereign State against another on account of damage caused by a falling space object.

Three other accidents had already occurred between 1964 and 1970. They had happened within a series of 22 launches of NPS satellites by the USA between 1961 and 1977[28]. The nuclear powered satellite SNAP 9A (System for Nuclear Auxiliary Power) Transit 5 BN-3 carrying on board a radio-isotopic generator burned up on re-entry in April 1964. However, 17,000 curies (2.2 lb) of its radio-nuclide fuel plutonium-238 - being one of the most enduring and deadly radio-active poisons known - were dispersed at high altitude above the East coast of Africa; until 1970 about 95% of this material descended to Earth. Yet, according to measurements through the end of 1970 and soil samples which had been collected at more than 60 sites to estimate global distribution of fallout from the accident, the respective amounts of plutonium which settled to Earth were not considered hazardous[29].

In this connection it has to be pointed out that the SNAP 9A fuel containment was designed to burn up on re-entry, so that the vaporization of the fuel source in the stratosphere was a *planned* manoeuvre - not an additional accident. But SNAP 9A was the last radio-isotope system of that design in the US space programme. All radio-isotope systems since have been designed for intact re-entry and recovery, which was made possible by a special containment system[30].

The second NPS accident occurred in 1968. SNAP 19 (also containing plutonium-238) was launched on board a NIMBUS weather satellite which was aborted due to a guidance error. The satellite's power source fell into the Santa Barbara Channel off the Californian coast and due to its containment was recovered intact from approx. 100 m depth of water[31]. Its fuel was re-used; no nuclear fuel had been released into the atmosphere or the ocean.

Apollo 13/SNAP 27 survived re-entry in April 1970 and re-entered the atmosphere over the South Pacific. It was lost on the bottom of the Tonga Trench in approx. 7,000 m depth of water and was not recovered[32].

At present no US satellites carrying active NPS on board are in use in near Earth orbits or planned to be launched there.

2.2   Satellite Orbits Before and During Re-entry

Satellites circling the Earth are bound to overfly the territories of quite a number of countries all over the world. During the final phase of their existence they gradually come down into the denser layers of the Earth's atmosphere and either burn up being dispersed in the form of fine particles, or - at least in part - reach the surface of the Earth. In the following section the main reasons for this behaviour shall briefly be set forth.

2.2.1   The Orbit and its Position in Space Relative to the Earth

When a satellite has been launched into an orbit around the Earth, this orbit can be characterized by a small number of parameters, among which are those indicating the position of the orbital plane in space. The most important of them regards the inclination of the plane with respect to the Earth's equator, *i.e.* the angle between the orbital plane and the plane of the equator.

Generally, the orbital plane rotates very slowly about the Earth's polar axis in one direction or the other, depending on the inclination. For some specific values of the inclination it is even constant with respect to the background stars in the sky, *i.e.* when the orbital plane either is perpendicular to the equator or coincides with it. For the present purpose, however, the position of the plane in space shall be considered as being fixed.

When the plane has an inclination of, for example, 65 degrees, this implies that the satellite is not able to overfly any point on Earth which has a latitude higher than 65 degrees North or 65 degrees South, but it can overfly any territory lying somewhere between these limits. This is due to the rotation of the Earth itself around its polar axis with a period of 24 hours, as is illustrated in Figure 1, showing five positions of the Earth's surface with respect to a certain satellite orbit at approximately five hour intervals.

The combination of the orbital motion of the satellite with the rotation of the Earth about its axis produces a ground trajectory on the Earth's surface which oscillates between the two extreme latitudes mentioned above, as shown in Figure 2. Due to the Eastward rotation of the Earth, each consecutive orbit is shifted to the West over a distance which depends on the ratio between the rotation period of the Earth with respect to the orbital plane, and the orbital period of the satellite. Thus, during one day the satellite describes a network of trajectories on the Earth's surface as shown in Figure 3. These trajectories cover the entire surface of the Earth between the two latitude limits mentioned above.

A satellite with an orbital revolution period of 90 minutes makes 16 revolutions per day. This corresponds to a shift of the trajectory from one revolution to the next of 2,500 km along the equator. If the number of revolutions per day is a round number, the grid of trajectories for one day is almost identical to the grid for the previous day. If this number is not a round number, the grid is shifted from one day to the next. In any case, it can be seen from Figure 3 that all countries whose territories are situated between the latitude limits of the given satellite's trajectory grid (except perhaps some small countries lying just between adjacent trajectories) are overflown by the satellite at least twice every day: once when the satellite is moving from South to North, and once when it is moving from North to South.

56

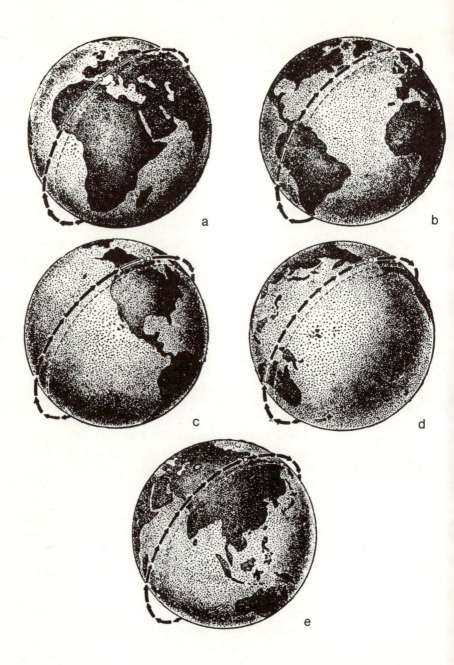

Figure 1
Satellite orbit around the Earth, with the Earth itself rotating Eastward underneath the orbit about its polar axis; a, b, c, d and e show positions of the Earth at
approximately five-hour intervals.

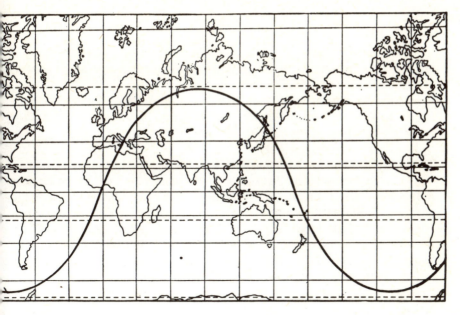

Figure 2
Satellite ground track across the Earth's surface for one orbital revolution.

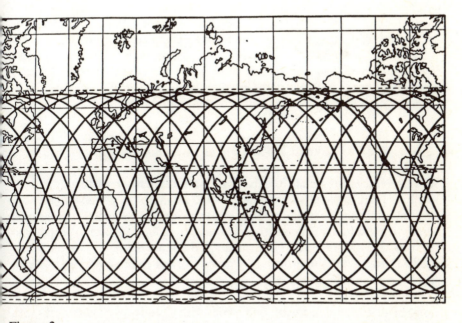

Figure 3
Network of ground tracks for fifteen consecutive orbits of a satellite described during one day. As a result of the Earth's rotation, each subsequent ground track is shifted approximately 24 degrees to the West with respect to the previous one.

Under ideal circumstances, such as an Earth with perfect spherical symmetry, and no other forces acting upon the moving satellite than the Earth's gravity, the orbit of a satellite would be perfectly constant in time. In reality, however, the Earth is not an ideal sphere, and there are several admittedly small disturbing forces acting upon a satellite circling the Earth. As a result the orbit is not constant, but varies in position, shape, and size.

The most important force for the purpose of the present discussion is the braking force generated by the resistance of the atmospheric air as the satellite moves through it. Generally, this braking results in a gradual decrease of the average altitude of the satellite above the surface of the Earth. The rate of decrease of the altitude depends upon the altitude itself and is higher at lower altitude, since the air density increases with decreasing altitude. At altitudes between, for example, 120 to 200 km, depending on some characteristics of the satellite itself, this descent rate becomes so high that the satellite is no longer capable of completing a full revolution around the Earth and comes down towards the Earth's surface. On the other hand, a satellite circling the Earth at an altitude of 1,000 km or more has a life expectancy of at least several thousands of years.

What happens during the descent of the satellite again depends on some of its characteristics. The air friction causing the descent also causes significant heating up of the satellite's structure, while in addition local forces may arise which tend to break up the structure into smaller fragments. If the satellite is sufficiently small, it will disintegrate and burn up completely during this re-entry phase of its orbital life. If it is larger, parts of it or, under certain conditions, even the whole satellite may reach the ground more or less intact. In that case the possibility that this may occur in a populated area, and that damage to persons or property may be the result, cannot be excluded.

2.2.3   The Re-entry of a Satellite and its Uncertainties

If the re-entry of a satellite into the Earth's atmosphere were a readily and accurately predictable phenomenon, it would no doubt be possible to identify the impact area of its fragments long in advance, to take adequate measures in order to exclude any damage to persons and to reduce damage to property to the unavoidable minimum. Unfortunately, this is not the case. As a rule, many of the factors determining the rate of descent of a satellite vary during its flight, partly in an unpredictable way.

First of all, the air density not only varies with altitude, but it also varies with time at a given position of the orbit, and thus the drag encountered by the satellite passing through that position varies. Some of these variations are regular: they depend, *e.g.*, on the satellite's position with respect to the globe, on the day of the year, and on the time of the day. Others are quite irregular: they depend on the general condition of the atmosphere as influenced by *e.g.* solar flares and similar disturbances. Up to now, such variations are not predictable.

Secondly, the number of air particles encountered by a satellite also depends upon its so-called cross-sectional area, which can be visualized as the area of the shadow cast by the satellite on a surface perpendicular to the flight direction when illuminated by a beam of light parallel to the flight direction. Generally, this cross-sectional area depends on the orientation of the satellite structure with respect to its flight direction, the only exception being a perfectly spherical satellite. For a particular satellite the variation of the cross-sectional area with its orientation may be a factor of two or even more. When the satellite's orientation is stabilized with respect to the flight path, or when it is changing in a well-known way, this is no problem, as in that case the cross-sectional area can be calculated for each point of the trajectory. In all other cases this is impossible. Normally, during the final stage of descent, when the satellite is heated up and strong disruptive forces on its structure may develop, any existing orientation stability or regularity is easily lost.

Usually, the descent trajectory of a re-entering satellite is best characterized by its expected lifetime at a certain moment, *i.e.* the period of time which is expected to elapse between that moment and impact. The effect of the variations discussed above is that this lifetime can, as a rule, be calculated with an uncertainty of 10 to 20 percent. Thus, if in a certain case the expected lifetime is 10 days, the actual lifetime will be between 8 and 12 days, and for an expected lifetime of 10 hours the actual lifetime will be between 8 and 12 hours. Consequently, just 10 hours before the estimated time of impact it is still only possible to indicate the orbit during which impact will probably take place, but not the precise part of this orbit. It should be recalled here that the length of the ground track of a satellite's orbit is equal to the circumference of the Earth, *i.e.* 40,000 km.

2.2.4   Some Examples

An extensive discussion of the problems to be encountered during the re-entry of a large satellite has been given by Professor D. Rex from the Technical University of Braunschweig, FRG [33], who analysed the re-entry and impact of Skylab in July 1979. We see that forecasts of the re-entry date made in April 1979, *i.e.* some 90 days in advance of the actual impact date of July 11, proved to be in error by about 20 days, or by more than 20%. A prediction dated June 29, *i.e.* twelve days before impact, proved to be in error by two days, or by some 15%. A prediction dated July 9, *i.e.* some 50 hours before impact, proved to be in error by over 3 hours, or by over 6%. Still, those three hours correspond to two full revolutions around the Earth.

Similar examples can be taken from the Soviet announcements concerning the fate of the Cosmos 1402 fragments. The first announcement by TASS published in 'Pravda' on January 8, 1983 only mentioned the intentional splitting up of the satellite into three fragments, only one of which had re-entered so far. On January 15, Academician O. Byelotserkovskij mentioned in an interview given on Moscow television and reproduced in 'Pravda' next day that the large structural fragment would re-enter during the last days of January and the reactor core in mid February. The predicted lifetime of some 15 days for the structure proved to be in error by about 6 days or 40%, and the lifetime of about 30 days for the core proved to be in error by some 6 days, or by about 20%. On January 21, the Permanent Mission of the USSR to the United Nations announced an expected impact of the structure for January 24 between 2 and 9 a.m. Moscow Time, *i.e.* three days later. Actual impact took place on January 24 at $1^h 10^m$ Moscow Time. Thus, the mean expected impact time of $5^h 30^m$ proved to be in error by more than 4 hours, or by some 6 percent. Similarly, on January 25 it was announced that re-entry of the reactor core could be expected between February 3 and 8, corresponding to a lifetime between 9 and 14 days and an uncertainty of some 20%. Actual impact took place on February 7 at $13^h 56^m$ Moscow Time[34].

Thus it is demonstrated that for an Earth-orbiting satellite which is approaching the end of its life, the remaining lifetime at any specific moment can only be estimated with an expected uncertainty of 10 to 20 percent. The only obvious exceptions to this rule are certain categories of manned or unmanned space vehicles, such as the US space shuttle orbiters, which are specifically designed to carry out and survive a completely guided re-entry and landing.

2.3   Existing Types of Nuclear Power Sources and their Use in Outer Space

Before drawing any final conclusions from the accidents outlined above or discussing the legal problems involved, a general survey will be given of the existing types of NPS and of the basic technical problems connected with their use in outer space.

2.3.1   Different Types of Power Sources Used in Outer Space

In outer space missions different objectives require different amounts of energy of various kinds. Space transportation normally requires very powerful sources, capable of producing vast amounts of energy in relatively short periods of time for the operation of their rocket propulsion motors. On the other hand, various instruments and housekeeping systems usually require less powerful systems, which need only produce small quantities of energy, but during much longer periods of time.

Several processes for the production of these different amounts of energy are currently being used or under consideration. So far the most important category of processes consists of chemical reactions, *e.g.* the combustion of suitable propellants in rocket motors, and the generation of electric energy in chemical batteries. Another category is that of the conversion of solar radiation into electric energy by means of photovoltaic generators or solar cells. At present, both of these categories are commonly used in space missions. However, they have specific characteristics that limit their use: chemical batteries have a restricted lifetime and, in addition, an inconvenient relation between energy capacity and battery weight. Solar cells have a rather limited capacity and, moreover, they only operate when being exposed to solar radiation. This implies that they cannot operate in the shadow of the Earth or some other celestial body and that their output decreases with increasing distance from the Sun ('deep space' missions). Furthermore, both systems are vulnerable to hostile environments such as external radiation (the Van Allen radiation belts of the Earth being a particular hazard for solar cells), meteorites, or excessive temperatures. Consequently, chemical batteries and solar cells cannot be used for certain types of space missions.

A third category of energy production processes involves the release of nuclear energy. Here, four different processes can be distinguished. First, there are a number of atomic nuclei (or nuclides) which decay spontaneously, emitting some sort of radiation in the process. These nuclides are often called radioactive isotopes. The word 'isotope' is derived from the Greek and means 'of equal position'. It is used in nuclear physics to indicate nuclides having a certain number of protons characteristic of a chemical element and consequently occupying a specific place in the so-called Mendeleyev periodic system of elements, but having different numbers of neutrons.

The second process is nuclear fission. Certain nuclides are capable of absorbing, under suitable conditions, a neutron, and splitting up into several fragments afterwards. The total mass of the resulting fragments is smaller than the mass of the original nuclide plus the captured neutron, and the mass difference (mass defect) is emitted in the form of several kinds of radiation. Among the fragments there are free neutrons which, in turn, can be captured. In this way a so-called chain reaction can develop, leading either to an explosive reaction (atomic bomb) or to a controlled reaction (nuclear reactor), depending on the conditions.

The third process is nuclear fusion, in particular the fusion of hydrogen nuclides into helium. This process is the principal source of energy for the radiation of the Sun. On Earth, it has so far only been used in the production of hydrogen bombs; the numerous large-scale efforts to effectuate controlled fusion reactions have not yet been successful.

The last process is the annihilation of matter and anti-matter, *e.g.* of an electron and a positron, or of a proton and an anti-proton.
This process is by far the most efficient one, as here the total combined mass of the interacting particles is transformed into radiation energy. Unfortunately, it has so far only been observed under laboratory conditions, and no technically feasible applications are expected for the near future.

Until now, only the first two processes discussed above have been applied in the construction of nuclear power sources (NPS) to be used in outer space. The radio-isotope thermo-electric generator (RTG) is based upon the radio-active decay of suitable nuclides, whereas the nuclear reactor uses a controlled fission reaction. Both are presently in use as energy suppliers on board various spacecraft, all of them together generating up to a thousand kW of electric power. So far, they have only been used for the operation of spacecraft systems and instruments, not for propulsion purposes.

Since 1961 the USA have launched 21 satellites and space stations carrying an RTG on board. Only one US satellite, SNAP 10A, which was launched in 1965 and is still in orbit, was equipped with a nuclear reactor producing over 0.5 kW of electric power during 43 days[35]. At present, a new type of reactor with a capacity of 10 to 100 kWe is being developed in the US SP-100 programme[36]. This reactor is supposed to be ready for use in the early 1990's. As to the Soviet space programme, it is assumed that, starting in late 1967, so far some 20 to 30 Cosmos satellites carrying a nuclear reactor have been launched, and that these launches will continue at a yearly rate between 2 and 4[37].

2.3.2 Radio-isotope Thermo-electric Generators (RTGs)

RTGs are composed of radio-active fuel surrounded by energy conversion and transmission systems. In theory, quite a number of radio-isotopes could be used as fuel for an RTG, but in practice only a few are suitable in view of the severe restrictions set by space missions[38].

One restriction concerns the conversion of the emitted radiation, first into heat, and then into electricity. In order to facilitate this conversion the radiation has to be easily absorbable. Since in most cases only the so-called alpha-radiation satisfies this demand, the successful candidate-isotope must be an alpha-emitter.
Thus, the choice is limited to a few radio-isotopes only, such as:
polonium (Po-210; half-time 138 d; specific power 135 W/g);
curium (Cm-242; half-time 163 d; specific power 100 W/g);
plutonium (Pu-238; half-time 87 d; specific power 0.54 W/g).
The 'half-time' of a radio-active nuclide is the period of time during which half of any number of nuclides present at a certain moment will decay.
Both polonium and curium have been used only for short-duration missions, due to their short half-times. Curium, in addition, has the disadvantage of intense gamma radiation and neutron fluxes which violate safety requirements during the construction and integration phases of the RTG. So, in most cases Pu-238 fuel is used for space RTGs, e.g. in the Apollo lunar missions and in the Viking, Pioneer and Voyager outer solar system space probes. The thermal power of these RTGs lies between 1,000 and 2,400 W (1 and 2.4 kW), and the resulting electric power between 70 and 150 W. If more power is needed in combination with a required lifetime of more than, e.g., one week, a nuclear reactor has to be employed.

2.3.3 Nuclear Reactors

A nuclear reactor derives its thermal energy from the controlled fission of some suitable atomic nucleus, such as the uranium isotope U-235. The term 'fission' denotes a process whereby the U-235 nuclide is transformed into U-236 by capturing a neutron. This nuclide is unstable and will split up into a few smaller fragments. Part of the energy liberated during the fragmentation process is thermal in nature, part of it, however, takes the form of ionizing radiation similar to that emitted by the decay of radio-active isotopes. Most of this radiation (both thermal and ionizing) can be absorbed as heat and subsequently be converted into electric energy[39].

As to the lifetime and power level of a nuclear reactor there are at present practically no limitations. An important factor in this respect is that the total weight of a nuclear reactor increases only little in relation to its power output. So, *e.g.*, with a certain type of reactor unit a power level increase from 1 to 4 kW corresponds to a weight increase from 300 to 400 kg. Usually a nuclear reactor is more attractive than any other power source in space for output levels above 25 kW. Nuclear reactors generating approximately 100 kW are already being developed and will possibly lead to a new era in space power technology.

2.4 Safety Measures Connected with the Use of Nuclear Power Sources in Outer Space

In view of the fact that both types of NPS contain strongly radio-active materials, such as plutonium, uranium, or their fission products, carefully designed safety measures have to be observed during all phases of their construction and lifetime.

It should be emphasized here that in this respect an NPS is fundamentally different from any other object to be used in a space vehicle: since an NPS is capable of emitting ionizing radiation it can be detrimental and even lethal to anybody coming near the emitting material.

If a satellite fragment should reach the ground after re-entry, it might damage somebody or something at impact, and in the case of its being a non-radioactive object nothing else would follow. However, in case it should be a radioactive fragment, a continuous danger to living organisms would remain for quite some time afterwards (from some months to several years). If a radio-active fragment fell down in or near a remote inhabited area without direct communication with the outside world, it might be found by local people unaware of the hazardous radiation it emits. In case this had happened with some of the most radio-active fragments of Cosmos 954, these people might easily have received more than lethal doses of radiation after only a few hours of close contact with the object.

Depending on the type of NPS and the fuel material to be used, the safety measures should cover the construction of the NPS, its integration into the spacecraft, the launching phase, the operational lifetime of the satellite, and the expected future development of its orbit. The last two of these phases only require attention in cases where the spacecraft might be expected to return to Earth at a time when the level of its ionizing radiation is still high enough to involve a danger to man. This is not the case with orbits at altitudes of at least about 1,000 km above the Earth and with deep space missions (*e.g.* to the Moon or the other planets) without planned return to Earth.

In order to assess the degree of damage to human beings as a result of exposure to ionizing radiation, it is necessary to know the effects of this radiation on living organisms. Radiation basically consists of particles (either electrically neutral or electrically charged) or photons (quanta of electromagnetic radiation with an energy which is proportional to the frequency of the radiation and inversely proportional to its wavelength). These particles and photons are generally capable of being absorbed by matter, or, more specifically, by the individual atoms and molecules of which it consists. Frequently, the absorption by a molecule will result in its dissociation, *i.e.* its breaking up into smaller molecules and/or individual atoms, whereas the absorption by an atom might result in its ionization, *i.e.* in the breaking away from the atom of one or more negatively charged electrons, as a result of which the atom is transformed into a positively charged ion. Radiation capable of producing this latter effect is called 'ionizing radiation'.

If an atom which has been ionized belongs to the molecular structure of a living organism, its properties with respect to the functioning of this organism will have changed drastically. Organisms normally contain tremendous numbers of atoms. If only a few of those are ionized, no noticeable harm will be done to the organism. As a matter of fact, all living organisms are permanently exposed to a small amount of radiation, either of cosmic origin or emitted by radio-active substances contained in the Earth's crust and atmosphere. Since these organisms were developed within this so-called 'natural radiation environment' or 'background radiation', it is obvious that they must be capable of overcoming any harm resulting from it. This is, however, no longer true for amounts of radiation which by far exceed this natural background.
In recent times, man has not only discovered the existence of naturally radioactive substances in nature (since a number of elements have both stable and radio-active isotopes, it is customary to call these substances 'radio-active isotopes'), but he has also developed techniques to isolate them and to produce them in high concentrations, thereby considerably enhancing their radiation intensity. In addition, he has developed methods to produce very intense artificial ionizing radiation, *e.g.* as a by-product of nuclear explosions or, in a less catastrophic way, through the controlled production of nuclear energy in nuclear reactors. Thus, a situation has arisen in which exposure to highly excessive amounts of radiation has become a real possibility. Therefore it is imperative to study the effects of ionizing radiation on man and to take measures to prevent him from being exposed to those effects which are found to be harmful.

Twice, in 1972 and in 1977, the United Nations Scientific Committee on the Effects of Atomic Radiation published a report on the 'Sources and Effects of Ionizing Radiation'. The following considerations are based on the latter of these two reports[40].

Two categories of effects of relatively low doses of radiation are considered in the report: those on the irradiated individual (somatic effects), and those on his/her progeny (genetic effects). Effects of heavy doses are not considered in this report. The aim of this study has been to estimate the frequency (or probability) with which certain harmful effects follow the exposure to a certain dose of radiation.

In most cases the harmful effects identified in the report consist of malignant diseases, such as several forms of leukaemia and cancer. Many of the results presented have been based on studies of surviving victims of the atomic bombs exploded over the Japanese cities of Hiroshima and Nagasaki in August 1945. In addition, a number of studies based on animal experiments have been considered. The results obtained from the Japanese victims are fairly accurate, since they involve a large group of individuals (several tens of thousands) exposed to a broad range of doses, and they had been observed for some thirty years at the time of the conclusion of the study. It should, however, be remarked here that recent reports state still new, unexpected after-effects, discovered nearly forty years after the exposure[41]. As to the results obtained with animals, these are substantially less accurate.

For the somatic carcinogenic effects the results are that for every rad (a dose of radiation equal to 0.01 Gray; 1 Gray = 1 wattsec./kg for the radiating object) absorbed 2 out of every 100,000 persons exposed will develop leukaemia, and about 10 will suffer from some other kind of malignant disease. Individuals exposed during their embryonal phase (*i.e.* between conception and birth) also show some after-effects, such as a reduction in body size. Here, however, the information available is far less conclusive.

Genetic effects usually comprise various physical and mental diseases and aberrations caused by mutations involving alterations in the elementary units of heredity localized within the chromosomes. The report estimates that for every rad of exposure nearly 200 out of every million live-born children (about a third of which are from the first generation) will show some form of genetic damage.

For higher doses it is estimated in a study by Professor Meissner[42] from the Research Institute for Experimental Biology and Medicine at Borstel (FRG) that the occurrence of radiation diseases increases from less than 1% at a dose of about 80 rem (a radiation dose comparable in most cases to the rad) to nearly 100% at 300 rem, whereas the expected death toll will increase from less than 1% at about 200 rem to nearly 100% at about 700 rem.

The studies mentioned above involve only known risks of ionizing radiation contacted by human individuals.

2.4.2   Safety Measures for RTGs

A radio-active thermo-electric generator is fuelled with naturally radio-active material, as described in sec. 2.3.2. This fuel emits ionizing radiation as soon as it has been produced and continues to do so throughout its subsequent life. For a given amount of fuel the level of its radiation decreases with time at a rate determined by the half-time of the radio-active isotope involved, *i.e.* by a factor of two after a period of time equal to this half-time. A similar decrease of its power output will follow, since the output of the RTG is proportional to the amount of radiation absorbed by the energy conversion system. So, after a period of one or at most a few half-times, the RTG will no longer produce enough energy to satisfy the demands of the spacecraft systems, thereby ending its operational lifetime. As, however, the output level of the ionizing radiation initially was exceedingly toxic, it will remain toxic even after having been reduced by several factors of two (after several half-times), *i.e.* for a period of time extending quite far beyond the end of the operational life of the spacecraft[43].

In order to maintain radiation safety the radio-isotope heat source of an RTG is shielded by a special containment system. It is designed to prevent, with a very high degree of reliability, the leakage of radio-isotope fuel both under ordinary and extraordinary conditions. Even in case the RTG should crash onto the surface of the Earth after its re-entry into the atmosphere, it is designed to remain intact and to be recovered safely. Should the RTG fall into water, it is designed to withstand corrosion for a sufficiently long period of time.

In spite of these precautions some cases might meet extremely unfavourable circumstances, such as an impact upon some very compact and hard object, which could lead to the destruction of the containment system and the subsequent leakage of radio-active material. Nevertheless, if the fuel container is well designed in conformity with the safety regulations, the probability of such a failure should be rather small. Moreover, it should be noted that radio-active emission from an RTG is not strongly penetrating and will, in general, not constitute a danger to persons, provided they do not come into close contact with it.

A safety problem of a more general character connected with the re-entry of an RTG is that of its recovery. In some cases one may be able to locate the RTG's impact point accurately enough, so that it can be recovered sufficiently soon afterwards. In other cases, however, if the exact impact site cannot be located immediately, detailed and expensive search and recovery operations will have to be carried out.

2.4.3 Safety Measures for Nuclear Reactors

One characteristic which is important for NPS safety considerations is that a nuclear reactor generates radio-activity by means of controlled fission of appropriate nuclides ('man-made' radio-activity). This means that a reactor will only emit ionizing radiation after it has been activated by starting the fission process, unlike an RTG which - since it produces 'natural' radio-activity - is always 'active', even during the construction phase. Thus, from the point of view of radiation safety, a nuclear reactor is absolutely safe from the very beginning of its construction up to the moment when it starts being operated. Only from this moment the reactor becomes radio-active and remains so for at least

several hundreds of years. Of course it is possible to close down the reactor after a certain period of time and thereby to stop the fission process. This, however, only prevents the reactor from increasing its level of ionizing radiation;
the level of radio-activity which already exists at that moment remains and de-
cays only slowly with time.

Another aspect regarding safety considerations for NPS is that, in case of an
accident, ionizing radiation emanating from a nuclear reactor has a wider
range than radiation from, *e.g.*, an RTG, and, corresponding to its higher power level, it will be much stronger. Thus, it is even more important than in the
case of an RTG that a fully activated nuclear reactor should be prevented from
crashing upon the Earth[44].

In the establishment of adequate safety regulations for this type of NPS a number of steps can be distinguished. First of all, it has to be ensured that a nuclear
reactor on board a satellite is not activated before the satellite's working orbit
has been reached. In this way, the possibility of any radiological hazard resulting from a launching failure can be excluded.

If the altitude of the working orbit is at least 1,000 km or more, there is practically no chance that an unscheduled re-entry of the satellite will take place.
The satellite will remain in orbit for at least about one thousand years, and, due
to natural orbital decay within such a period of time the ionizing radiation
emitted by the reactor has dropped to a sufficiently low level to exclude any radiological hazard that might result from a re-entry.

If, however, the working orbit lies substantially below the 1,000 km safety limit
and an unscheduled return is expected, or if the satellite is scheduled to return
to Earth intact either from a 'safe' or from an 'unsafe' orbit, special precautions
will have to be taken to ensure that no radiological hazard may accompany the
return of the satellite.
A solution to this problem can be to separate the radio-active parts from the
rest of the satellite and to boost them up to a safe long-duration orbit in order
to prevent their return to Earth, at least for the next one thousand years. In that
case, only the non-radio-active parts of the satellite will re-enter the Earth's atmosphere, probably burning up in the process. Since 1978, after the Cosmos
954 accident, this procedure has evidently been adopted for most of the Soviet
Cosmos satellites carrying NPS[45]. If this manoeuvre fails, and a return to Earth
of the satellite's radio-active parts becomes unavoidable, back-up procedures
may ensure the dispersion of the reactor fuel into fine particles at a sufficiently
high altitude to prevent their rapid return to Earth. Two methods are considered to be practicable in this respect. The first method consists of the separa-
tion of the reactor core containing the fuel from the reactor itself: during re-entry the core is heated up by aerodynamic friction and is vaporized. In the second case, dispersion is achieved by means of a chemical reaction leading to the
dissolution of the fuel, followed by the ejection and scattering of the solution
products.

For the time being the advantages and disadvantages of these procedures are not fully understood. While they have the positive effect of preventing a nuclear reactor's intact re-entry and impact on the ground, they have the disadvantage of not being able to *destroy* the radio-activity completely: they only disperse the radio-active material, which then slowly descends to the ground. So far, there has been no evidence that such radio-active clouds produce significant and disquieting increases beyond the natural background radiation level. On the other hand, as long as this possibility can theoretically not be excluded, safety measures still have to be taken. This, for example, was the case with the SNAP 9A accident[46] when extensive investigations were carried out for years to ensure that no damage would be caused by the liberated radio-active cloud.

2.5   The Probability of Accidents Involving NPS in Outer Space

In the preceding sections we have outlined in general terms some aspects of the use of nuclear power sources in outer space. We have discussed the construction of NPS, the development of outer space missions, some of the hazards connected with the use of NPS, as well as some safety measures designed to prevent accidents. In the following section we will consider the question of the chances that such accidents may actually occur, and the probable number of victims involved in them.

It has to be pointed out, however, that our deliberations are based on two essential preconditions:

1.   that the use of NPS is accompanied by the application of all of the safety measures which are recognized at present (see sec. 2.4 above)

2.   that the conditions for the use of NPS are at least as good as at present (optimal staff, most modern launching site, sufficient financial security for the respective project to be carried out, etc.).

When judging the statements made in the following with regard to the probability of an NPS accident, these two factors have to be borne in mind.

A major difficulty encountered in the determination of an accident probability for NPS is that so far only a few tens of them have been launched by both of the large space powers (as has been described in secs. 2.1.1.3, 2.1.2, and 2.3.1 above). In the USA, from 1961 until 1983, 22 launches involving an NPS have taken place: only one of them was a nuclear reactor, all the others were RTGs. In two cases a failure occurred during the launching phase, resulting in the burning up of one of the RTGs in the atmosphere and the safe recovery of another from the ocean. A third RTG was buried in the South Pacific at the end of the aborted Apollo 13 lunar mission. Of the remaining 19, 5 were placed on the Moon during successful Apollo lunar missions, 6 are being used in deep space for interplanetary missions to Mars, Jupiter, and beyond, and 8 were successfully launched into long-duration Earth orbits with lifetimes of 500 years or more[47].

Officially, much less is known about the use of NPS in the space programme of the USSR. Usually the official launching announcement of a Soviet space vehicle does not indicate whether or not it is provided with an NPS. Some Western observers, however, have found indications that in 1965 two RTGs were launched with Cosmos 84 and Cosmos 90, and that from 1967 to 1984, 25 Cosmos satellites with nuclear reactors were launched, apart from two launching failures observed in 1969 and 1973[48]. These 25 satellites are of the Radar Ocean Reconnaissance type. One of them was Cosmos 954, which re-entered over Canadian territory in January 1978, another was Cosmos 1402, for which the back-up dispersal method had to be used.

In view of this lack of empirical data, the discussion of accident probabilities for NPS has to be mainly of a theoretical nature. A fairly detailed study of this problem was presented in January 1980 in a working paper submitted by the United Kingdom of Great Britain and Northern Ireland to the Scientific and Technical Sub-Committee of the United Nations Committee on the Peaceful Uses of Outer Space. To our knowledge no other studies have been published in this field. Therefore the following deliberations are largely based on this working paper[49].

2.5.1   Adopted Characteristics of Typical NPS

It is evident that the extent of the risks involved by an NPS in outer space depends on a number of factors, *i.e.* the type, the dimensions, the power output, and the construction of the NPS. In the UK working paper[49] two typical NPS are considered:

1. an RTG containing 5 kg of plutonium Pu-238 with an activity of 70,000 curies producing 2,000 watts of thermal energy and, with an overall efficiency of about 5%, some 100 watts of electric energy

2. a nuclear reactor containing 50 kg of uranium U-235 alloy with an output of 100 kW of thermal energy and 6 kW of electric energy, having reached a stable radio-activity level after 50 days of operation at constant power level.

As explained above, in the case of an RTG both the launching phase *and* the re-entry phase have to be considered from the point of view of radiation safety risks. For the launching phase several stages have been identified at which specific failures may occur, leading to the abortion of the mission. The probability that at least one of these failures will occur is estimated to be approximately 6%. Even so, only in 0.1% of the launching failures a contamination of the lower atmosphere through an explosion of the isotope fuel has to be expected. As soon as a suitable orbit has been reached by the satellite, the probability that radio-active fuel material will disperse either into the atmosphere or onto the ground (at impact) is estimated not to exceed 0.5%. This is the case since RTGs are specifically designed to survive both a launching failure and an unintentional re-entry (see sec. 2.4.2 above).

Since in the case of nuclear reactors the radiological hazards are related to the fission products rather than to the original fuel material, it may be assumed that, if a reactor is not activated before the satellite has reached its working orbit, only the re-entry phase will involve a radiation safety risk.

In contrast to RTGs, reactors are specifically designed to be dispersed upon re-entry into the higher layers of the atmosphere. The risks encountered herein involve various possible failures of this aim of dispersion. To minimize these risks safety measures include (if necessary) transfer of the satellite to a long-duration orbit after the end of its operational life in order to postpone re-entry to a time when the reactor's radio-activity will have decayed to a sufficiently low level, or ejection of the reactor fuel in order to ensure complete dispersion into fine debris high up in the atmosphere. Intact impact upon the ground is not considered an acceptable option here, because it might result either in the contamination of an area of several square kilometers, or in the explosion of the fuel, followed by the dispersal of large radio-active fragments of the reactor.

2.5.2 Release and Dispersion of Radio-active Debris

Although, as mentioned above, an RTG is usually designed to survive re-entry intact, there is a small, but non-negligible probability that this aim might not be achieved, and that part or all of the radio-active fuel contents will be dispersed in the atmosphere or near the ground. The consequences thereof depend upon the size of the particles resulting from the dispersal process: generally, most of the plutonium oxide fuel will produce particles with dimensions exceeding 100 microns (1 micron or μm equals 0.001 mm). It is assumed that during a re-entry failure at least 90% of the fuel is dispersed in the atmosphere; after a launching failure or after a failure upon impact on the ground following an intact re-entry, at most about 1% of the fuel are expected to be dispersed by prevailing winds.

As to nuclear reactors it should be recalled here that reactors are not activated until they have reached their intended orbits (see sec. 2.4.3 above). Consequently, they do not involve any radiation hazard after a launching failure. Therefore, the safety designs of nuclear reactors primarily aim at preventing the reactor from reaching the ground after re-entry. To this purpose metallic fuels are used which melt easily and burn to very small particles at sufficiently high altitude, and the satellite structure and subsystems are arranged in such a way as not to protect the core from burning up. With this design it is assumed that most if not all of the fuel is dispersed into particles smaller than about 10 microns. If it fails to do so (after an unintentional more or less intact re-entry), the result might be the fragmentation of the reactor core into a number of highly radio-active pieces, as well as the release of respirable particles into the air.

The dispersion pattern of debris produced in the atmosphere depends upon the size of the particles and the place where they were produced. Dispersion can occur at altitudes anywhere between the ground and some 100 km. Small particles (*i.e.* smaller than 10 microns) are likely to remain in the air where they were formed, following the prevailing air circulation patterns, before, in the end, they slowly precipitate to lower levels. It is assumed that radio-activity resulting from such dispersion in most cases only slightly exceeds natural radiation levels. Larger particles (100 microns or more) tend to reach the Earth within hours after their production, thereby contaminating a large area along the ground track of the satellite, determined in size and location by the prevailing winds.

In consideration of the factors explained above, the UK working paper distinguishes three categories of debris:

1. coarse debris covering an area some tens of kilometers wide and some hundreds or thousands of kilometers long

2. fine debris introduced into the higher atmosphere

3. fine debris released at ground level into the atmosphere.

For each of these categories the contamination probabilities of the environment have been assessed for different geographic and climatological conditions, taking into account the frequency of their occurrence on the Earth. However, we shall not go into these details.

2.5.3 Global Distribution Probabilities

So far, we have considered several technical aspects of the use of nuclear power sources in outer space, and particularly those which are relevant to the possible contamination of the Earth by ionizing radiation. In this sub-section we will deal with the question of how such contamination might affect the world's population in general and any individual in particular.

Generally, two ways in which a person can be exposed to ionizing radiation have to be distinguished: the exposure of the whole body to a field of radiation in its neighbourhood; and the inhalation of tiny radio-active particles from the surrounding air. The first situation is most likely to occur after a nearby impact of radio-active fragments, or after the release of dense clouds of radio-active particles subsequent to an impact. In this case, a person continues to accumulate a radiation dose until he leaves the contaminated area. The second situation will occur some time after the release of fine radio-active particles into the higher atmosphere, when these particles will have migrated slowly to air masses at ground level. Such an event leads to an increase of the natural background radiation level. Of course, in the first situation it is also possible that radio-active particles may be inhaled, but in that case it usually is the exposure to the radiation field which is the dominant factor.

The effect of the contamination hazards described above strongly depends upon the local population distribution. Some 70% of the surface of the Earth are covered by water and thus, apart from the accidental passage of ships, not populated. On land, the population density varies from a few inhabitants per km² in desert-like areas to several thousands per km² in large urban areas. Since, as we have seen in sec. 2.2.3, it is generally impossible to predict with any accuracy the location of the expected re-entry site, the impact probabilities for all existing population distributions have to be taken into account.

Apart from statistical considerations, it also has to be borne in mind that the actual effect of exposure to ionizing radiation, at least in a number of cases, depends rather strongly on the individual behaviour of the persons involved. If they are sufficiently aware of the existing dangers, they will take care to avoid any contact with located, possibly radio-active fragments and seek shelter until the fragments have been recovered by competent authorities. If they are not aware of the radiation hazard, they might search for fragments in order to collect them and to keep them *e.g.* as souvenirs, thereby running the risk of exposing themselves to lethal doses of radiation. In case that impact should occur in a populated region of a developing country, people might even become exposed to lethal doses of radiation before the site of impact has been located and rescue teams arrive on the spot to remove the radio-active fragments.

2.5.4 Results of Probability Estimates

The UK working paper[49] presents estimates of the possible hazards resulting from the use of nuclear power systems in outer space missions, based upon the considerations discussed above. The results are given in the form of the probability (f) that more than a given number of people (N) would die in either short or long term in consequence of the launching of a single NPS. Short term or early deaths involve people who die within a year as a result of exposure to lethal doses of radiation; long term or delayed deaths involve people who develop lethal diseases such as cancer or leukaemia after exposure to non-lethal doses and who die several years later. Furthermore, a distinction has been made as to types of NPS and types of missions (terrestrial or extra-terrestrial). A nuclear reactor used in an extra-terrestrial mission does not involve a radiation hazard: it is not activated until it has successfully completed the launching phase and is on its way into deep space.

The results given in Figure 4 represent a compilation of a number of figures provided by the working paper. In order to facilitate the understanding of this Figure it should be mentioned that, if $f = 10^{-3}$ for $N = 10^0$ (which is the same as $N = 1$), the probability is 0.001 that at least one person will die as a result of the launching of one single RTG, or, to put it differently, if one thousand RTG's are launched, it is almost certain that at least one person will die in consequence of these launches.

For comparative purposes the Figure includes data on the actual occurrence of unnatural deaths from other causes than NPS accidents. The original UK figure showed five separate curves: one each for aircraft accidents, marine accidents, railway accidents, fires and explosions, and mining accidents. All of

these five curves lie within the hatched area in the upper right part of Figure 4.
A sixth curve for accidents due to meteorite impacts is shown separately.

The NPS curves (RTG and reactor) can only be compared with the others provided there is only one single launch per year for each type of mission. If this is not the case, the curve for the corresponding type of mission should be multi-

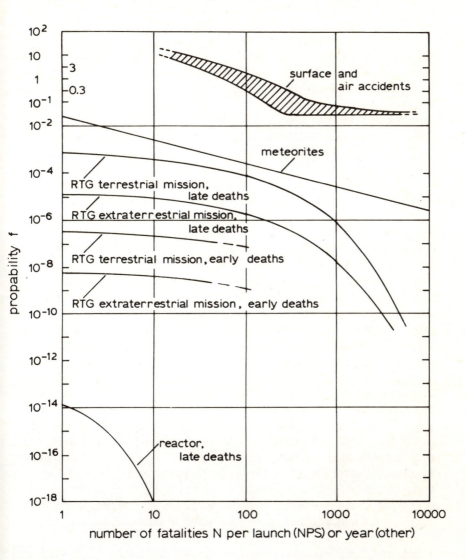

Figure 4
Estimates of the number of fatalities resulting from different types of accidents. Those involving the use of an NPS in outer space (labeled 'RTG' or 'reactor') give the probability (vertical scale) that at least N deaths (horizontal scale) will occur during one single mission of the indicated category. Early deaths are those occurring within one year after the accident; late deaths occur more than 1 year after it. For comparison, the number of casualties per year resulting from a number of other categories of accidents are included.

plied by the actual number of launches per year. In the logarithmic representation of the Figure this means shifting the curve upward (or downward) across a distance corresponding to the number of launches per year as indicated in the upper right hand corner of the Figure.

2.6   Summary of Safety Considerations; Conclusions

Before summing up the conclusions regarding safety considerations, it has to be stressed again that these conclusions can only be drawn provided that all safety measures for the use of NPS have been taken and satellites which are equipped with NPS have been launched and operated under optimal but realistic conditions. Given these circumstances, it can be stated that at present the probability of deaths resulting from an NPS accident is very small: it is less than one for every thousand efforts to launch a space vehicle equipped with an NPS. Even if these thousand launches all occurred within one year, the total number of deaths to be expected as a result would only just become comparable to the number of casualties from other, common type accidents. Since it seems highly unlikely that for NPS-carrying space vehicles a launching frequency of the order of one thousand per year will be attained in the foreseeable future, the present casualty risk seems to be acceptable, at least for the time being.

Still, this conclusion is drawn from the *statistical* point of view. While, on the one hand, civilizationary damages only affect the victims immediately concerned in an accident, NPS accidents, on the other hand, may under certain conditions also concern subsequent generations and their environment[50]. With some kinds of radio-active damage harmful effects have been observed through to the third generation. For this reason the two types of accidents are not in every case comparable as regards the *nature* of the risks and the specific type of consequences involved.

Moreover, some of the factors included in the procedures by which the present probability figures were obtained could under certain circumstances lead to less favourable figures in the future. The present estimates were based upon two distinct NPS: an RTG with an electric power output of 100 watts, and a nuclear reactor with an electric power output of 6 kilowatts. Particularly as to the nuclear reactor it may well be possible that much more powerful devices of that type will be developed and used in the future, *e.g.* reactors with an output of 100 kW, as they are being developed in the US SP-100 programme[36]. This development may aggravate the casualty risk in case of failures.

When evaluating this casualty risk, however, not only statistical aspects should be taken into account. It should also be considered that the *risk involved in an activity must remain in an acceptable proportion to the benefit resulting from it*[51]. With a great number of common type risks this proportion is given in so far as the risk and the benefit of the activity are confined to the nation that creates them. Even under extreme conditions the risk might at most involve the neighbouring State or neighbouring States.

Yet, in the case of NPS satellites which circle the Earth in low orbits the situation is different. Again the receiver of the benefits of the activity normally is the

launching State and, under certain conditions, other States co-operating with
it. The risk, however, involves *all* of the States that are overflown by the satellite in its given orbit. Thus, a situation arises in which these States, although they are not being consulted or even informed in advance, and although they themselves will, as a rule, not derive any benefit from those launches (in cases where nuclear powered space vehicles are intended to be used for military purposes one can even say that the opposite is true), will automatically be exposed to any risk connected with the re-entry of such an NPS into the Earth's atmosphere.

It follows that any risk/benefit calculation regarding NPS satellites must not be judged on the same level with risk/benefit calculations for other, common type activities. In view of the special character of nuclear power sources it seems imperative that their use in outer space be governed by carefully designed and detailed international regulations.

2.7. Deliberations in the United Nations: UNCOPUOS Scientific and Technical Sub-Committee[52]

The debate relating to the use of NPS in outer space within the Scientific and Technical Sub-Committee was opened in 1978 - immediately after the Cosmos 954 accident - and has been treated as a priority item since 1980.
In the following, we shall give an outline of the discussions in this Sub-Committee and a summary of its conclusions and recommendations since 1978. In order to avoid repetition, specific details of the debate as regards technical aspects and problems relating to the use of NPS in outer space shall not be restated in this section; for detailed information see secs. 2.2 - 2.5 above.

2.7.1 Sessions in 1978[53] and 1979[54]

In 1978, the NPS discussion was initiated by the Cosmos 954 accident, which had occurred about 10 days before the first meeting of the Sub-Committee's 1978 session. There was a heated debate about the implications of this event and especially about the steps to be taken as a possible response to these implications. Several proposals were made to this purpose, as *e.g.* the establishment of an *ad hoc* working group for the safety aspects of the use of NPS in outer space and a *moratorium* for nuclear reactors in near Earth orbits until an investigation about the risks involved would have been carried out and safety measures would have been elaborated. But, in spite of the request of most delegations that the Sub-Committee should take immediate action during its 1978 session, a consensus could not be reached.

In 1979, the Scientific and Technical Sub-Committee finally established a Working Group on the Use of NPS in Outer Space in accordance with General Assembly Resolution 33/16 of November 10, 1978. The Working Group discussed the technical aspects relating to the use of NPS (types of NPS, prediction of the re-entry path of malfunctioning NPS-satellites, etc.) as well as possible safety measures for NPS.

76 On the basis of these deliberations the Working Group came to the following agreements, which are laid down in paras. 13, 14, 15 of its report:

1. Appropriate measures for radiation protection should be derived principally from the existing, and internationally accepted, basic standards recommended by the International Commission on Radiological Protection (ICRP) in particular ICRP Document No. 26. These measures should be taken for protection during *all phases* of an orbital mission of a spacecraft with nuclear power sources: launch, parking orbit, operational orbit or re-entry (Para. 13) (emphasis added)

2. The safety of radio-isotope systems is being assured by designing them to contain the radio-isotope for all normal and abnormal conditions. The design should ensure minimal leakage of the radio-active contents and must at least meet the limits recommended by the ICRP *in all circumstances* including launch accidents, re-entry into the atmosphere, impact and prolonged water immersion (Para. 14) (emphasis added)

3. Reactor systems should be started and operated in orbits sufficiently high to give time for radio-active materials to decay to a safe level in space after the end of mission. *In this way the dose equivalents at the time of re-entry could be guaranteed in all circumstances to be within the limits recommended by the ICRP for non-accident conditions.* If reactors are intended for use in low orbits where the radio-active materials do not have sufficient time to decay to an acceptable level, safety depends on the start of the operation in orbit and the success of boosting nuclear power sources to a higher orbit after operation is completed. In the event of an unsuccessful boost into higher orbit the system must in all circumstances be capable of dispersing the radio-active material so that when the material reaches the Earth the radiological hazard conforms to the recommendations of the ICRP (Para. 15) (emphasis added).

The Working Group recommended that assistance should be provided in training on hazard evaluation following the re-entry of an NPS, and on performing pertinent search and recovery and emergency planning operations. This assistance in training should be given through appropriate international channels to the personnel of the States requesting it (para. 31).

Finally the Working Group came to the following conclusion:

1. NPS can be used safely in outer space provided that the safety considerations mentioned above (paras. 13, 14, 15) are met in full

2. The decision to use NPS in outer space should be based on technical considerations provided that safety requirements can be met while satisfying mission requirements.

The conclusion of the NPS Working Group in the Scientific and Technical Committee stating that NPS can be used 'safely' in outer space seems to be basically correct for the time being. Of course, it has to be understood that 'safe' does not mean 'absolutely safe'; even if all safety measures are applied to the use of NPS, the risk involved will under present conditions never be zero - although it will be relatively small compared with other, common type risks[55]. Therefore, the Working Group's conclusion that NPS can be used 'safely' has to be interpreted in the sense that the risk involved in the use of NPS is supposed to be 'acceptable'.

The use of the term 'acceptable', however, is extremely problematic, as it depends on a number of factors such as *e.g.* a risk-benefit analysis. This analysis might not be the same for the launching State as for other States which do not participate in the particular space programme, since only the launching State draws a positive net *benefit* from the use of NPS. Nevertheless, the *risk* involved in the use of an NPS does not only affect the launching State but all States which are overflown by the spacecraft equipped with the NPS. As the Working Group's conclusion does not make a distinction in this respect either, we have to interpret the term 'safely' once more, in the sense that it does not only apply to the launching State but to all members of the international community.

But, even if we agree with this interpretation of the Working Group's conclusion, we have to make the reservation that this conclusion might be judged quite differently in case the present conditions for the use of NPS should change; *e.g.* if the power level of nuclear reactors were 6-10 times higher than it is at present (such developments might already be expected for the 1990's)[56], or if the number of NPS satellites in near Earth orbits were increased. These factors might considerably augment the risk involved by NPS as regards the Earth's population and environment and consequently influence any conclusions about the acceptance of this risk and the 'safe' use of NPS in general (as explained in sec. 2.5 above). Such possible developments, however, were neither reflected in the conclusions drawn by the Working Group in 1979 nor in those of the following sessions.

As to paras. 13, 14, 15 of the Working Group's report, which are referred to in the above-mentioned Working Group's conclusion, more problems arise. They shall be explained in the following.

The safety measures mentioned in paras. 13-15 refer to the internationally accepted basic standards recommended by the ICRP, and especially to ICRP Document 26[57]. This document formulates the fundamental principles upon which appropriate radiation protection measures can be based - although detailed guidance as to their application (*e.g.* regulations or codes of practice) is not given.

78   In para. 12 of Document 26 the following system of dose limitation is recommended:

1.   No practice shall be adopted unless its introduction produces a positive net benefit

2.   All exposures shall be kept as low as reasonably achievable, economic and social factors being taken into account

3.   The dose equivalent to individuals shall not exceed the limits recommended for the appropriate circumstances by the Commission.

As to exposure limits for populations, paras. 129-132 recommend that the annual dose equivalent limit for workers should be 50 mSv (5 rem) body dose or equivalent doses to parts of the body. The annual dose equivalent limit for the most highly exposed members of the public (critical group) should be 5 mSv from all man-made sources.

Regarding the application of ICRP Document 26 on the use of NPS in outer space, and especially the recommended maximum radiation exposure levels, there does not seem to be any problem, provided that the NPS is working under normal conditions. In case of an accident, however, reference to the ICRP exposure levels does not always seem to be realistic. Of course it is *desirable* that the ICRP radiation levels should not be exceeded even under abnormal conditions. But this can never be guaranteed in case of an accident under extremely unfavourable conditions. Here the Cosmos 954 accident might again be cited as an example: one fragment of the satellite, which was found about one month after its crash over Canada, had the (lethal) radiation level of 500 r/h, which is 100 times higher than the maximum annual radiation level of 5 rem permitted for the most highly exposed members of the public[58]. This accident happened in spite of the fact that all precautionary measures had been taken. Consequently, it cannot be ensured that according to para. 15 of the Working Group's report '... dose equivalents ... be guaranteed *in all circumstances* to be within the limits recommended by the ICRP ...'(emphasis added).
Moreover, the authors of ICRP Document 26 themselves were well aware of the limitations of their recommendations and of the impossibility to guarantee safe dose limits in case of accidents, as is testified in paras. 133, 134, 135, 242, and 243.

Therefore it is evident that although the Working Group's conclusion applies to all phases of an orbital mission - accidents included - the conclusion only considers accidents under *ideal* circumstances, *i.e.* accidents with which all safety measures provided for such an emergency will work correctly and with which the ICRP recommendations can be observed. An accident, however, which does not present such an ideal case, is not dealt with in the Working Group's conclusion - even though the examination of this specific problem would have been of great importance to the future work of the Outer Space Committee.

In 1980 the Working Group discussed the following items:

1.   Elaboration of an inventory of the safety problems involved in the use of nuclear power sources in outer space

2.   Implementation of the International Commission on Radiological Protection (ICRP) recommendations for populations and the environment in the context of space vehicles utilizing NPS

3.   Evaluation of existing methods in understanding orbital mechanics to determine if improvements may be made in predicting re-entry phenomena

4.   Definition of technical considerations with regard to a format for notification.

Furthermore, the discussion of the Working Group's previous session was continued.

As to item 2 of the NPS discussion (implementation of the ICRP recommendations) the Working Group re-affirmed the agreement laid down in para. 13 of its previous report of 1979. As a next step, the Working Group agreed that in each case, prior to launch, an assessment of the collective and individual dose equivalent commitments had to be carried out for all planned phases of a space mission with an NPS.

Appropriate guidelines were provided in ICRP Publication 26, paras. 129-132, on exposure of populations. The Working Group recommended that the ICRP dose limits should *not be exceeded during any phase of an NPS mission* (para. 12 of the 1980 report).

Furthermore, the Working Group re-affirmed the statement previously agreed upon in para. 15 of its 1979 report (relating to operational safety measures and safety design of nuclear reactors).

As to item 4 of the NPS discussion (notification), the Working Group agreed that it was the responsibility of those States which launch space vehicles utilizing NPS to conduct safety tests and evaluations.

Finally, the Working Group re-affirmed its conclusion of 1979 in a slightly modified version stating that 'NPS can be used safely in outer space provided that all necessary safety requirements are met'.

When looking at this conclusion we realize that this statement was not linked any closer to the paras. 13-15 of the 1979 report as it was the case in the 1979 conclusion. However, the agreements laid down in paras. 13 and 15 of the 1979 report (referring to the ICRP recommendations) were re-affirmed separately. So the problems outlined above in sec. 2.7.2 remained.

In 1981 the following items were discussed in the NPS Working Group:

1. Types of NPS

2. Recommendations of the ICRP

3. Notification

4. Orbit Prediction

5. Search and Recovery.

As to item 2 of the discussion (recommendations of the ICRP) the Working Group re-affirmed its agreement relating to operational safety measures and the safety design of nuclear reactors (para. 15 of the 1979 report). However, the Working Group made a slight modification in the last sentence of the agreed text, saying that the radiological situation should conform to the ICRP recommendations 'when relevant'. An explanation for this change might be seen in the passage following the agreement in the 1981 report of the Working Group: 'The Working Group noted that ICRP Publication 26 does not provide specific guidance for accidents and emergencies although it does address in general terms the circumstances in which remedial action might be taken'.

Furthermore, the Group repeated its agreement of 1979, as laid down in para. 13 of its report, relating to appropriate measures for radiation protection. With regard to dose limits recommended by the ICRP the Working Group re-affirmed its recommendation laid down in para. 12 of the 1980 report.

As to item 3 of the discussion (notification), the Working Group agreed on the following notification format:

1. *System parameters*
    * 1.1 Name of launching State or States including the address of the authority which may be contacted for additional information or assistance in case of accident
    * 1.2 International designation
    * 1.3 Date and territory or location of launch
      1.4 Information required for best prediction of orbit lifetime, trajectory and impact region
    * 1.5 General function of spacecraft

2. *Information on the radiological risk of nuclear power source(s)*
      2.1 Type of NPS: radio-isotopic/reactor
      2.2 The probable physical form, amount and general radiological char-

---

* Denotes the requirements in the Convention on the Registration of Objects Launched in Outer Space (art. IV)

acteristics of the fuel and contaminated and/or activated components likely to reach the ground. The term 'fuel' refers to the nuclear
material used as the source of heat or power.

This notification format is of great practical importance, as no international regulation exists which is specifically designed for cases where a malfunctioning satellite re-enters the Earth's atmosphere. Only the General Assembly Resolution 33/16 requests 'launching States to inform States concerned in the event that a space object with nuclear power sources on board is malfunctioning with a risk of re-entry of radio-active materials to the Earth'[61]. As to details of such an information, however, the resolution remains silent. In 1983, this format became the basis of the discussions of the Legal Sub-Committee when elaborating legal norms relating to the use of NPS in outer space. During this session, agreement was reached in the Legal Sub-Committee about this text, and it was also unanimously agreed upon during the session of the Main Committee in 1983[62].

As to item 5 of the Working Group's debate (search and recovery), the Group repeated its recommendation of 1979, as laid down in para. 31 of its report. Finally, the Working Group re-affirmed its conclusion that 'NPS can be used safely in outer space provided that all necessary requirements are met'.
After the conclusion of the 1981 session, the NPS Working Group was suspended as in its own view it had concluded its work. Nevertheless, the item NPS remained on the agenda of the Scientific and Technical Sub-Committee.

2.7.5 Sessions 1982 through 1984[63,64,65]

After the suspension of the NPS Working Group in 1981, the use of NPS was still discussed within the Sub-Committee on a priority basis. Especially in 1983 the debates were influenced by recent events, *i.e.* the crash of Cosmos 1402 (part 3 of the satellite re-entered the Earth's atmosphere during the session of the Scientific-Technical Sub-Committee). But no agreement could be reached relating to the technical aspects of the use of NPS, or possible safety measures which could prevent future NPS accidents, or at least reduce possible harmful consequences for the population of the Earth and its environment (*e.g.* a *moratorium* for the use of NPS in near Earth orbits until internationally agreed legal regulations would have been adopted).

In 1984, the NPS Working Group was, finally, reconvened in order to study a number of problems which *i.a.* had become relevant after the Cosmos 1402 accident in 1982/83.
These were

1. Safety aspects relating to the use of NPS in outer space

2. Monitoring and intervention in case of releases of radio-active material

3. Questions relating to notification of States in case of an NPS accident.

82 On the basis of the discussions of these topics the Working Group recommended that the Secretary-General be requested to invite Member States to submit any views and suggestions they might have concerning questions to be considered in further studies by the Working Group during the next session of the Sub-Committee. In that context, the Working Group identified the following subjects relating to radiological risks and environmental impact, safety and reliability, information and emergency planning:

1. Accumulation of radio-active material dispersed in the upper atmosphere as a consequence of re-entry

2. Physical and chemical composition, injection, transport and dispersion of various radio-active nuclides in the space and time domains

3. Question of assessing the safety and reliability of the use of nuclear power sources

4. Methods, form and frequency of communication of notification

5. Emergency procedures and action plans in case of unplanned re-entry of NPS.

From these items, which are to be dealt with by the NPS Working Group, especially item no. 1 might be of growing relevance to the deliberations on the probability of NPS accidents and the discussion of effective safety measures for the use of NPS. As already pointed out in our safety considerations it is often stated that an NPS can burn up 'completely' upon re-entry into the Earth's atmosphere. For evidence, the SNAP 9A accident and the re-entry of Cosmos 1402 are referred to (see secs. 2.1.2 and 2.1.1.2 above). Still, this term does *not* imply that the radio-active fuel contained in the NPS is likewise destroyed. It is only dispersed into fine particles in the upper atmosphere and descends to the Earth in the form of a radio-active cloud. This has been confirmed by measurements taken after the above-mentioned accidents. Scientists *assume* that the respective quantities of radio-active material descending on different parts of the Earth in these and similar cases are negligible. However, no studies of this problem have been published so far. Particularly the question whether and to what extent harmful consequences will have to be expected if

— a greater number of NPS re-enters the Earth's atmosphere per year and

— the respective NPS contains larger quantities of radio-active material

lacks analysis. (As is known, nuclear reactors with an output of approx. 100 kW are already being constructed, while at present reactors with a power output of 10-15 kW are employed.) Studies of the NPS Working Group in this field might be of great importance to the future NPS discussion.

Apart from the identification of subjects to be further studied by the Sub-Committee, the Working Group re-affirmed its conclusions contained in its previous reports, particularly in that of its 3rd session. In this session a notification format and procedure had been drawn up which were used as a basis for the elaboration of a consensus text in the 1983-session of the Legal Sub-Committee (see secs. 2.7.4 above and 2.8.5 below). This work will be continued under item no. 4, which will be studied by the NPS Working Group in 1985.

2.8 Deliberations in the UNCOPUOS Legal Sub-Committee[66]

2.8.1 Sessions 1978 through 1980[67,69]

The discussion of problems relating to the use of NPS in outer space was taken up in the Legal Sub-Committee in 1978 - the year of the Cosmos 954 accident. However, in 1978 and 1979 the issue was neither dealt with by a special working group of the Legal Sub-Committee nor even under a separate item of the agenda, but during the general debate and the discussion of "other matters". Consequently, the time available for the discussion of this topic was seriously restricted.

In 1978, the first NPS working paper[68] was presented to the Legal Sub-Committee. It was supported by 15 countries, namely Australia, Belgium, Canada, Chile, Colombia, Egypt, the Federal Republic of Germany, Iran, Italy, Japan, Kenya, Mexico, Sierra Leone, Sweden, and the United Kingdom. These countries requested the Sub-Committee to review existing international instruments with the objective of recommending any necessary additional legal measures (e.g. a further convention) concerning the use of NPS in outer space. As principal matters requiring examination and appropriate subsequent action, three issues were put forward:

1. the establishment of *safety measures* in the form of effective international standards, safeguards, and limitations for the use of NPS in outer space

2. the elaboration of detailed *notification* obligations for the launching State

3. the development of additional legal measures relating to *emergency assistance* for search, recovery and clean-up operations with respect to the re-entry of a spacecraft with an NPS on board.

In addition, the above-mentioned working paper contained the request that the Legal Sub-Committee should presently begin substantive discussion, particularly of those questions which did not require special scientific and technical study, as for example the issues of notification and emergency assistance. This would have ensured that the work of the Scientific-Technical Sub-Committee was not interfered with.

Still, the working paper was not discussed in the 1978 session of the Legal Sub-Committee, since the Sub-Committee felt uncertain about its mandate as regards the examination of legal aspects for the use of NPS. Even in 1979 it was

84   still disputed whether or not this problem should be discussed in the Legal Sub-Committee, and whether or not the elaboration of supplementary norms relating to the use of NPS was really necessary.

According to General Assembly Resolution 34/66 of December 5, 1979, the Legal Sub-Committee finally took up the NPS discussion in 1980, under the agenda item 'Review of existing international law relevant to outer space activities with a view to determining the appropriateness of supplementing such law with provisions to the use of NPS in outer space.

The discussion was opened by the Canadian delegation, which submitted a working paper already formulating legal norms for the use of NPS in outer space[70]. The paper may be summed up as follows:

Part A: *Information Concerning the Use of NPS*
           It contains provisions imposing the obligation on the launching State of an NPS satellite to notify the Secretary-General of the United Nations of a planned launch and to provide certain technical data and information on the type of NPS to be used

Part B: *Notification Prior to Re-entry*
           In case of the re-entry of an NPS satellite into the Earth's atmosphere the Secretary-General as well as potentially concerned States are to be notified. The launching State shall be obliged to provide any information that is required in order to take measures for the recovery of the nuclear power source and for the protection of the population against potential hazard

Part C: *Assistance to States*
           Containing provisions for the co-operation between and the assistance to States in case of the re-entry of an NPS satellite into the Earth's atmosphere

Part D: *Radiation Exposure Levels*
           It regulates *i.a.* the doses of radiation allowed to be emitted by an NPS satellite in case of an accident as well as technical and operational safety measures for the use of NPS in general.

The elaboration of supplementary legal norms regulating the use of NPS was supported by nearly all of the Western States, including the USA. The USSR, however, supported by most though not all socialist States, did not see any need to elaborate supplementary NPS norms. In her opinion, all of the problems potentially arising in connection with the use of NPS could adequately be handled with already existing legal norms. France, too, held the opinion that this topic should not yet be dealt with in the Outer Space Committee.

When considering the question whether or not the elaboration of supplementary norms for the use of NPS is necessary, we have to bear in mind that according to international law and space law in particular we do not have any special regulations for the use of NPS in outer space. In fact, there is no distinction made between the use of NPS satellites and any other space object - or to be more precise: between the use of NPS in outer space and any other kind of power source. Of course, we already have a number of legal norms which are of great importance to the use of NPS in outer space, as for instance Art. VII of the Outer Space Treaty and Art. II of the Liability Convention. They provide *i.a.* for the liability of the launching State - and according to the Liability Convention even *absolute* liability - for any damage caused on the surface of the Earth. According to the provisions of the Registration Convention, it is also ensured that the launching State of the space object can be identified, and a claim for compensation can be put forward to the liable party.

Yet, nowhere in space law specific regulations can be found that would account for safety measures which - in the first line - aim at the *prevention* of NPS accidents[71] instead of only taking care of the consequences resulting from such accidents.
As already pointed out in our safety considerations (see secs. 2.3 and 2.4, above), NPS accidents can be prevented under certain conditions. For instance, in cases where nuclear reactors are employed in so-called 'deep space' missions the possibility of an NPS accident can be excluded altogether if the reactor is not activated before the satellite has reached a sufficiently high and therefore 'safe' orbit, and if it is ensured that the NPS will not re-enter the Earth's atmosphere.

In other cases, however, *e.g.* if NPS are used in near Earth orbits, it is impossible completely to exclude the risk of an NPS accident. Still the risk may be reduced considerably, first of all through the application of a number of already recognized technical safety measures for the construction of NPS (see secs. 2.4.2 and 2.4.3 above). Even in cases in which an NPS has re-entered the Earth's atmosphere and a nuclear contamination seems to be unavoidable, it is still possible to limit the damage resulting from such an accident to a minimum. This could be ensured *i.a.* by timely and sufficiently detailed information about the type of NPS employed and the radio-active fuel used, so that immediate clean-up and recovery operations can be carried out effectively. Furthermore, international co-operation could ensure that emergency assistance is given to those States who are not able to have these operations carried out by their own authorities. Additional problems may result from the fact that even if emergency assistance is given to developing countries, they might not be able to carry the expenses connected with the necessary operations. Of course, these countries can claim compensation from the launching State, which legally is obliged to refund the full amount of expenses. In the meantime, however, *i.e.* from the date of the accident to the date when the claim between the launching State and the injured State will have been settled, the costs generally have to be borne by the injured State. In this connection the Cosmos 954 accident should be recalled (see sec. 2.1.1.1, above), which cost the Canadian Government approximately 14 million Can $ for search and recovery operations. It took almost two years until the Soviet Union agreed to pay only part of this sum, namely 3 million Can $ - without express acknowledgement of legal liability. Such problems could *i.a.* be solved, at least to a certain extent, by compulsory insurance for certain outer space activities and by the establishment of an international fund which would be employed to satisfy claims for compensation in case of NPS accidents.

As we have seen, NPS accidents involve a great number of legal problems which cannot be solved by the application of already existing legal norms alone. This leads to the conclusion that a detailed discussion of these problems and the elaboration of supplementary norms in order to ensure the safe use of NPS in outer space is both necessary and possible. Quite a number of NPS accidents have already occurred, illustrating the particular dangers involved in the use of NPS. Therefore, we should not wait for further accidents to happen, in retrospective view of which criteria would be found for the establishment of safety measures that - if they had been taken earlier - would have prevented these accidents or reduced the damage caused by them.
In its 1981 session the Legal Sub-Committee started its work on this issue.

2.8.3   1981 Session[72]

In 1981 the Legal Sub-Committee established a working group which should consider the 'possibility of supplementing the norms of international law relevant to the use of NPS in outer space' according to General Assembly Resolution 35/14 of November 3, 1980.

However, in spite of this mandate the debate did not center exclusively on the question whether such norms were necessary or not but already on specific details of a legal regulation.

Discussion was based on a new paper submitted by Canada, which in fact only was a slightly modified version of the Canadian paper of the previous year[73]. Further working papers had been submitted by Venezuela[74] and Italy[75].

The Venezuelan paper did not contain a textual proposal - it rather constituted an essay arguing in detail the need to supplement space law with additional NPS regulations. Still, the requests put forward in the paper largely corresponded to those of the Canadian working paper.
The Italian paper, on the other hand, regarding Part A paras. 1 and 2 of the Canadian paper proposed that the notification of the Secretary-General as well as the provision of information as formulated in A. 2 should be taken care of already two months prior to the launch of an NPS satellite (instead of only one month prior to launch, as requested in the Canadian paper). Moreover, the States potentially concerned in the re-entry of an NPS satellite into the Earth's atmosphere should not be notified as late as the moment when the re-entry can

be predicted with sufficient certainty (so the Canadian paper), but as far as possible already prior to the launch of the satellite. At least regarding these two initial issues the Italian proposal seemed hardly practicable for the time being. Since most of the NPS satellites involving a hazard because they circle in near Earth orbits are reconnaissance satellites, they are launched as occasion demands in case of international crises (*e.g.* Afghanistan). Consequently, the launch of an NPS satellite may not in every case be foreseen by the launching State two months in advance.

In addition, the Italian paper contained an amendment to the section 'Assistance to States' and an additional section E to the Canadian working paper. Section E stressed that NPS regulations in no way affected liability regulations provided by space law - which actually should go without saying.

In connection with the discussion of section D of the Canadian working paper (Radiation Exposure Levels) the USA, the United Kingdom, the Netherlands, and Brazil stated that they could accept a regulation according to which the launching State of an NPS satellite would be obliged to ensure that the radiation emitted in case of an NPS accident is restricted to a minimum. However, they stressed the view that the Canadian proposal (sec. D para. 1, first sentence) requesting that radiation exposure should not exceed the exposure levels recommended by the ICRP during all phases of space flight - accidents included - were neither acceptable nor technically practicable. They pointed out that the ICRP regulations quoted in the Canadian working paper only provided for normal operational conditions of NPS, not, however, for accidents which under certain conditions might involve losing control of the quantity of nuclear radiation emitted[76]. In this connection they stated that the second sentence of section D was equally unrealistic: it contained the request that *no radiation exposure* at all should occur in situations where a space object or debris of a space object landed outside the territory of the launching State.

2.8.4   1982 Session[77]

Discussion during this session mainly concentrated on the following issues:

1. The question whether NPS satellites should not be permitted to operate in near Earth orbits

2. Determination of maximum amounts of radiation to be emitted by an NPS satellite even in case of an accident

3. Assistance to States provided by the launching State in case of an NPS accident

4. Liability of the launching State in case of an NPS accident over foreign territory.

The Canadian working paper already submitted to the Sub-Committee in

88   1981 once again provided the basis for the deliberations in the Outer Space Committee.

Canada opened the discussion with two basic requests[78]:

(a)   NPS satellites should not be employed in near Earth orbits, and

(b)   future NPS regulations should in any case determine permissible maximum amounts of radiation. The ICRP safety regulations should be taken as a guideline.

Both of these issues were commented on in detail by the USA. As to (a) they held the opinion that NPS satellites could not on principle be banished from near Earth orbits, since certain activities could not be carried out without NPS and with e.g. solar energy instead. However, they proposed the following rules in order to restrict the danger of nuclear contamination:

(i)   The decision whether to use NPS in a given activity or not should in any case be a 'technical' one, i.e. NPS should only be used for satellites when no other power system can be employed

(ii)   In case radio-isotope batteries are used for power supply they should be designed in such a way as to prevent the release of any radio-activity with sufficient certainty - even in case of a crash. Such a design is already known by a so-called 'containment' or 'immobilization' system being used in US outer space missions

(iii) If an NPS satellite is powered by a reactor, this reactor should not be activated before the satellite has reached a sufficiently high orbit i.e. an orbit in which the satellite's lifetime amounts to several thousand years so that it cannot involve any danger to the Earth's population

(iv)   NPS satellites circling near Earth orbits should be equipped with a safety system boosting up the satellite into a higher and therefore safer orbit in case of malfunction.

The US statement was especially important for the distinction it made between the two types of nuclear power sources. As pointed out in section 2.3.1 above, the USA at present employs radio-isotope batteries, whereas the USSR mainly employs nuclear reactors. Since both of these systems have different safety designs, it seems to be reasonable to relate different types of safety regulations to the different types of NPS when setting up NPS regulations.

This, of course, may involve that after not too long a period of time technological progress will have outdated part of these regulations. As, however, it appears to be rather unlikely at present that NPS satellites will generally be banished from near Earth orbits, it seems to be desirable to elaborate sufficiently detailed NPS safety regulations.

As to the Canadian request for application of the ICRP safety regulations on
NPS accidents, which was supported by a working paper by Sweden[79], it was
repeatedly pointed out that the maximum amount of radiation determined in
ICRP Publication 26 only provides for NPS operating under *normal* conditions, but not for accidents. Moreover, it would be impossible to employ NPS
without any risk at all[80]. In order to solve this problem, the USA proposed to
focus on the category of 'acceptable risk' rather than that of 'maximum
amount of radiation'. Experts of the International Atomic Energy Agency
(IAEA) should be consulted in this matter. (It should be noted here, however,
that the IAEA's field of activity is mainly that of the *regular* use of nuclear energy and not that of accident conditions.)

Part C of the above-mentioned Canadian paper made up the major issue of the
1982 NPS discussion. It concerned the questions of assistance to States, especially developing countries, and State responsibility in case of nuclear accidents.

With regard to assistance to States the USSR held the opinion that the search,
recovery, and clean-up operations should not only constitute the duty but also
the *privilege* of the launching State of a re-entered NPS satellite. Thus it would
be ensured that the launching State would not have to pay excessive costs, and
also that the satellite would be recovered speedily and competently. This could
not be the case if other States than the launching State would undertake these
operations, since they were not acquainted with foreign satellites' construc-
tions. (This request seems to be closely linked to the experiences the USSR
made when Cosmos 954 crashed over Canada in 1978: on that occasion the
Soviet satellite was recovered by Canada and the USA without consulting Soviet experts, although the Soviet Union had offered assistance[81].)
However, Western States and also the developing countries (above all Indonesia, Brazil[82], and Nigeria[83]) strongly opposed this demand, claiming the sovereignty of the State concerned. They proposed that the State concerned should
have the right to carry out clean-up operations on its own account or through
experts of its choice, while the costs for these operations should be borne by the
launching State.
In connection with the problem of the launching State's liability in case of an
NPS accident, the interpretation of the term 'damage' was discussed. Argentina, Chile, and Brazil requested that the launching State should be liable for all
damages caused by clean-up operations as well as for 'direct' and 'indirect' damages. In this context it should be noted that the definition of 'damage' as contained in Art. I of the Liability Convention might in fact be too general and
therefore not satisfactory, especially with regard to damages resulting from radio-active contamination. For this reason it might be preferable *e.g.* to include
in the definition of 'damage' in Art. I especially those damages which are typical of nuclear accidents, such as expenses for clean-up operations including recovery and storage of radio-active NPS debris[84]; damages resulting from nuclear contamination including delayed damages affecting people, therein considering under certain circumstances psychical harm equal to physical damage. In our opinion it should be ensured in any regulation that all of these damages can be traced back in adequate causality to an NPS accident. This, how-

90   ever, at present is not provided by the terms 'direct' and 'indirect' damage as suggested in the above-mentioned proposals.

2.8.5   1983 Session[85]

The NPS discussion in 1983 centered on the Cosmos 1402 incident. The Legal Sub-Committee based its debate on a new Canadian working paper[86] consolidating the three previous Canadian papers of 1980 to 1982. Furthermore, two working papers were submitted by the Federal Republic of Germany. The first one[87] contained an amendment to the Canadian proposal. The second one[88] gave a detailed account of the experience gained in tracking Cosmos 1402 for several months and the difficulties had in deciding in good time which safety measures were to be taken for the protection of the population. According to the FRG information *e.g.* on the type and the quantity of the radio-active material on board Cosmos 1402 and on the containment system of the satellite's reactor, was insufficient. These experiences raised the request for timely, comprehensive, and continuously updated information to be given by the launching State to those States potentially concerned and to the Secretary-General of the United Nations in case of the malfunctioning of an NPS satellite. With more detailed and precise information, the States potentially concerned should be able to calculate their risks in adequate proportion and to decide which safety measures were necessary for the protection of their population and environment.

Some of the proposals of the FRG working paper were the following:

— The Secretary-General of the United Nations should be informed as soon as the re-entry of a nuclear power source is foreseeable, following some malfunction on board a satellite. Immediately after this malfunction information should be provided so that there is time enough for thorough preparation and information

— Apart from the items included in the format for notification as laid down by the Working Group of the Scientific-Technical Sub-Committee in 1981 there should be timely information on the planned or predicted sequence of re-entry, as well as on the construction of the reactor fuel and its expected fate during re-entry.

The Federal Republic of Germany claimed that only by the provision of such information the Governments would be enabled to reduce their precautionary measures.

The USSR put forward her criticism, not so much concerning the proposals but concerning Part II of the FRG working paper relating to the experiences made in tracking and track prediction. She voiced her surprise that the Federal Republic of Germany on the one hand demanded detailed information, but on the other hand she obviously had ignored or disbelieved information provided by the USSR on Cosmos 1402. Already on January 8 and 16, 1983 the Soviet

newspaper 'Pravda' had reported the splitting up of the satellite into a radio-
active and a non-radio-active part (see section 2.1.1.2 above). As a response
to this the Canadian delegation pointed out that the item under discussion in
the Legal Sub-Committee was an *official* notification to be provided by the
launching State to the Secretary-General of the United Nations and concerned States.

Agreement was reached that the work of the Legal Sub-Committee should
concentrate on the question of notification prior to re-entry. A distinction was
made between notification format and procedure. As to the format, the text already agreed upon in the NPS Working Group of the Scientific-Technical
Sub-Committee in 1981 was accepted without modification[89]. At the end of
difficult negotiations, both the notification format and procedure had been
elaborated, and the following text was unanimously agreed upon:

> 'Any State launching a space object with nuclear power sources on
> board should timely inform States concerned in the event this space ob-
> ject is malfunctioning with a risk of re-entry of radioactive materials to
> the earth. The information should be in accordance with the following
> format:
> 1.   *System parameters*
> 1.1   Name of launching State or States including the address of the
>   authority which may be contacted for additional information or
>   assistance in case of accident
> 1.2   International designation
> 1.3   Date and territory or location of launch
> 1.4   Information required or best prediction of orbit lifetime, trajec-
>   tory and impact region
> 1.5   General function of spacecraft
>
> 2.   *Information on the radiological risk of nuclear power source(s)*
> 2.1   Type of NPS: radio-isotopic/reactor
> 2.2   The probable physical form, amount and general radiological
>   characteristics of the fuel and contaminated and/or activated
>   components likely to reach the ground. The term 'fuel' refers to
>   the nuclear material used as the source of heat or power.
> This information should also be transmitted to the Secretary-General
> of the United Nations'.

This agreement had to be appreciated as the first important step towards an
amendment of international law relating to the use of NPS in outer space.

After the agreement on the text the USSR made the following statement:

1.   The consensus text in no way prejudiced the legal status of the international instrument which would in the end contain this text

2.   As to section 1.4 of the consensus text the USSR interpreted it as follows:
'In reading point 1.4 it should be ballistical coefficient which is sometimes

called mean-coefficient of deceleration, as well as projected time and area of re-entry of object into dense layers of atmosphere with the possibility of further updating of the forecast'.

2.8.6   1984 Session[90]

During the 1984 session, efforts were made to elaborate a set of legal principles relating to the use of NPS in outer space which should serve as a basis for future discussions in the Legal Sub-Committee. To this purpose Canada, China, and Sweden submitted a working paper on safety measures concerning radiological protection[91]. According to a proposal by the Netherlands, this paper was restructured and a distinction was made between precautionary safety measures (Section I), action to be taken before the possible re-entry of a space object carrying an NPS (Section II), action to be taken after the re-entry of a space object carrying an NPS (Section III), and assistance to States (Section IV)[92]. (Due to the shortness of time, however, an appropriate text for Secs. III and IV could not yet be elaborated.) Regarding the proposal as a whole, though, no consensus could be reached in the Committee. The same was the case with the working paper submitted by Sweden[93], which, too, dealt with radiological protection measures, as well as with the working paper submitted by the Federal Republic of Germany[94]. The latter aimed at reopening last year's discussion (1983) of the notification procedure prior to re-entry of a malfunctioning NPS satellite..

This lack of consensus in the NPS discussion was mainly due to the attitude of the Soviet Union, who held the position that there was no need to elaborate additional NPS norms in international law. Furthermore, she pointed out that the NPS Working Group within the Scientific and Technical Sub-Committee had taken up its work again, and suggested that the Legal Sub-Committee should postpone the elaboration of legal norms until the studies in that Working Group had been concluded.

Looking at the results of the 1984 session it can be observed that the more time elapses since the last NPS incident, the more the readiness to achieve an agreement on legal norms relating to the use of NPS in outer space decreases. As already pointed out (secs. 2.1.1 and 2.1.2 above), the United States do not use NPS in near Earth orbits at present. As to the USSR, she had stopped launching NPS satellites in near Earth orbits after the Cosmos 1402 incident in 1982/83. On June 29, 1984, however, according to Western sources, the Soviet Union launched Cosmos 1579[27a], a nuclear reactor powered ocean surveillance satellite. This shows that the Soviet Union is not willing to stop using NPS in near Earth orbits. In the same way, the fact that powerful nuclear reactors presently are under development in the United States (sec. 2.3.1 above) stresses the need for an elaboration of relevant legal norms for the use of NPS in outer space.

1. As to the history of this event see *Questions Relating to the Use of Nuclear Power Sources in Outer Space*, Report presented by Canada, UN Doc. A/AC.105/C.1/L.106 of January 25, 1979; a complete account of the accident is given in Gummer/Campbell/Knight/Richard, Cosmos 954, *The Occurrence and Nature of Recovered Debris*, Hull (Quebec, Canada) 1980; and: Canada: *Claim against the Union of Soviet Socialist Republics for Damage Caused by Soviet Cosmos 954*, January 23, 1979 and March 15, 1979, International Legal Materials, Vol. XVIII, 1979, p. 899 ff. The latter publication is of special interest as it contains also the diplomatic correspondence between Canada and the USSR after the Cosmos 954 accident
2. See sec. 2.1.2 above
3. As to details concerning the radioactive effects on human organism see sec. 2.4.1 above
4. Information furnished to the UN Secretary-General as contained in UN Doc. A/AC.105/INF.368 of November 22, 1977 and *COSPAR Information Bulletin* 81, April 1978, p. 98
5. *Aviation Week and Space Technology*, October 3, 1977, p. 27; Reese, Townsend R./Vick, Charles P., *Soviet Nuclear Powered Satellites, Journal of the British Interplanetary Society* Vol. 36, 1983, p. 457
6. Krey, P.W./Leifer, R./Benson, W.K./Dietz, L.A./Hendrikson, H.C./Coluzza, J.L., *Atmospheric Burn-up of the Cosmos 954 Reactor, Science* Vol. 205, August 10, 1979, p. 583 ff.; Rich, Vera, *The Facts about Cosmos 954, Nature* Vol. 271, February 9, 1978, p. 497; Reese/Vick, *op. cit. supra* note 5
7. UN Doc. A/AC.105/INF.368 of November 22, 1977; Jasani, Bhupendra, *Outer Space - A New Dimension of the Arms Race*, Stockholm 1982, Appendix 1C, p. 345
8. Rich, *op. cit. supra* note 6, p. 498
9. *Questions Relating to the Use of Nuclear Power Sources in Outer Space*, UN Doc., *op. cit. supra* note 1, p. 2
10. Canada: *Claim against the USSR, op. cit. supra* note 1, Annex A, No. 4, p. 902
11. Taylor, H.W./Hutchinson, E.A./McInnes, K.L./Svoboda, J., *Cosmos 954: Search for Airborne Radioactivity on Lichens in the Crash Area, Northwest Territories, Canada, Science* Vol. 205, September 29, 1979, p. 1383 ff.; Gummer/Campbell/Knight/Richard, *op. cit. supra* note 1, iii and Appendix D, pp. 46
12. Gummer/Campbell/Knight/Richard, *op. cit. supra* note 1, p. 29 ff
13. *Questions Relating to the Use of Nuclear Power Sources in Outer Space*, UN Doc., *op. cit. supra* note 1, p. 2; Gummer/Campbell/Knight/Richard, *op. cit. supra* note 1, p. 1
14. *Canada and USSR Settle Claim for Damages by Cosmos 954*, Canadian Department of External Affairs, Communiqué No. 27, released on April 2, 1982, reprinted in the Annex to this chapter
15. *Canada and USSR Settle Claim, op. cit. supra* note 14, see Annex to this chapter
16. Covault, Craig, *U.S. Assesses Hazard of Cosmos Fuel, Aviation Week and Space Technology*, January 31, 1983, p. 20; Rich, Vera, *Soviet Satellite Falling to Earth, Nature* Vol. 301, January 1983, p. 188
17. Budiansky, Stephen, *Nuclear Reactors in Space - One has Come Down, but More are Still to Come, Nature* Vol. 301, February 10, 1983, p. 458; Covault, *op. cit. supra* note 16
18. Covault, *op. cit. supra* note 16, p. 21; Hewish, Mark, *Atoms Power the Space Spies, New Scientist*, January 20, 1983, p. 158; see also the experiences made by the Federal Republic of Germany during the Cosmos 1402 incident as reported in UN Doc. A/AC.105/C.2/L.138 of March 28, 1983, reproduced in the Annex to this chapter
19. Hewish, *op. cit. supra* note 18
20. Hewish, *op. cit. supra* note 18
21. Information furnished to the UN Secretary-General on January 18, 1983 as contained in UN Doc. ST/SG/SER.E/72/Add.1 of January 20, 1983, see Annex to this chapter
22. See account given by the Federal Republic of Germany, *op. cit. supra* note 18
23. Information furnished to the UN Secretary-General as contained in UN Doc. ST/SG/SER.E/72/Add.2 of January 21, 1983, see Annex to this chapter
24. Information furnished to the UN Secretary-General on January 25, 1983 as contained in UN Doc. ST/SG/SER.E/72/Add.3 of January 27, 1983, see Annex to this chapter
25. Information furnished to the UN Secretary-General on February 7, 1983 as contained in UN Doc. ST/SG/SER.E/72/Add.4 of February 9, 1983, see Annex to this chapter
26. Covault, *op. cit. supra* note 16, p. 20; Covault, Craig, *Soviet Nuclear Spacecraft Poses Reentry Danger, Aviation Week and Space Technology*, January 10, 1983 p. 18; see also the account given by the Federal Republic of Germany, *op. cit. supra* note 18
27. Covault, *op. cit. supra* note 16, p. 19; Hewish, *op. cit. supra* note 18; Reese/Vick, *op. cit. supra* note 5, p. 461

94   27a. Covault, Craig, *Spaceplane Called a Weapons Platform, Aviation Week and Space Technology*, July 23, 1984, p. 71 and July 9, 1984

28.   *Uses of Radioactive (Nuclear) Materials by the United States of America for Space Power Generation*, UN Doc. A/AC.105/L.102 of March 15, 1978

29.   *Astronautics Year*, April 17-22, 1964, Ref.: 4.64, and May 22-26, 1964, Ref.: 5.55; *Astronautics and Aeronautics*, March 1, 1972, (NASA SP-4017, Washington 1974) p. 80; Hardy, Edward P., Jr./Krey, Philip W./Volchok, Herbert L., *Global Inventory and Distribution of Pu-238 from SNAP 9A*, Health and Safety Laboratory, U.S. Atomic Energy Commission, New York, 1972

30.   As to details on this type of safety design see section 2.4.2 of this chapter

31.   *Uses of Radioactive (Nuclear) Materials by the United States, op. cit. supra* note 28, p. 2 and Attachment 5, pp. 1 and 5

32.   *Uses of Radioactive (Nuclear) Materials by the United States, op. cit. supra* note 28, p. 2 and Attachment 5, pp. 1 and 8

33.   Rex, Dietrich, *Der Wiedereintritt grosser Satelliten in die Erdatmosphäre - Risiko und Vorausberechnung (Re-entry of large satellites into the Earth's atmosphere - risk and precalculation. With summary in English)*, Zeitschrift für Flugwissenschaft und Weltraumforschung Vol. 4, 1980, p. 354

34.   See notification furnished to the UN Secretary-General *op. cit. supra* note 25

35.   See sec. 2.1.2 of this chapter

36.   *Aeronautics and Space Report of the President*, Washington 1980, p. 12; this report is reprinted in: Gorove, Stephen, *US Space Law, National and International Regulation* Vol. I, New York 1983, section I.A.6, p. 12; Klass, Philip J., *Agencies Agree on Space Power Effort, Aviation Week and Technology*, February 21, 1982, p. 22; Buden, David/Bennett, Gary L., *On the Use of Nuclear Reactors in Space, Physics Bulletin* Vol. 33, December 1982; Klass, Philip J., *Space-Based Power Plan Deadline Near, Aviation Week and Space Technology*, December 12, 1983, p. 63 ff.

37.   See sec. 2.1.1.3 of this chapter

38.   Löb, H.W., *Nuclear Energy in Space, Earth-Oriented Applications of Space Technology*, Vol. 2, No. 1, 1982, pp. 1-16; Ross, Donald M., *Radiation Sources Carried by Space Vehicles*, in: Campbell, *Medical and Biological Aspects of the Energies of Space*, Columbia University Press, New York 1966, pp 130-153

39.   Buden/Bennett, *op. cit. supra* note 36, pp. 432-434; Brooks, E.H. et al., *Radiation Environment About the Nerva Reactors, IEEE Transactions on Nuclear Science*, February 1966, pp. 663-669

40.   United Nations Scientific Committee on the Effects of Atomic Radiation, 1977 Report to the General Assembly: *Sources and Effects of Ionizing Radiation*

41.   *New Scientist*, July 14, 1983, p. 83

42.   Meissner, Johannes, *Natürliche und zivilisatorische Strahlenbelastungen und Strahlenrisiken, Materia Medica Nordmark* 30, Jan./Feb. 1978; *Recommendations of the International Commission on Radiological Protection (ICRP)*, adopted January 17, 1977, ICRP Publication 26, *Annals of the ICRP* Vol. 1, No. 3, 1977, Oxford/New York/Frankfurt 1977; Bünemann, Dietrich, *Faktensammlung zur Kerntechnik*, Kerntechnische Gesellschaft, Bonn 1981

43.   As to safety measures taken for RTGs in US space flight see Campana, R.J., *SNAP-15A Radio-Isotope Thermo-Electric Generator, IEEE Transactions on Nuclear Science*, February 1966, p. 270 ff.; *Questions Relating to the Use of Nuclear Power Sources in Outer Space*, US Working Paper, *Studies on Technical Aspects and Safety Measures of Nuclear Power Sources in Outer Space*, UN Doc. A/AC.105/C.1/WG.V/L.8 of January 23, 1980; *Uses of Radioactive (Nuclear) Materials by the United States, op. cit. supra* note 28, p. 3 ff.

44.   As to safety measures taken for nuclear reactors in Soviet space flight see Reese/Vick, *op. cit. supra* note 5; *Questions Relating to the Use of Nuclear Power Sources in Outer Space*, Union of Soviet Socialist Republics Working Paper, *Studies on Technical Aspects and Safety Measures of Nuclear Power Sources in Outer Space*, UN Doc. A/AC.105/C.1/WG.V/L.10 of January 25, 1980.
       As to safety measures for reactors in US space flight see Buden/Bennett, *op. cit. supra* note 36; Ureda, B.F., *Snapshot Launch Operations, IEEE Transactions on Nuclear Science*, February 1966, p. 254 ff.

45.   Covault, *op. cit. supra* note 16, p. 21; Reese/Vick, *op. cit. supra* note 5, p. 459

46.   See sec. 2.1.2 of this chapter above and *op. cit. supra* note 29

47.   *Uses of Radioactive (Nuclear) Materials by the United States, op. cit. supra* note 28

48.   Reese/Vick, *op. cit. supra* note 5, p. 461

49.   UN Doc. A/AC.105/C.1/WG.V/L.11 of January 28, 1980 and Add.1

50. See sec. 2.4 above
51. As to the cost-benefit analysis for the use of nuclear power in general see Karam, R.A., and Morgan, K.Z. (eds.), *Energy and the Environment, Cost-Benefit Analysis*, Supplement I to ENERGY, Georgia Institute of Technology Series in Nuclear Engineering, Pergamon Press, New York/Toronto/Oxford/Sydney/Braunschweig/Paris 1976
52. As to a detailed summary of the debates between 1979 and 1981 see Christol, Carl. Q., *The Use of Nuclear Power Sources in Outer Space, Zeitschrift für Luft- und Weltraumrecht* 1981, p. 47 ff.; and the same: *The Modern International Law of Outer Space*, New York 1982, p. 765 ff.
53. The report of the Sub-Committee about its NPS debate in 1978 is contained in UN Doc. A/AC.105/216 of March 6, 1978, p. 28 ff.
54. The report of the NPS Working Group about its 1979 session is contained in UN Doc. A/AC.105/238 Annex II of February 26, 1979
55. See sec. 2.6 above
56. *Op. cit. supra* note 36
57. *Op. cit. supra* note 42
58. See sec. 2.1.1 of this chapter above
59. The report of the Working Group about its 1980 session is contained in UN Doc. A/AC.105/267 Annex II of February 15, 1980
60. The report of the Working Group about its 1981 session is contained in UN Doc. A/AC.105/287 Annex II of February 13, 1981
61. Reprinted in: Jasentuliyana, Nandasiri, and Lee, Roy S.K., Manual of Space Law 1981, Vol. IV, p. 536
62. See sec. 2.8.4 above
63. The report of the Sub-Committee is contained in UN Doc. A/AC.105/304 of January 25, 1982
64. The report of the Sub-Committee is contained in UN Doc. A/AC.105/318 of February 24, 1983
65. The report of the NPS Working Group is contained in UN Doc. A/AC.105/C.1/L.139 of February 17, 1984
66. As to a detailed summary of the debates between 1979 and 1982 see Christol, *op. cit. supra* note 52, p. 770 ff.; and: Benkö, Marietta, *Weltraumrecht in den Vereinten Nationen - Die Arbeit des Weltraumausschusses in den Jahren 1979 bis 1981, Zeitschrift für Luft- und Weltraumrecht (ZLW)* 1981, p. 278 ff.; for 1982 see the same, ZLW 1982, p. 335 ff.; for 1983 see the same, and Klaus Damian, ZLW 1983, p. 242 ff. The last-mentioned three articles have been used as a basis for the preparation of parts of this chapter.
    As to the legal aspects of the use of NPS see i.a. the following publications: Jasentuliyana, Nandasiri, *A Perspective of the Use of NPS in Outer Space, Annals of Air and Space Law* 1979, p. 519 ff.; Reijnen, G.C.M., *Utilization of Outer Space and International Law*, Amsterdam/Oxford/New York 1981, p. 41 ff.; Danielson, Sune, *An Interdisciplinary Approach in the Regulation by the UN of Activities in Outer Space - Some Technical Considerations*, in: *Space Activities and Implications - Where From and Where To at the Threshold of the 80's*, McGill University, Montreal 1981, p. 103 ff.; Schwartz, Bryan, and Berlin, Mark L., *After the Fall: An Analysis of Canadian Legal Claims for Damage Caused by Cosmos 954*, in: *McGill Law Journal* Vol. 27, November 1982, p. 676 ff.
67. The report of the 1978 session of the Legal Sub-Committee is contained in UN Doc. A/AC.105/218 of April 13, 1978, p. 5; as to the 1979 session see: UN Doc. A/AC.105/240 of April 10, 1979, p. 10
68. UN Doc. A/AC.105/C.2/L.115, reproduced in Annex IV to the 1978-report of the Legal Sub-Committee, *op. cit. supra* note 67
69. The report of the 1980 session of the Legal Sub-Committee is contained in UN Doc. A/AC.105/271 of April 10, 1980
70. UN Doc. A/AC.105/C.2/L.126 of February 6, 1980, reproduced in Annex III to the Sub-Committee's 1980 report, *op. cit. supra* note 69
71. In fact there are international conventions providing for the prevention of nuclear accidents; among these are
    — the ('Vienna') Convention of May 21, 1963, on Civil Liability for Nuclear Damage
    — the ('Paris') Convention on Third Party Liability in the Field of Nuclear Energy (incorporating the provisions of the Additional Protocol of January 28, 1964).
    A collection of multilateral conventions on civil liability for nuclear damage is contained in: International Atomic Energy Agency, Legal Series No. 4, rev. ed., Vienna 1976. These conventions, however, only account for nuclear accidents as regards civil liability, for which limits of liability can be established. They do not account for the liability of States which is laid down in the Outer Space Treaty as well as in the Liability Convention. Moreover, according to their wording the conventions are not applicable to NPS satellites

96   72. The report of the 1981 session of the Legal Sub-Committee is contained in UN Doc. A/AC.105/288 of April 20, 1981

73. UN Doc. A/AC.105/C.2/L.129; as to the Canadian working paper of 1980 see supra note 70

74. UN Doc. WG/NPS(1981)/WP.1, reproduced in the Sub-Committee's 1981 report, *op. cit. supra* note 72

75. UN Doc. WG/NPS(1981)/WP.2, reproduced in the Sub-Committee's 1981 report, *op. cit. supra* note 72

76. As to details of this problem see sec. 2.7.2 above

77. The report of the 1982 session of the Legal Sub-Committee is contained in UN Doc. A/AC.105/305 of February 24, 1982

78. UN Doc. WG/NPS(1982)/WP.2, reproduced in Annex II to the Subcommittee's 1982 report, *op. cit. supra* note 77

79. See Canadian working paper A/AC.105/C.2/L.134 of February 15, 1982, reproduced in Annex II to the Sub-Committee's 1982 report, *op. cit. supra* note 77

80. See deliberations in sec. 2.7.2 above

81. *Canada and USSR Settle Claim for Damages by Cosmos 954, op. cit. supra* note 1; and see Annex to this chapter; Gummer/Campbell/Knight/Richard, *op. cit. supra* note 1, p. 2; Canada: *Claim Against the USSR, op. cit. supra* note 1, Annex B: Texts of diplomatic communications between the Department of External Affairs and the Embassy of the USSR, p. 915

82. UN Doc. WG/NPS(1982)/WP.3/rev.1 of February 12, 1982, reproduced in the Sub-Committee's 1982 report, *op. cit. supra* note 77

83. UN Doc. WG/NPS(1982)/WP.4 of February 11, 1982, reproduced in the Sub-Committee's 1982 report, *op. cit. supra* note 77

84. Background: After the Cosmos 954 accident 79 pieces of debris were found along a stretch of 600 km in length, all of them being radio-active, except two. In addition, about 4,000 very small particles were found. All the pieces and particles taken together amounted to a total weight of 68 kg - the biggest piece of satellite debris has to be taken special care of after its recovery, Canada repeatedly requested the USSR to take charge of the remnants of Cosmos 954. The USSR, however, refused to do so declaring that 'the objects do not present interest to the Soviet side as such and consequently the Canadian side can continue to dispose with them at its own discretion'. Canada: Claim Against the USSR, *op. cit. supra* note 1, p. 916 ff., 922

85. The report of the 1983-session of the Legal Sub-Committee is contained in UN Doc. A/AC.105/320 of April 13, 1983

86. UN Doc. A/AC.105/C.2/L.137 of March 28, 1983, reproduced in the Annex to this chapter

87. UN Doc. WG/NPS(1983)/WP.1 of March 31, 1983, reproduced in Annex II Appendix to the Sub-Committee's 1983 report, *op. cit. supra* note 85

88. UN Doc. A/AC.105/C.2/L.138 of March 28, 1983, reproduced in the Annex to this chapter

89. See sec. 2.8.3 above, and UN Doc. A/AC.105/C.1/L.126 of February 1981

90. The report of the 1984 session of the Legal Sub-Committee is contained in UN Doc. A/AC.105/337 of April 12, 1984

91. UN Doc. WG/NPS(1984)/WP.3 of March 28, 1984

92. UN Doc. WG/NPS(1984)/WP.4 of March 29, 1984

93. UN Doc. WG/NPS(1984)/WP.1 of March 23, 1984

94. UN Doc. A/AC.105/C.2/L.146 of March 26, 1984.

COSMOS 954: PROTOCOL BETWEEN THE GOVERN-
MENT OF CANADA AND THE GOVERNMENT OF THE
USSR OF APRIL 2, 1981 FOR THE SETTLEMENT OF ALL
MATTERS CONNECTED WITH THE DISINTEGRATION
OF COSMOS 954 IN JANUARY 1978

The Government of Canada and the Government of the Union of Soviet Socialist Republics, have agreed as follows:

ARTICLE I

The Government of the Union of Soviet Socialist Republics shall pay to the
Government of Canada the sum of three million Canadian dollars
(C$ 3,000,000.00) in full and final settlement of all matters connected with
the disintegration of the Soviet satellite "Cosmos 954" in January 1978.

ARTICLE II

The Government of Canada shall accept the payment of the sum of three million Canadian dollars (C$ 3,000,000.00) in full and final settlement of all those
matters referred to in Article I hereof, including the claim advanced by Canada in this respect.

ARTICLE III

This Protocol shall enter into force on the date of signature.

IN WITNESS WHEREOF the undersigned, duly authorized by their respective Governments, have signed this Protocol.

DONE in duplicate at Moscow this second day of April 1981, in the English,
French and Russian languages, all texts being equally authentic.

For the Government of Canada   For the Government of the Union of
                                    Soviet Socialist Republics

INTRODUCTION

1. This Statement sets forth Canada's claim for compensation for damage the result of the intrusion into Canadian air space of a Soviet space object, the Cosmos 954 satellite, and the deposit on Canadian territory of hazardous radioactive debris from the satellite. The claim is presented pursuant to the 1972 *Convention on International Liability for Damage caused by Space Objects* and the international practice of states. The Statement outlines the facts giving rise to the claim, the legal principles applicable to the claim, the compensation claimed and certain reservations entered by Canada.

THE FACTS

2. The Soviet space object, the Cosmos 954 satellite, hereinafter also referred to as the satellite, was placed in orbit by the Union of Soviet Socialist Republics on September 18, 1977. The Secretary-General of the United Nations was officially informed of the launching, as reported in United Nations document No. A/AC.105/INF. 368 of November 22, 1977. According to the Note of March 21, 1978 of the Embassy of the Union of Soviet Socialist Republics in Ottawa, the satellite carried on board a "... nuclear reactor working on uranium enriched with isotope of uranium-235". On January 24, 1978, the satellite entered the earth's atmosphere intruding into Canadian air space at about 11:53 A.M. Greenwich Mean Time to the north of the Queen Charlotte Islands on the west coast of Canada. On re-entry and disintegration, debris from the satellite was deposited on Canadian territory, including portions of the Northwest Territories, Alberta and Saskatchewan.

3. Within minutes of the re-entry and the intrusion of the satellite into Canadian air space the Government of the United States of America made an offer of technical and material assistance to assist Canadian emergency operations. This offer of assistance was accepted immediately by the Government of Canada.

4. In the course of the day January 24, 1978, an official of the Department of External Affairs expressed to the Ambassador of the Union of Soviet Socialist Republics in Ottawa the surprise of the Government of Canada that the Government of the Union of Soviet Socialist Republics had failed to give Canada notice of the possible re-entry of the satellite into the earth's atmosphere in the region of Canada and subsequently, of the imminent re-entry of the satellite. The Canadian official put questions to the Ambassador concerning the satellite and, noting information as to the presence of a nuclear reactor on board the satellite, requested that precise responses be provided urgently. The questions posed on that occasion were reiterated on January 27, 1978 and are recorded in the Department of External Affairs Aide-Memoire of February 8, 1978 presented to the Embassy.

5. Later on January 24, 1978, the Ambassador of the Union of Soviet Socialist Republics advised an official of the Department of External Affairs that the satellite had been expected to enter the dense layers of the atmosphere on January 24, 1978 and, in case it did not burn out completely in the atmosphere, the possibility that some of its parts would fall in the area of the Aleutian Islands was not excluded. The Ambassador asserted that there should not be any sizeable hazard and that in places of impact there could only be insignificant local pollution requiring very limited measures of disactivation. He also stated that the construction of the nuclear reactor on board the satellite envisaged its complete destruction on re-entry of the satellite into the dense layers of the atmosphere. On that occasion, the Ambassador expressed his Government's readiness to render urgent assistance by sending to Canada a group of specialists to ameliorate the possible consequences and evacuate remnants of the satellite. Canadian officials replied that their urgent need was for immediate and complete answers to the questions posed earlier on January 24, 1978.

6. In the Note of March 21, 1978, the Embassy informed the Department of External Affairs that the active zone of the nuclear reactor on board the satellite "... was a set of heat-emitting elements with a berillium reflector" and that "The reactor's design provided for destruction of the reflector at the entry into dense layers of the atmosphere to be followed by the total destruction of the reactor's active zone".

7. The Government of the Union of Soviet Socialist Republics failed to provide timely and complete replies to the questions posed by Canada on January 24, 1978 despite the reiteration of the request for information on several occasions, in particular in the Department of External Affairs' Aide-Memoire of February 8, 1978, in its Note of February 28, 1978 to the Embassy and in its Note of April 13, 1978 to the Embassy. The Government of Union of Soviet Socialist Republics ultimately provided some information in the Notes of the Embassy dated March 21, 1978 and May 31, 1978. This information, particularly that in the latter Note, contributed to the Canadian evaluation of the required course of action.

8. Upon the intrusion of the satellite into Canadian air space and with the apprehension of the deposit of hazardous radioactive debris from the satellite on Canadian territory, the Canadian Armed Forces and the Atomic Energy Control Board of Canada undertook operations directed at locating, recovering, removing and testing the debris and cleaning up the affected areas. The purpose of these operations was to identify the nature and extent of the damage caused by the debris, to limit the existing damage and to minimize the risk of further damage and to restore to the extent possible the affected areas to the condition that would have existed if the intrusion of the satellite and the deposit of the debris had not occurred. The operations took place in two phases: Phase I from January 24, 1978 to April 20, 1978 and Phase II from April 21, 1978 to October 15, 1978. The total cost incurred by the various Canadian Departments and Agencies involved in Phase I of the operations was $ 12,048,239.11 of which $ 4,414,348.86 are included in Canada's claim. The total cost incurred during Phase II of the operations was $ 1,921,904.55

of which $ 1,626,825.84 are included in Canada's claim. In sum, Canada claims from the Union of Soviet Socialist Republics payment in the amount of $ 6,041,174.70.

9. During the operations described in paragraph 8, debris from the satellite was found in areas of the Northwest Territories and the Provinces of Alberta and Saskatchewan. Lists describing the location of the debris are set forth in annexes to the Department of External Affairs Notes dated February 8, 1978, March 3, 1978 and December 18, 1978, to the Embassy of the Union of Soviet Socialist Republics. Inscriptions in the Cyrillic alphabet can be distinguished on one of the fragments recovered.

10. The Canadian authorities determined that all but two of the fragments recovered were radioactive. Some fragments located proved to be of lethal radioactivity. It was necessary for the debris to be handled with great care as it is well established that radioactive material can have serious physiological effects and in some cases can be fatal. The debris recovered was sent to the Canadian Government's Whiteshell Nuclear Research Establishment at Pinawa, Manitoba. There tests were carried out on the debris, the results of which provided valuable information that was of assistance with regard to the operations and confirmed that highly radioactive and dangerous debris from the satellite had been deposited on Canadian territory.

11. The Government of Canada informed the Secretary-General of the United Nations of the discovery of debris from the satellite as is indicated in United Nations documents A/AC.105/214 and 214/Corr.1 of February 8, 1978; A/AC.105/217 of March 6, 1978 and A/AC.105/236 of December 22, 1978.

12. In addition to general admissions as to the origin of the Cosmos 954 satellite, the Government of the Union of Soviet Socialist Republics confirmed the Canadian conclusion as to the origin and identity of the recovered debris by admissions contained in the statement made on February 14, 1978 in the Scientific and Technical Subcommittee of the Committee on the Peaceful Uses of Outer Space by Academician Fedorov, a representative of the Union of Soviet Socialist Republics. In addition, the Note from the Embassy of the Union of Soviet Socialist Republics in Ottawa dated May 31, 1978 includes admissions to the effect that debris found in the Northwest Territories of Canada originated from the satellite.

13. It is thus beyond doubt on the basis of the operations described above and on the basis of admissions by representatives of the Union of Soviet Socialist Republics that the debris found in the areas covered by the operations originated from the Soviet space object identified as the Cosmos 954 satellite.

THE LAW

14. Canada's claim is based jointly and separately on (a) the relevant interna-

tional agreements and in particular the 1972 *Convention on International Liability for Damage caused by Space Objects,* to which both Canada and the Union of Soviet Socialist Republics are parties, and (b) general principles of international law.

(a) International Agreements

15. Under Article II of the *Convention on International Liability for Damage caused by Space Objects,* hereinafter also referred to as the Convention, "A launching State shall be absolutely liable to pay compensation for damage caused by its space object on the surface of the earth....". The Union of Soviet Socialist Republics, as the launching State of the Cosmos 954 satellite, has an absolute liability to pay compensation to Canada for the damage caused by this satellite. The deposit of hazardous radioactive debris from the satellite throughout a large area of Canadian territory, and the presence of that debris in the environment rendering part of Canada's territory unfit for use, constituted "damage to property" within the meaning of the Convention.

16. The intrusion into Canadian air space of a satellite carrying on board a nuclear reactor and the break-up of the satellite over Canadian territory created a clear and immediate apprehension of damage, including nuclear damage, to persons and property in Canada. The Government of the Union of Soviet Socialist Republics failed to give the Government of Canada prior notification of the imminent re-entry of the nuclear powered satellite and failed to provide timely and complete answers to the Canadian questions of January 24, 1978 concerning the satellite. It thus failed to minimize the deleterious results of the intrusion of the satellite into Canadian air space.

17. Under general principles of international law, Canada had a duty to take the necessary measures to prevent and reduce the harmful consequences of the damage and thereby to mitigate damages. Thus, with respect to the debris, it was necessary for Canada to undertake without delay operations of search, recovery, removal, testing and clean-up. These operations were also carried out in order to comply with the requirements of the domestic law of Canada. Moreover, Article VI of the Convention imposes on the claimant State a duty to observe reasonable standards of care with respect to damage caused by a space object.

18. The operations described in paragraph 8 above would not have been necessary and would not have been undertaken had it not been for the damage caused by the hazardous radioactive debris from the Cosmos 954 satellite on Canadian territory and the reasonable apprehension of further damage in view of the nature of nuclear contamination. As a result of these operations, the areas affected have been restored, to the extent possible, to the condition which would have existed if the intrusion of the satellite and the deposit of the debris had not occurred. The Departments and Agencies of the Government of Canada involved in these operations incurred, as a result, considerable expense, particularly with regard to the procurement and use of services and

102 equipment, the transportation of personnel and equipment and the establishment and operation of the necessary infrastructure. The costs included by Canada in this claim were incurred solely as a consequence of the intrusion of the satellite into Canadian air space and the deposit on Canadian territory of hazardous radioactive debris from the satellite.

19. In respect of compensation for damage caused by space objects, the Convention provides for "... such reparation in respect of the damage as will restore ... [the claimant] to the condition which would have existed if the damage had not occurred" (Article XII). In accordance with its Preamble, the Convention seeks to ensure" ... the prompt payment ... [under its terms] of a full and equitable measure of compensation to victims of such damage" (Fourth preambular paragraph). Canada's claim includes only those costs which were incurred in order to restore Canada to the condition which would have existed if the damage inflicted by the Cosmos 954 satellite had not occurred. The Convention also provides that "The compensation which the launching State shall be liable to pay for damage under this Convention shall be determined in accordance with international law and the principles of justice and equity..." (Article XII). In calculating the compensation claimed, Canada has applied the relevant criteria established by general principles of international law and has limited the costs included in its claim to those costs that are reasonable, proximately caused by the intrusion of the satellite and deposit of debris and capable of being calculated with a reasonable degree of certainty.

20. The liability of the Union of Soviet Socialist Republics for damage caused by the satellite is also founded in Article VII of the *Treaty on Principles Governing the Activities of States in the Exploration and Use of Outer Space, including the Moon and Other Celestial Bodies*, done in 1967, and to which both Canada and the Union of Soviet Socialist Republics are parties. This liability places an obligation on the Union of Soviet Socialist Republics to compensate Canada in accordance with international law for the consequences of the intrusion of the satellite into Canadian air space and the deposit on Canadian territory of hazardous radioactive debris from the satellite.

(b) General Principles of International Law

21. The intrusion of the Cosmos 954 satellite into Canada's air space and the deposit on Canadian territory of hazardous radioactive debris from the satellite constitutes a violation of Canada's sovereignty. This violation is established by the mere fact of the trespass of the satellite, the harmful consequences of this intrusion, being the damage caused to Canada by the presence of hazardous radioactive debris and the interference with the sovereign right of Canada to determine the acts that will be performed on its territory. International precedents recognize that a violation of sovereignty gives rise to an obligation to pay compensation.

22. The standard of absolute liability for space activities, in particular activities involving the use of nuclear energy, is considered to have become a general principle of international law. A large number of states, including Canada and

the Union of Soviet Socialist Republics, have adhered to this principle as contained in the 1972 *Convention on International Liability for Damage caused by Space Objects*. The principle of absolute liability applies to fields of activities having in common a high degree of risk. It is repeated in numerous international agreements and is one of "the general principles of law recognized by civilized nations" (Article 38 of the Statute of The International Court of Justice). Accordingly, this principle has been accepted as a general principle of international law.

23. In calculating the compensation claimed, Canada has applied the relevant criteria established by general principles of international law according to which fair compensation is to be paid, by including in its claim only those costs that are reasonable, proximately caused by the intrusion of the satellite and deposit of debris and capable of being calculated with a reasonable degree of certainty.

COMPENSATION CLAIMED

24. On the basis of the facts asserted and the legal principles referred to herein, the Government of Canada claims payment from the Government of the Union of Soviet Socialist Republics of the sum of $ 6,041,174.70.

RESERVATIONS

25. The Government of Canada hereby enters reservations as follows:

(a) The Government of Canada reserves its right to present additional claims for compensation to the Government of the Union of Soviet Socialist Republics in respect of damage not yet identified or determined or damage which may occur in the future as a result of the intrusion of the Cosmos 954 satellite into Canada's air space and the deposit of hazardous radioactive debris from the satellite on Canadian territory;

(b) The Government of Canada reserves its right to claim from the Government of the Union of Soviet Socialist Republics all costs that Canada may be obliged to incur in the event of the establishment of a Claims Commission under the provisions of the 1972 *Convention on International Liability for Damage caused by Space Objects* and the presentation by Canada of its claim to such a Claims Commission; and

(c) The Government of Canada reserves its right to claim from the Government of the Union of Soviet Socialist Republics payment of interest at an appropriate rate on the amount of compensation declared payable by a Claims Commission, such interest to accrue from the date of the decision or award of the Claims Commission.

COSMOS 1402: EXPERIENCES MADE BY THE GOV-
ERNMENT OF THE FEDERAL REPUBLIC OF GER-
MANY DURING THE RE-ENTRY OF COSMOS 1402 IN
1982/83 AS REPORTED TO THE UNITED NATIONS IN
UN DOC. A/AC.105/C.2/L.138 OF MARCH 28, 1983

...

II. Experience from the Re-Entry of a Nuclear Powered Satellite

The typical situation of any country before and during the re-entry of a satellite
with NPS can be illustrated by the history of the COSMOS-1402 event and the
precautionary measures taken in the Federal Republic of Germany. Some important conclusions can be drawn from this event with respect to the necessity
of early notification and full information as well as to the benefits of international co-operation.

In January/February of this year, the satellite COSMOS-1402 bearing a nuclear reactor re-entered into the earth's atmosphere. It had been separated into
the three objects A, B and C. The dates of their re-entry were as follows:

Object A on 23 January 1983

Object B on 30 December 1982

Object C on 7 February 1983

Start-up of operations

During the first days of January 1983, authorities in the Federal Republic of
Germany became aware of the fact that, following some malfunction on board
COSMOS-1402, there was the risk of its re-entry into the earth's atmosphere
together with its nuclear reactor. Bearing in mind the consequences of such an
event experienced in Canada in 1978, where some hundred mostly radioactive
pieces of debris were spread over a 600-km length of the subsatellite track, the
authorities in the Federal Republic of Germany decided to go ahead with pre-
planned precautionary measures in order to be prepared for protecting the
population should this become necessary. At that time, there was no information on how that specific case would develop, especially as there was no evidence that it would be different from the COSMOS-954 accident in Canada.
Under those circumstances the precautionary measures taken by the Federal
Republic of Germany were justified.

On 12 January 1983, several German scientific institutions with considerable
manpower and facilities started tracking the two objects A and C - while object
B had decayed already - and calculating their further orbital decay. In addition, orbital elements of the two objects were received from the National Aeronautics and Space Administration (NASA), enhancing the reliability of the

orbital predictions. The results of these predictions, especially the predicted groundtracks flown over by the satellite over Europe and estimates of the re-entry date, were collected by the German Ministry of the Interior and distributed by telex bulletins not only to all federal authorities involved in the Federal Republic of Germany but also to the authorities of most neighbouring countries in Europe.

In distributing its results and in replying to inquiries from other countries the Federal Republic of Germany followed the recommendations discussed so far in the bodies of the United Nations with respect to NPS accidents.

Tracking of object A

Of the two objects A and C, the object C was considered initially only as a minor fraction without importance, since its size was between 10 and 100 times smaller than object A. Also, it was not known at that time that the satellite had been separated into the fragments intentionally and not by accident. Therefore the main tracking and calculating activities were concentrated on object A. But by 18 January it became evident from the orbital data, that object C was a very compact part (i.e. small but very heavy), which well could represent the core of the nuclear reactor or a part of it. Two days later, on 20 January, the Union of Soviet Socialist Republics confirmed by notification to the Secretary-General of the United Nations that object C was the reactor core. So the question arose whether all the prediction activities for object A had been in vain. On the other hand, there was no information on how much of the structure material of object A had been activated by neutron radiation from the reactor core. While it was clear that the radioactivity produced in object A by activation would be much less than the activity in the reactor core, there was still considerable uncertainty about this due to lack of information. So it had to be decided to track also object A until its final descent on 23 January at 2220 hours universal time (equal to Greenwich mean time). If the satellite had stayed in its orbit only 1 hour and 10 minutes longer, it would then have crossed the Federal Republic of Germany, posing a risk to this territory, at least with respect to the level of information then available.

By timely information, probably most of the tracking and prediction activities spent on object A could have been saved.

Tracking of object C

After the decay of object A the activities were concentrated on object C. The question whether it would totally burn up during re-entry was still open since there was no information on the materials and the physical sizes of the object (containment or single parts, etc.). For another two weeks the institutions involved in tracking and orbital predictions had to be assigned to that task and all the data transmission and international distribution of the results were continued as described before. Until 4 February the final re-entry of object C was predicted for the night hours between 7 February and 8 February, in conformity with predictions in other countries. Then an unforeseeable eruption on the sun (solar flare) occurred, which produced an increase of atmospheric density of the earth. From then on the final re-entry of object C was predicted for times centring around noon on 7 February (universal time). But the time period of uncertainty was considerable.

The consequences of this uncertainty and the resulting nearly world-wide threat can best be discussed together with figures 1 and 2 attached to this paper. Figure 1 shows the subsatellite tracks flown over by object C during the last three hours before its final re-entry (and also the tracks which it would have passed within three hours after its final re-entry if it had not re-entered at that time). Figure 2 shows the tracks over Europe within the same time period in an enlarged scale, some instants of passage being indicated in universal time (UT = GMT).

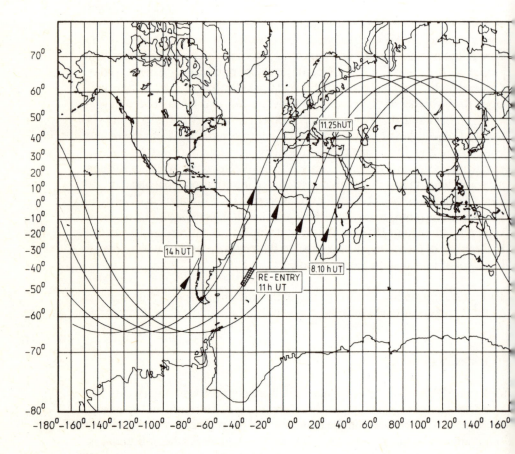

Figure 1
Groundtracks of Cosmos 1402 (Object C) on Feb 7th 1983.
Two Revolutions before and after Actual Decay

The actual re-entry occurred over the southern Atlantic Ocean at about 11.00 hours UT. Only about 25 minutes later the satellite would have passed the border area between Austria and the Federal Republic of Germany. So the German precautionary measures had to be maintained until the very end.

In the early morning of the re-entry day, 7 February, the uncertainty of the predicted re-entry time was still ± three hours, corresponding to the groundtracks shown in figures 1 and 2. At that time all the countries underneath those tracks were subject to the risk of being afflicted by the re-entry.

In the evening before the re-entry, the uncertainty of the predicted re-entry time was even ± eight hours, which corresponds to more than five orbits before and after the actual re-entry. So, then, nearly every country of the world was under one of the ground tracks. This uncertainty was to some extent enhanced by the preceding solar flare and would be less than half as wide under normal circumstances.

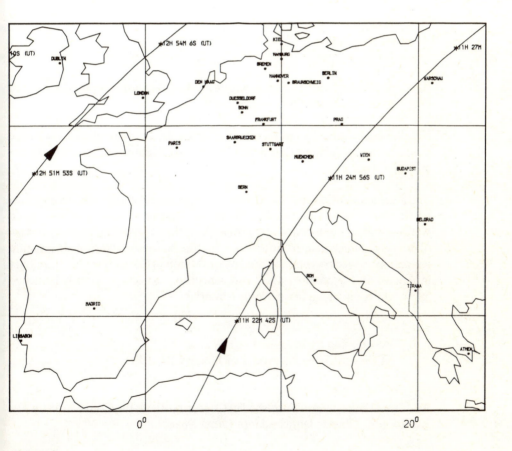

Figure 2
Groundtracks of Cosmos 1402 (Object C) on Feb 7th 1983.
Two Tracks following the Actual Decay

It can be seen from this example that every re-entry of a satellite with NPS raises world-wide concern, justified by the geometry of the ground tracks flown over by the re-entering object within the predicted uncertainty period of the final re-entry.

Timely notification and comprehensive information given by the launching State about all circumstances influencing the expected further history of the event would help to reduce this concern.

INFORMATION FURNISHED BY THE USSR TO THE UNITED NATIONS SECRETARY-GENERAL ABOUT COSMOS 1402

Information as Contained in UN Doc.
ST/SG/SER.E/72 from December 29, 1982

Information Furnished in Conformity with the Convention on Registration of Objects launched into Outer Space

Note verbale dated 14 December 1982 from the Permanent Mission of the Union of Soviet Socialist Republics to the United Nations addressed to the Se-cretary-General

The Permanent Mission of the Union of Soviet Socialist Republics to the Unit-ed Nations presents its compliments to the Secretary-General of the United Nations and, in conformity with article IV of the Convention on Registration of Objects Launched into Outer Space, has the honour to transmit information concerning space objects launched by the Union of Soviet Socialist Republics in August and September 1982 and concerning objects previously launched into earth orbit which are no longer in orbit.

Information as contained in UN Doc.
ST/SG/SER.E/72/Add.1 of January 20, 1983

Additional Information Furnished in Conformity with the Convention on Re-gistration of Objects launched into Outer Space

Note verbale dated 18 January 1983 from the Permanent Mission of the Un-ion of Soviet Socialist Republics to the United Nations addressed to the Secre-tary-General

REGISTRATION DATA ON SPACE OBJECTS LAUNCHED BY THE USSR IN AUGUST 1982

1. In August 1982, the USSR launched the following space objects:

No.	Name of space object	Date of launching	Basic orbit characteristics					General purpose of space object
			Apogee (km)	Perigee (km)	Inclination (degrees)	Periode (minutes)		
1	2	3	4	5	6	7		8
1741	COSMOS-1398	3 August	262	225	82.3	89		Investigation of the upper atmosphere and outer space
1742	COSMOS-1399	4 August	371	179	64.9	89.7		Investigation of the upper atmosphere and outer space
1743	COSMOS-1400	5 August	675	631	81.2	97.6		Investigation of the upper atmosphere and outer space
1744	SOYUZ T-7	19 August	280	228	51.6	89.5		Transport to the SALYUT-7 orbital station of a crew comprising L. I. Popov, A. A. Serebrov and S. E. Savitskai to conduct scientic and technical research and experiments
1745	COSMOS-1401	20 August	282	226	82.3	89.3		Investigation of the natural resources of the earth in the interests of various branches of the national economy of the USSR and international co-operation
1746	MOLNIYA-3	27 August	40814	494	62.8	736		Operation of the long-range telephone and telegraph radio communication system in the USSR, and transmission of Central Television programmes to stations in the Orbita network and within the framework of international co-operation
747	COSMOS-1402	30 August	279	254	65	89.6		Investigation of the upper atmosphere and outer space

All objects were launched from territory of the USSR.

2. The following space objects ceased to exist in August 1982 and were no longer in earth orbit at 2400 hours Moscow time on 31 August:

SOYUZ T-5 (1982-042A) PROGRESS-14 (1982-070A) COSMOS-1396 (1982-075A) COSMOS-1398 (1982-077A)

COSMOS-1398 (1982-077A)

REGISTRATION DATA ON SPACE OBJECTS LAUNCHED BY THE USSR IN SEPTEMBER 1982

1. In September 1982, the USSR launched the following space objects:

No.	Name of space object	Date of launching	Basic orbit characteristics					General purpose of space object
			Apogee (km)	Perigee (km)	Inclination (degrees)	Periode (minutes)		
1	2	3	4	5	6	7		8
1448	COSMOS-1403	1 September	380	216	70.4	90.2		Investigation of the upper atmosphere and outer space
1449	COSMOS-1404	1 September	394	211	72.9	90.2		Investigation of the upper atmosphere and outer space
1450	COSMOS-1405	4 September	456	438	65	93.3		Investigation of the upper atmosphere and outer space
1451	COSMOS-1406	8 September	253	222	82.3	89.0		Investigation of the natural resources of the earth in the interests of various branches of the national economy of the USSR and international co-operation
1452	COSMOS-1407	15 September	364	181	67.2	89.2		Investigation of the upper atmosphere and outer space
1453	COSMOS-1408	16 September	679	645	82.5	97.8		Investigation of the upper atmosphere and outer space
1454	EKRAN	16 September	35580	35580	0.3	1426		Transmission of Central Television programmes to a network of receivers for collective use
1455	PROGRESS-15	18 September	258	195	51.6	88.7		Transport of various cargoed to the SALYUT-7 orbital station
1456	COSMOS-1409	22 September	39340	613	62.8	709		Investigation of the upper atmosphere and outer space
1457	COSMOS-1410	24 September	1522	1500	82.6	116		Investigation of the upper atmosphere and outer space
1458	COSMOS-1411	30 September	384	208	72.9	90.1		Investigation of the upper atmosphere and outer space

All objects were launched from territory of the USSR.

2. The following space objects ceased to exist in September 1982 and were no longer in earth orbit at 2400 hours Moscow time on 30 September:

COSMOS-144 (1967-018A)   COSMOS-1399 (1982-078A)   COSMOS-1401 (1982-081A)   COSMOS-1403 (1982-085A)

The Permanent Mission of the Union of Soviet Socialist Republics to the United Nations presents its compliments to the Secretary-General of the United Nations and, in accordance with article IV of the Convention on Registration of Objects Launched into Outer Space, has the honour to transmit the enclosed notification.

The Permanent Mission of the USSR to the United Nations takes this opportunity to renew to the Secretary-General of the United Nations the assurances of its highest consideration.

Notification to the Secretary-General of the United Nations

In accordance with article IV, paragraph 2, of the Convention on Registration of Objects Launched into Outer Space, which specifies that each State of registry of a space object may, from time to time, provide the Secretary-General of the United Nations with additional information concerning a space object carried on its registry, the following additional information is provided concerning the COSMOS-1402 satellite, launched into orbit in the Soviet Union on 30 August 1982.

COSMOS-1402, carrying on board a small nuclear energy unit of the reactor type, completed its programme of work and, on command from earth, ended its active existence on 28 December 1982. The safety system with which the satellite was equipped then split it into three fragments, one of which burnt up on entry into the dense layers of the atmosphere on 30 December 1982. The two remaining fragments consist of the main part of the satellite structure and the reactor core, which has been separated from it. Before the satellite was split into fragments, the reactor was shut off on command from earth.

According to preliminary calculations, the main part of the satellite structure will enter the dense layers of the atmosphere during the last few days of January and the core separated from the reactor will enter those layers in mid-February 1983. The extraction of the core from the reactor ensures that the core will burn up in the dense layers of the atmosphere and be dispersed into fine particles.

Radio communication with the main part of the satellite structure, maintained for two days after the satellite was split into fragments, confirmed the fact that the reactor had been shut off and its core had been separated. The fragments of COSMOS-1402 are being observed in order to forecast the most probable time and place of their entry into the dense layers of the atmosphere.

Radiation after the fragments of COSMOS-1402 enter the dense layers of the atmosphere will be within the limits recommended by the International Commission on Radiological Protection.

Information as contained in UN Doc.
ST/SG/SER.E/72/Add.2 of January 21, 1983

Additional Information Furnished in Conformity with the Convention on Registration of Objects Launched into Outer Space

Note verbale dated 21 January 1983 from the Permanent Mission of the Union of Soviet Socialist Republics to the United Nations addressed to the Secretary-General

The Permanent Mission of the Union of Soviet Socialist Republics to the United Nations presents its compliments to the Secretary-General of the United Nations and, in accordance with article IV of the Convention on Registration of Objects Launched into Outer Space, has the honour to transmit the enclosed notification to supplement the notification from the Permanent Mission contained in its note of 18 January 1983.

The Permanent Mission of the USSR to the United Nations takes this opportunity to renew to the Secretary-General of the United Nations the assurances of its highest consideration.

Notification to the Secretary-General of the United Nations

According to more precise data furnished by the competent Soviet authorities at 7 a.m. Moscow time, 21 January 1983, the fragment of the COSMOS-1402 satellite's structure consisting of its main part without the core of the nuclear reactor has a ballistic coefficient of 0,00453 square metres per kilogram of weight; its altitude at apogee is 206 kilometres, and at perigee 187 kilometres.

The entry of the above-mentioned fragment of the COSMOS-1402 satellite's structure into the dense layers of the atmosphere is expected between 2 a.m. and 9 a.m. Moscow time, 24 January 1983, over the area of the Arabian Sea.

Information as contained in UN Doc.
ST/SG/SER.E/72/Add.3 of January 27, 1983

Additional Information Furnished in Conformity with the Convention on Registration of Objects Launched into Outer Space

Note verbale dated 25 January 1983 from the Permanent Mission of the Union of Soviet Socialist Republics to the United Nations addressed to the Secretary-General

The Permanent Mission of the Union of Soviet Socialist Republics to the United Nations presents its compliments to the Secretary-General of the United Nations and, in accordance with article IV of the Convention on Registration of Objects Launched into Outer Space, has the honour to transmit the enclosed notification to supplement the notification from the Permanent Mission contained in its note of 18 January 1983.

Notification to the Secretary-General of the United Nations

In accordance with article IV, paragraph 2, of the Convention on Registration of Objects Launched into Outer Space, the following additional information is provided concerning the COSMOS-1402 satellite, launched into orbit in the Soviet Union on 30 August 1982.

According to data furnished by the competent Soviet organizations monitoring the flight of COSMOS-1402, the fragment of the satellite consisting of the main part of its structure entered the dense layers of the atmosphere over the central area of the Indian Ocean at 1.10 a.m. Moscow time, on 24 January 1983, and ended its existence.

The satellite's other fragment - the core of the energy unit reactor - will, according to projections, enter the dense layers of the atmosphere between 3 and 8 February 1983 and will burn up completely.

Information as contained in UN Doc.
ST/SG/SER.E/72/Add.4 of February 9, 1983

Additional Information Furnished in Conformity with the Convention on Registration of Objects Launched into Outer Space

Note verbale dated 7 February 1983 from the Permanent Mission of the Union of Soviet Socialist Republics to the United Nations addressed to the Secretary-General

The Permanent Mission of the Union of Soviet Socialist Republics to the United Nations presents its compliments to the Secretary-General of the United Nations and, in accordance with article IV of the Convention on Registration of Objects Launched into Outer Space, has the honour to transmit the enclosed notification to supplement the notification from the Permanent Mission contained in its note of 25 January 1983.

Notification to the Secretary-General of the United Nations

In accordance with article IV, paragraph 2, of the Convention on Registration of Objects Launched into Outer Space, the following additional information is provided about the COSMOS-1402 satellite, launched into orbit in the Soviet Union on 30 August 1982.

According to data from the competent Soviet organizations which have been monitoring the flight of COSMOS-1402, on 7 February 1983, at 1356 hours Moscow time, a fragment consisting of the reactor core of the nuclear energy unit entered the dense layers of the atmosphere over the southern part of the Atlantic Ocean and was completely burnt up.

From that time, COSMOS-1402, launched in the Soviet Union on 30 August 1982, completely ceased to exist.

WORKING PAPERS SUBMITTED TO THE UNCOPUOS LEGAL SUB-COMMITTEE

Canada: Working Paper as Contained in UN Doc. A/AC.105/C.2/L.137 of March 28, 1983

Use of nuclear power sources in outer space

The present working paper represents a consolidation of the previous Canadian working papers as contained in documents A/AC.105/C.2/L.129, A/AC.105/C.2/L.134 and A/AC.105/C.2/L.135. It contains ideas that are put forward for the purpose of structuring and facilitating further our deliberations on promoting the developments of principles relevant to the use of nuclear power sources (NPS) in outer space.

A. Information concerning the use of nuclear power sources

1. Each launching State should furnish to the Secretary-General of the United Nations, at least one month prior to launching, the planned date and time of launching of a space object containing a nuclear power source. All changes in the planned date of launching should be communicated to the Secretary-General as soon as practicable.

2. Each launching State should provide the Secretary-General of the United Nations, at least one month prior to launching, with information relating to generic design, safety tests conducted, basic orbital parameters, and primary and back-up devices, systems and procedures. Each launching State should also provide a safety evaluation statement, including an analysis of accident probability, sufficiently comprehensive to assure the international community that the nuclear power source can be utilized safely.

3. The Secretary-General should transmit this information to all Members of the United Nations as early as possible prior to launching.

4. Each launching State should also provide this information for those space objects containing nuclear power sources which have already been launched into and remain in earth orbit.

B. Safety measures regarding radiological protection

1. States should ensure that their use of space objects containing nuclear power sources meets generally accepted international guidelines for radiological protection; inter alia, the radiological risks involved should conform to the recommendations of the International Commission on Radiological Protection. In particular, the intended benefits to those people incurring radiological risks must adequately compensate for such risks.

2. In any case, States using NPS in outer space should ensure that the radiological risks involved do not exceed (...).

3. States should endeavour to ensure that radiation exposure in all phases of a space mission involving use of NPS, including accident situations, does not exceed 0.5 rem per year for members of the general public.

4. Where the type of nuclear power source utilized makes it unfeasible to prevent the release of nuclear radiation under re-entry conditions, earth orbits should be used which are sufficiently high to allow radio-active materials to decay before re-entry to a level that would meet the conditions set out in paragraph 1. Reactors should not be activated until the space vehicle has reached a safe operating altitude.

5. If a launching State considers it necessary to use NPS in outer space in a way inconsistent with generally accepted international guidelines for radiological protection, it should announce that it is doing so for reasons of national security.

6. The launching State should not use more than (X) nuclear reactor(s) in low-earth orbit at the same time and should not launch more than (X) nuclear reactor(s) a year intended for low-earth orbit.

7. Space objects in low earth orbit containing nuclear reactors should be equipped with at least two back-up systems to boost the object into higher orbit in cases where the object is not to be returned to earth in a controlled re-entry. Where the space object is to return to earth at the completion of its mission, the level of control should at least meet the standards for manned spacecraft.

8. The amount of radioactive fuel contained in space objects should not exceed (...).

1. Whenever it becomes possible to predict with reasonable certainty that a space object containing a nuclear power source will imminently re-enter the earth's atmosphere, the launching State should notify the Secretary-General of the anticipated re-entry and provide him with information adequate to enable Member States to assess the likelihood and consequences of a particular re-entry and to carry out preparations for search and recovery of the nuclear power source and protection of their population. That notification should be in accordance with the following format:

1. *System parameters*

* 1.1   Name of launching State or States including the address or the authority which may be contracted for additional information or assistance in case of accident
* 1.2   International designation
* 1.3   Date and territory or location of launch
  1.4   Information required for best prediction of orbit lifetime trajectory and impact region
* 1.5   General function of spacecraft

---

* Denotes the requirements in the Convention on Registration of Objects Launched into Outer Space (art. IV).

2. *Information on the radiological risk of nuclear power source(s)*

2.1   Type of NPS: radio-isotopic/reactor
2.2   The probable physical form, amount and general radiological characteristics of the fuel and contaminated and/or activated components likely to reach the ground. The term 'fuel refers to the nuclear material used as the source of heat or power.

2. The Secretary-General should transmit this information to all Members of the United Nations as early as possible.

3. In situations where the timely transmission of this information via the Secretary-General is not possible, the launching State should communicate the information direct to those States likely to be affected. States at most risk should be informed first.

D. Assistance to States

1. The State launching a space object containing a nuclear power source that is about to re-enter the earth's atmosphere in an uncontrolled manner, should co-operate to the greatest extent feasible with States along the orbital path of the object in monitoring the object. In doing so, the launching State should bear in mind the need for prompt notification with sufficient information so as

to allow those States likely to be affected to assess the situation, in particular in order to take necessary precautionary measures. States other than the launching State possessing space monitoring and tracking facilities should co-operate for the same purpose with States along the orbital path of the object.

2. The State launching a space object containing a nuclear power source that is about to re-enter the earth's atmosphere in an uncontrolled manner should offer to provide all necessary assistance to States likely to be affected by the re-entry or impact of the space object or its component parts. When an uncontrolled re-entry has occurred, the launching State, in accordance with the provisions contained in article 5, paragraph 4, of the 1968 Agreement on the Rescue of Astronauts, the Return of Astronauts and the Return of Objects Launched into Outer Space, should promptly provide necessary assistance to eliminate possible danger of harm if requested to do so by States over whose territory or areas of jurisdiction the space object disintegrated or on whose territory or areas of jurisdiction debris has landed.

3. Other States or international organizations with relevant technical capabilities should, to the extent feasible, be prepared to provide necessary assistance if requested to do so by the affected States. In this connection, States and international organizations should consider co-operating to establish an international registry that would list those countries and international organizations with expertise available in this field, the type of expertise available and those agencies or branches in which it is available. States, particularly launching States of space objects containing nuclear power sources, should also co-operate to establish appropriate training programmes to assist States to prepare for and deal with re-entering space objects containing nuclear power sources. The special needs of developing countries for assistance in developing their capacity to take precautionary measures and to remedy the effects of an uncontrolled re-entry or impact of a space object containing a nuclear power source should be borne in mind.

E. State responsibility

1. The State launching a space object containing a nuclear power source should bear international responsibility in accordance with international law, including the relevant outer space conventions.

2. Such responsibility should include the obligation of the launching State to offer to provide all necessary assistance to States likely to be affected by the re-entry or impact of its space object containing a nuclear power source; promptly to provide the necessary assistance to eliminate possible danger of harm if requested to do so by the affected States; and, in accordance with the 1972 Convention on International Liability for Damage Caused by Space Objects, to pay compensation for all damage caused by the nuclear power source, including all reasonable expenses for search and clean-up, and damages related to measures taken to prevent and limit radiation exposure and related to the number of people exposed and the degree of exposure.

3. Nothing in these principles shall have the effect of reducing the responsibility of States under international law, including the relevant outer space conventions.

4. States launching nuclear power sources into outer space should consider establishing an independent internationally administered fund for the purpose of satisfying claims for compensation.

5. If damage is caused to other States by the return to earth of a space object containing NPS, punitive (treble) damages should be paid.

Canada, China, Netherlands and Sweden: Working Paper as contained in UN Doc. WG/NPS(1984)WP.4 of 29 March 1984

SAFETY MEASURES CONCERNING RADIOLOGICAL PROTECTION

I. *Precautionary safety measures*

1. States should ensure that their use of space objects containing nuclear power sources meets generally accepted international guidelines contained in the recommendations of ICRP regarding exposure to ionizing radiation. This implies in particular that (a) no practice shall be adopted unless its introduction produces a positive net benefit; (b) all exposures shall be kept as low as reasonably achievable, economic and social factors* being taken into account; and (c) the dose equivalent to individuals shall not exceed the limits recommended for the appropriate circumstances by the Commission.

2. A careful analysis of these issues should be undertaken by the launching States prior to the use of NPS in space. The results of such an analysis should be communicated in a timely manner to other States to the extent feasible.

3. Where the type of nuclear power source utilized makes it unfeasible to prevent the release of radioactive materials under re-entry conditions, States should use earth orbits which are sufficiently high to allow radioactive materials to decay before re-entry to a level that would meet the conditions set out in ICRP publication 26. Reactors should not be activated until the space vehicle has reached a safe operating altitude.

---

* These terms are meant to indicate the cost effectiveness of radiation protection measures and to take into account public perceptions of radiation exposure.

4. In case of a possible re-entry of a space object into the atmosphere, leading to dispersal of radioactive material, it is recommended that States monitor the event, assess the situation and decide on the need for safety measures.

5. In order to make it possible for States to take safety measures, advice and assistance should be made available upon request by the launching State and other States in a position to do so to States concerned, in particular developing countries, bearing in mind the Radiation Emergency Plan of IAEA.

III. *Action to be taken after re-entry of a space object carrying an NPS*

IV. *Assistance to States*

QUESTIONS RELATING TO THE DEFINITION/DELIMITATION OF OUTER SPACE AND OUTER SPACE ACTIVITIES AND THE CHARACTER AND UTILIZATION OF THE GEOSTATIONARY ORBIT

by M. Benkö and W. de Graaff

Introduction

The question of the definition and/or delimitation of outer space, which will be referred to in this chapter as the delimitation question, is one of the oldest problems in the field of space law. Already in 1959 this item was discussed by the *ad hoc* Committee on the Peaceful Uses of Outer Space, and it still is on the agenda of the UNCOPUOS Legal Sub-Committee[1]. Since 1984 it has even been a priority item for which a special working group was established[2].

In the legal debate a great number of solutions to the delimitation question have been put forward. This may already be indicated by the fact that the Secretariat of the UNCOPUOS Legal Sub-Committee issued two background papers about this problem; approx. 60 pages were needed alone for the presentation of the proposals which were under deliberation until 1977[3]. Still, up to the present no consensus could be reached - although five international instruments were elaborated by UNCOPUOS in the field of space law. None of these instruments contains a definition and/or delimitation of outer space or outer space activities. As to details of the present debate see sec. 3.2 below.

In order to facilitate the work of the Legal Sub-Committee, the question of delimitation was also examined by the Scientific and Technical Sub-Committee. However, in 1967 the Sub-Committee arrived at the conclusion that at that time no scientific and technical criteria could be found which would permit a precise and lasting definition of outer space[4] and which would be acceptable to all States. This situation is still unchanged, in spite of a number of well-documented proposals and studies submitted since that time. The delimitation question remains a problem to be solved by the UNCOPUOS Legal Sub-Committee.

In 1976 a new problem was added to the delimitation issue, related to the *character and the use of the geostationary orbit*. A number of developing countries voiced their concern that the geostationary orbit might one day be over-crowded by the industrial nations as a result of the practice of the 'first come, first served' - concept. They feared that orbit positions would no more be available to developing countries who at that time did not yet employ satellites in the geostationary orbit. On December 3, 1976, eight Equatorial countries (Brazil, Colombia, Congo, Ecuador, Indonesia, Kenya, Uganda, and Zaire) issued the so-called 'Bogotà Declaration'[5]. They claimed that the geostationary orbit located at an approximate distance of 35,800 km over the Earth's equator is a 'national resource corresponding to their (the Equatorial countries') national terrestrial, sea and insular territory'. Therefore they claimed sovereign rights for the part of the geostationary orbit situated over their territories. This implied - according to their view - that the stationing of satellites within this section of the geostationary orbit should be subject to their prior and express consent[6].

This position, which is still upheld by a number - though not all - of the Equatorial States, added several new aspects and perspectives to the delimitation debate from the legal as well as from the political point of view (see sec. 3.4 below).

In the following, after a short survey of the relevant scientific aspects, we shall give a summary of the *present* discussion of the agenda item 'matters relating to the delimitation of outer space and to the character and utilization of the geostationary orbit' within the UNCOPUOS Legal Sub-Committee.

3.1   The Delimitation Question: Some Scientific and Technical Aspects

3.1.1   Basic Differences between Air Space and Outer Space

From the ancient times onward, man has dreamt of the possibility of leaving the surface of the Earth and moving about in the space above. A well-known testimony of this desire is the story about Daedalus and Icarus, who tried to escape from their imprisonment in Minoan Crete and fly in the air, just as birds do, by attaching artificial wings to their arms. Later, man actually succeeded in realizing his dream; first by building balloons filled with hot air, afterwards by constructing motor-driven aircraft, and finally, during the last three decades, by launching spacecraft into what is called outer space. As he did so, he set rules to govern his conduct in the newly opened domain, however, so far without explicitly establishing its frontiers separating it from other domains, in particular from air space, the domain used by balloons, aircraft, and similar devices and governed by the rules of air law.

At the present time, there is a clear and unambiguous distinction between balloons and aircraft on the one hand and spacecraft on the other hand, just as a clear distinction exists between vehicles moving on the solid ground and ships floating on the water. The fundamental distinction is that balloons and aircraft derive their motion capability in some way or other from the properties of the surrounding air, whereas a spacecraft must be capable of moving in space without any support whatsoever from the air, the only exception being its planned, intact, and safe return to the ground. Of course, these distinctions do not preclude the existence of hybrid vehicles which can move both on land and on water, or both in the air and on land, or both in the air and on water, or both in space and in the air.

A practical consequence of these distinctions between aircraft and spacecraft is that aircraft possess a relatively high degree of freedom in their motions. Their direction, *e.g.*, can be changed at will, the only condition being that the horizontal speed of their fixed or rotating wings remains sufficiently high to produce the airlift necessary to prevent the craft from falling to the ground. This is not the case with a spacecraft. Once a spacecraft has been injected into its orbit (*i.e.* after the motor of the last stage of the launching rocket has shut down), it has to move continuously in a specific orbit around the Earth, which is (apart from minor perturbances) completely determined by the injection parameters: the position of the injection point above the Earth and the magnitude and direction of the injection velocity. Unless the spacecraft is equipped with powerful rocket motors and sufficient amounts of fuel, it is impossible to alter its orbit in any significant way. Due to the rotation of the Earth underneath the orbit once a day, its ground trajectory will in the course of time cross the territory of almost every State between the northern and southern latitude corresponding to the orbit inclination (see Figs. in chapter 2, sec. 2.2.1, above).
The question arises, at what altitudes balloons and aircraft on the one hand, and spacecraft on the other, can perform their respective motions. The airlift necessary for balloons and aircraft to remain up in the air decreases with decreasing air density, and, since the air density decreases with increasing altitude, the same is true for the airlift. On the other hand, the propulsive force of an aircraft motor also decreases with the air density and, consequently, with the altitude. In practice, balloons and aircraft remain well below 60 km of altitude.

The same density which is so essential for the flight of balloons and aircraft is rather a disadvantage to the motion of spacecraft. The air drag exerts a braking force on a moving spacecraft, thereby diminishing its velocity. This force is proportional to the air density and thus increases with decreasing altitude. Since a decrease in velocity leads to a decrease in orbital altitude, the braking force and the resulting deceleration will gradually increase until a point is reached where the spacecraft will no longer be able to complete a full orbit around the Earth. It will then return to Earth, either intact, in case of a carefully prepared, planned re-entry (all manned missions and some unmanned ones), or in the form of debris, in case of natural decay (most unmanned missions). The altitude of this 'point of no return' depends upon the structure of the spacecraft and in particular upon its so-called ballistic coefficient or drag coefficient. This coefficient is the effective cross-sectional area per unit mass in the flight direction of the spacecraft, usually given in square meters per kilogramme of mass. It may vary considerably from one spacecraft to the other, between large values for light, hollow ones and small values for heavy, massive ones. Even for one and the same spacecraft it may depend upon the attitude of the craft with respect to its flight direction.

The laws of physics determining the motion of spacecraft in the atmosphere are well known and completely reliable[7]. However, some of the quantities included in those laws, such as the air density as a function of altitude, do vary in a way which is not always accurately predictable.

Nevertheless, it has been found[8] that only in very exceptional cases spacecraft can orbit the Earth at altitudes lower than between 90 and 100 km. Therefore, if the altitude of a spacecraft reaches such a value at perigee, it will be bound to decay within the next orbit. This is equivalent to saying that no orbital spaceflight is possible at altitudes lower than between 90 and 100 km (the perigee is the point where the orbit is nearest to the Earth, while the apogee is farthest away from the Earth).

3.1.2   Spacecraft Trajectories at Launch and Re-entry

At *launch*, the air drag opposes the lift force of the rocket motor, thereby reducing its effectiveness, particularly in the lower, denser layers of the atmosphere. In order to minimize this reduction, the launch trajectory is chosen in such a way that the rocket will pass through the denser layers in the shortest possible time at the lowest possible speed. For this purpose, the trajectory is chosen to be very steep, with elevations of some 70 degrees above the horizon or more, up to an altitude between 10 and 20 km. Afterwards, at altitudes where the air density has become sufficiently low, the flight direction is gradually changed to lower elevations in order to proceed to the ultimate, nearly horizontal orbital injection trajectory. Figure 1 shows a typical ascent trajectory for a three-stage carrier rocket. It can be seen that the space vehicle reaches altitudes above 100 km at a horizontal down-range distance from the launching site not exceeding a few hundred kilometers. This shows that space objects which are launched into outer space do not have to cross foreign air space at altitudes below 100-110 km under regular conditions, because any space object, irrespective of its destination, reaches the altitude of 100 km already at a distance of only a few hundred km from its launching site. A slightly different situation may arise with the use of the *spaceplane*, which will be able to take off from and land on any conventional runway[9] like an airplane.

However, Fig. 1 shows a different problem arising from the launching of satellites: the burnt-out stages of the carrier rocket fall back to Earth at distances between a few hundred and several thousands of kilometers (*e.g.* of the Saturn 5 launch vehicle used for the Apollo missions to the Moon, the second stage impacted at surface distances between 4,000 and 5,000 km down-range). Also the heat shield of the satellite will fall back to Earth at a considerable distance from the launching site. In this connection we have to bear in mind that particularly the first and second stages of these rockets may be very heavy. For the Saturn 5 launch vehicle they had masses of about 50 and 6 tons, respectively, and for the Ariane stages these figures were 13 and 3 tons. For this reason, the location of launching facilities and the trajectories of spacecraft launched have been carefully selected to ensure a ground trajectory either over the High Seas or over the territory of the launching State itself.

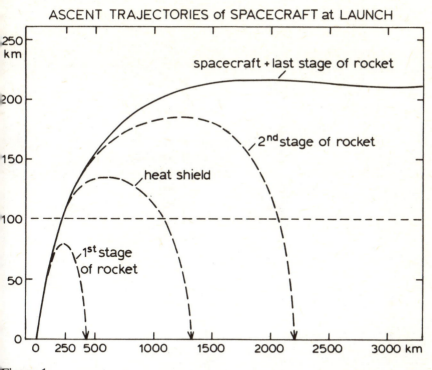

Figure 1

Typical example of an ascent trajectory for a three-stage launching rocket, showing the approximate down-range impact distances of the discarded rocket stages and other fragments. In some cases the down-range distance of the last stage may be up to 5,000 km.

Serious problems might arise from the possible impact of spent rocket parts on foreign territory, if a State whose territory does not include any suitable location satisfying the safety regulations normally imposed on launching sites should nevertheless wish to construct its own facility and to launch its own satellites. In this case, the co-operation of any State potentially affected by such an enterprise has to be ensured, since safety measures will have to be taken by this State, *e.g.* evacuation of certain areas, or arrangements to clear the flight path below the space object from international aviation[10]. Moreover, the foreign State concerned might wish that spacecraft trajectories in the range of which satellite parts can still impact on the Earth should not lead over populated areas.

In case of a satellite's *re-entry* to the Earth the situation is different. As can be seen from Fig. 2, altitudes below 100 km are typically reached at surface distances of some 2,000 km from the expected touchdown area, even for completely different types of spacecraft and different types of descent trajectory profiles. For spacecraft like the space shuttle or the spaceplane these distances will be much longer: the space shuttle even has to cross an area of about 7,000 km below the altitude of 100 km before landing[11].

126

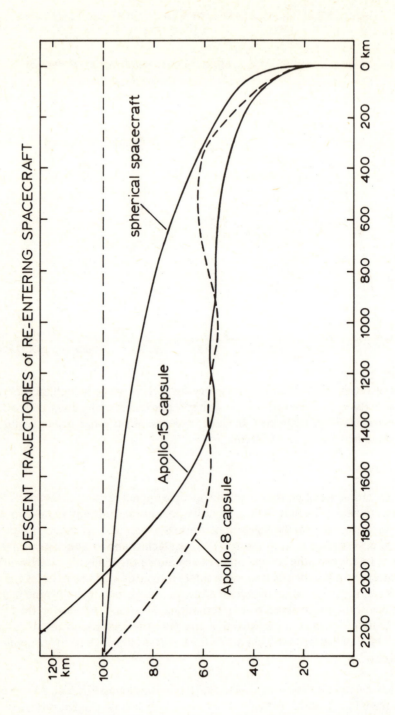

Figure 2
Typical examples of descent trajectories for various types of re-entering spacecraft.

This shows that the question relating to the passage of space objects through foreign air space mainly becomes relevant in the case of *re-entry*. As we can see from Fig. 2, spacecraft has to fly a distance of approx. 1,700 km at altitudes around 60 km - well below the lowest perigee altitude of spacecraft explained above. Yet, those trajectories still lie above the domain used by balloons and aircraft, so that no serious interferences with normal air traffic are to be expected in this case. However, at distances less than a few hundred km from the landing point, *i.e.* during the last ten to fifteen minutes before landing, the altitude is lower than 60 km, and precautions have to be taken to avoid interference with the air traffic.

As a last remark relating to Figs. 1 and 2, it should be noted that in both Figures the vertical scale is ten times larger than the horizontal scale in order to show the relevant features of the trajectories in more detail. The actual trajectories are far more shallow than would appear at first glance from these Figures.

3.2 Present State of the Legal Debate and Suggested Solutions within UNCOPUOS

As a solution to the delimitation question in the legal field mainly two approaches are under consideration: the spatial and the functional approach.

3.2.1 The Spatial Approach

The spatial approach attempts to establish the lower boundary of outer space. As to the altitude of such a demarcation no less than eight possible criteria have been identified in the two background papers prepared by the Secretariat of the UNCOPUOS Legal Sub-Committee in 1970 and 1977[3]. They were listed as follows:

A. Demarcation based upon the equation of the upper limit of national sovereignty with the concept of 'atmosphere'
B. Demarcation based on the division of atmosphere into layers
C. Demarcation based on the maximum altitude of aircraft flight (theory of navigable air space)
D. Demarcation based on aerodynamic characteristics of flight instrumentalities (von Kármán line)
E. Demarcation according to the lowest perigee of an orbiting satellite
F. Demarcation based upon the Earth's gravitational effects
G. Demarcation based on effective control
H. Demarcation based upon the division of space into zones.

There were also theories based on combinations of the various approaches. For several years now, however, only one of these theories, namely that mentioned under point E above, has still been advocated by those States who favour a spatial delimitation[1,3]. The other delimitation theories are no more under discussion, so that we shall refrain from analysing them in this context. As to details thereof, we refer to the above-mentioned background papers prepared by the Secretariat of the UNCOPUOS Legal Sub-Committee[3], as well as to the great number of excellent studies in space law literature.

Returning to the spatial delimitation theory which is being debated at present in the Outer Space Committee - *i.e.* delimitation according to the lowest perigee of an orbiting satellite at an altitude of approx. 100-110 km above sea level -, a number of arguments have been expressed in favour of this theory.

First of all, it is argued that it would satisfy the demands of free space flight and space exploration, for it defines outer space as the region in which a satellite can still describe a full orbit around the Earth. At altitudes *below* 100-110 km this is impossible, since due to the air drag the satellite would burn up or re-enter the Earth's atmosphere.

Secondly, the needs of international civil aviation would be taken care of, because this delimitation lies well above the maximum altitude where an aircraft as such can operate, which is at present well below 60 km above sea level. Thus - as a rule - interferences between air traffic and outer space activities, as well as between the different legal regimes which are applicable to air space and outer space, can be avoided.

Thirdly, this theory would be in agreement with the actual practice, because so far no State has protested against satellites passing over its territory at altitudes above 100-110 km (under regular, *i.e.* non-accident, conditions)[15].

The most recent demand for a spatial delimitation was laid down in a working paper from April 4, 1983, which was submitted by the USSR to the UNCOPUOS Legal Sub-Committee[12]. In connection with this demand, the USSR claims the right of 'free (peaceful) passage' for spacecraft below this limit through foreign air space for the purpose of take-off and landing. The object of this claim seems to be the access to outer space without let or hindrance, combined with a right of passage through foreign air space.

The above-mentioned USSR working paper from April 4, 1983[12] reads as follows:

Approach to the delimitation of air space and outer space

1. The boundary between outer space and air space shall be established by agreement among States at an altitude not exceeding 110 km above sea level, and shall be legally confirmed by the conclusion of an international legal instrument of a binding character.

2. This instrument shall also specify that a space object of any State shall retain the right of innocent (peaceful) passage over the territory of other States at altitudes lower than the agreed boundary for the purpose of reaching orbit or returning to earth.

The term 'peaceful' passage, which replaces the term 'innocent' passage in an
earlier version of the working paper, was explained by the USSR delegation as
being a passage which does not cause adverse effects in the territory of the
State whose air space is crossed[13]. As to the legal basis of such passage rights,
however, no comments were made.

3.2.2   The Functional Approach

According to the functional approach to the delimitation question, the legal
regime governing outer space should be based primarily on the *nature* and the
type of particular space activities[3]. A distinction is made between aeronautical
and astronautical activities, wherein the latter should be subject to space law -
irrespective of the altitude at which they are carried out.
Such an approach would render it unnecessary to solve the theoretical dispute
of whether there is a boundary between air space and outer space and where it
should be located. Instead, however, the functional solution raises problems
concerning the definition of the terms 'space activity' and 'space flight', as well
as the distinction between aircraft and spacecraft. For example, a consequence
of the functional approach might be that a spacecraft would be exclusively subject to the rules of space law from launch to landing, even when it crosses the
sovereign air space of a foreign State.

It is argued that the functional approach would permit a definition of objectives and missions for space activities, and that regulations could be established
to avoid possible interferences between activities peacefully carried out and
activities which could have adverse consequences for human life on Earth.
However, a substantial proposal, offering a functional solution to the problem
of delimitation has not been submitted to the Legal Sub-Committee during the
last few years. For this reason, attention is focused here on the spatial approach.

3.2.3   A Third Approach to the Delimitation Question

During the last few decades a substantial number of contributions to the study
of the delimitation problem have been made, not only by national delegations,
but also by international organizations and by individual authors. Among
these are studies which address the scientific and technical aspects of the establishment of a boundary between air space and outer space, as discussed in
section 3.1 of this chapter. It has been demonstrated that the motion of aircraft
and spacecraft is governed by different physical principles: support from the
atmospheric air in the case of aircraft; absence of any such support in the case
of spacecraft. It has also been demonstrated that different environmental conditions are required for these principles to operate: a sufficiently high air density in the case of aircraft motion; sufficiently low air density in the case of spacecraft motion.

At present (and for the near future) the domains of space where these environmental conditions are met do not overlap, or even touch. Admittedly, it is difficult to define a sharp, accurately measurable boundary where one domain ends, or where the other domain begins, particularly so since the air density not only varies with altitude but, at a given altitude, also with time. Moreover, some space vehicles operate during one part of their mission as a spacecraft and during another part as an aircraft (the US space shuttle is an example of this category). On the other hand, even in this case the transition from one domain to the other is accompanied by violent interactions with the environment, such as heating of the vehicle due to air friction, and loss of radio communication with the outside world which, as a rule, take place at altitudes between 100 and 50 km.

Therefore, some delegations[14] advocate a third approach to the delimitation of outer space, taking as a basis some of these arguments as well as the fact that so far no international complications have arisen from the lack of a well-defined lower boundary of outer space (apart from the problem of the geostationary orbit to be mentioned later in this chapter). They propose, at least for the time being, to refrain from any definition of this lower boundary and to continue the present practice in which the laws of outer space operate without it.

3.3 Comments

3.3.1 Arguments Pro and Contra Delimitation

From the previous sections of this chapter it is clear that, in spite of the long period during which the delimitation problem has already been discussed within UNCOPUOS, even with respect to the basic question - *i.e.* whether a delimitation of outer space is necessary or not - there is no universal agreement between the States involved.

This is mainly due both to the not yet clearly predictable political and economic implications of the problem, as well as to its scientific and technical nature. Particularly the latter constitutes a difficulty to decision makers, who often do not have the scientific and technical background to fully appreciate all of the aspects involved.

3.3.2 Arguments in Favour of Delimitation

3.3.2.1 State Sovereignty and its Limitations

As a decisive argument speaking in favour of a definition/delimitation, the basic difference between the legal status of air space and outer space has been pointed out: while every State has complete and exclusive sovereignty over the air space of its territory, national sovereignty cannot be extended to outer space. According to Art. I of the Outer Space Treaty this region *'shall be free for exploration and use by all States . . . '*, and Art. II of the Treaty provides that 'outer space, including the moon and other celestial bodies, is not subject to national appropriation by claim of sovereignty, by means of use or occupation, or by any other means'. This points out the necessity of a delimitation from the legal point of view.

The argument finds support in the discussions about the character and utilization of the geostationary orbit, where Equatorial countries claim sovereign rights at an altitude of approx. 36,000 km above the equator (see sec. 3.4 below). These discussions, or those of a similar nature, probably could have been prevented if the question of delimitation had been settled earlier.

3.3.2.2 Possible Damage Resulting from the Passage of Spacecraft through Foreign Air Space

So far, no practical problem has arisen from the fact that no delimitation has been agreed upon: no State has protested against satellites overflying its territories (under regular, *i.e.* non-accident, conditions), claiming that its sovereignty had been violated[15]. However, the situation may change.

Under normal conditions - *i.e.* non-accident conditions - satellites overfly the territory of foreign States at altitudes of several hundreds or even thousands of kilometers; the minimum altitude of space objects is never below 100-110 km above sea level. At present, launching sites all over the world are situated in such a way that space objects can be launched either over the High Seas or over the territory of the launching State, so that space objects usually reach a much higher orbit than 100-110 km above sea level before they pass over another State[16]. In case of a spacecraft's planned re-entry, foreign States are not overflown below the altitude of 100-110 km either, since the return trajectories are selected in such a way that these altitudes are reached either over the territory of the launching State or again over the High Seas.
This, probably, is the explanation of the fact that conflicts have not yet arisen between launching States and States whose territories have been overflown under normal conditions.
However, the situation might change if satellites should pass over foreign territory at much lower altitudes. Theoretically, this would be possible, *e.g.* if new launching sites were constructed in areas which do not lie at a sufficient distance of neighbouring States and from where it is not possible to launch or retrieve spacecraft over the High Seas, or if a new category of spacecraft were to be developed. Space objects then might have to pass over foreign territory at altitudes lower than 100-110 km - especially in case of their re-entry (as to spacecraft trajectories at launch and re-entry see sec. 3.1.2 above). In this case neighbouring States might wish to protect their safety interests, claiming their sovereign air space violated by the launching State. Such safety interests might regard *e.g.* the security of civil aviation, which might be affected by the passage of a spacecraft at altitudes lower than 60 km.
Even if it does not seem to be realistic that new launching sites will be constructed in the near future, there are indications that some States do not exclude such a possibility altogether. One indication may be the demand which was already raised in the UNCOPUOS Legal Sub-Committee, claiming that

space objects should have the right of free passage through foreign *air space* for the purpose of take-off from and landing on the territory of the launching State[12,13].

In this context 'air space' is understood as being the area over a State's territory up to an altitude of 100-110 km above sea level[17]. This demand seems to fit exactly the situation anticipated above.

And still, even if new launching sites or new types of spacecraft will not be built in the near future, the possibility regarding the passage of spacecraft over foreign territory at altitudes below 100-110 km may not be excluded altogether. This is due to the fact that there are already space objects such as the US space shuttle[18], which can land like an aircraft on a regular runway of an airport. It should be emphasized, however, that the space shuttle orbiter, after having been brought into its descent and landing trajectory, is not capable of manoeuvring like a motor-driven aircraft, but only of carrying out a gliding movement towards the runway like a sailplane. Up to now, the space shuttle has neither landed outside the USA nor overflown foreign States below 100-110 km during its space missions, and there is no indication that such an operation will be planned without the consultation of the States overflown. (In May-June 1983, the shuttle orbiter Enterprise visited several European airports, mounted on top of a Boeing 747 carrier aircraft. During this visit, a direct passage over the inner city of Paris was prohibited by the local authorities for safety reasons[19].) It might be interesting to mention that in 1983 it had been agreed between the USA and the Federal Republic of Germany that the shuttle was permitted to land on the civilian airport Cologne/Bonn[10] in case an emergency situation should occur during the flight to outer space on November 28, 1983 of Shuttle STS 9 carrying Spacelab 1[19]. A similar arrangement was made for the military Zaragosa Air Base in Spain. If an emergency landing had taken place in the FRG, the shuttle would have crossed Western European air space (mainly British and Dutch) at altitudes below 60 km (see sec. 3.1.2 above).

At the same time provisions were made to reduce the risk that due to propulsion failures during the launch phase of this mission the external tank could impact in countries like Scotland, the GDR, the Soviet Union, Turkey, Iraq, Iran, and Saudi Arabia. Fortunately, no serious problems occurred during this mission: there was no need to use a European emergency landing site, and the external tank hit the ocean south of Australia as planned, some 25,000 km from the launching site.

A space transportation system which will be similar to the US space shuttle is already being developed in the USSR[20], and other such options are under study in Japan and in some European countries.

3.3.2.3   The Spaceplane, a New Development

According to recent reports, the United States Air Force has taken steps to promote the development of a so-called spaceplane, capable not only of landing like an aircraft (as the shuttle does), but also of taking off from a conventional runway like an aircraft and accelerating directly from there into Earth orbit. It is expected that such a spaceplane will be available for US military space missions in the 1990's. It will be capable of carrying payloads of up to some 10 tons into any Earth orbital plane, independent of a launching site[9].

So far, no details have been given about the expected construction and performance of such a spaceplane, apart from a reference to the 'production of new structural and thermal materials and the recent development of the space shuttle main engine'[9]. This seems to indicate that the essential new feature of the spaceplane concept will be an adaptation of the shuttle system with the purpose of replacing the present vertical take-off from a launching pad with a horizontal take-off from a conventional runway. Apparently, the new vehicle will contain a conventional rocket propulsion system similar to that of the shuttle and will, after take-off, be brought into a steeply ascending trajectory in order to enable an efficient use of the rocket motors which will boost the plane into its destined Earth orbit.

Just as the shuttle, it will during each mission have only one possibility of entering into a transfer trajectory back to Earth, where it is very likely to land in a way similar to the shuttle's, with the possible addition of a better manoeuvring capability as an aircraft at lower altitudes. After landing, it will have to be refurnished and refuelled before the next take-off. It is unlikely, however, that it will be able to combine the orbital capabilities of a spacecraft with the full, unrestricted manoeuvring capabilities of a conventional aircraft at low altitudes.

Still, the new vehicle will undoubtedly act as a spacecraft during one part of its mission, and as an aircraft during other parts. It will be a hybrid type of vehicle, operating mainly in outer space but partly also in air space, under certain conditions maybe even in the air space of a foreign State. This development can be considered an argument against a functional approach to the delimitation problem and in favour of an agreed demarcation between sovereign air space and outer space which shall be 'free for exploration and use by all States' (Art. I of the Outer Space Treaty).

3.3.3   Arguments against Delimitation

3.3.3.1   Practical Experience without Delimitation up to the Present

The leading argument against the necessity of a delimitation points out that all legal problems which have arisen until present have been solved without an agreed solution to the delimitation question. The reason for this is the fact that *e.g.* in case of accidents the application of the relevant provisions of the Outer Space Treaty and of the Liability Convention does not depend on the location *where* the accident happened, namely in air space or in outer space. It is only relevant that the damage has been caused by a *space object*.

As to this point Art. VII of the Outer Space Treaty provides:

> Each State Party to the Treaty that launches or procures the launching of a space object into outer space, including the moon and other celestial bodies, ... is internationally liable for damage to another State Party ... by such an object or its component parts on the Earth, *in air space or in outer space, including the moon and other celestial bodies* (emphasis added).

The same principle holds for the application of the Registration Convention and the Rescue Agreement. In both cases the obligation of States can be determined clearly without the necessity of defining the terms 'air space' and 'outer space'.

This situation seems to be satisfactory for the time being because the major legal issues arising from the exploration and the use of outer space are primarily questions relating to the liability of States in case of accidents, as well as the registration of space objects and notification of States about space activities which are being carried out. Since the number of space objects launched into outer space is increasing, and from the statistical point of view every single day a satellite re-enters the Earth's atmosphere[21] (although in most cases burning up upon re-entry), these questions remain among the most important problems in space law.

Nevertheless, it is quite possible that in the future problems may arise which cannot be solved without a delimitation, as already indicated in sec. 3.3.2 above.

3.3.3.2 Gradual Transition between Air Space and Outer Space

As a second argument against a delimitation, reference is made to the UN-COPUOS Scientific and Technical Sub-Committee's conclusion from 1967, in which it is stated that there was consensus in the Scientific and Technical Sub-Committee that it was not possible at that time to identify scientific or technical criteria which would permit a precise and lasting definition of outer space[4].

In a strict sense, this conclusion is still correct. Although, as we have seen in sec. 3.1.1, air space and outer space are two clearly distinguishable environmental domains in which normal movements of vehicles are governed by fundamentally different physical principles, it is true that the transition from one domain to the other is a gradual one and not a clearly recognizable, sharply defined one. Furthermore, as we have already seen, some of the relevant properties of the Earth's atmosphere such as density and temperature vary both with time and with position above the Earth's surface. Therefore, any definition of a boundary between the two domains involving precise values of these properties would lead to a delimitation at variable altitudes.

As an objection to this argument it can be pointed out that for the present time and for the near future the two domains in actual practice do not overlap. Thus - from the scientific and technical point of view - it would be feasible to select a boundary at a precise and constant altitude somewhere within the transition zone, *e.g.* at 100 km or near it[7].

3.3.3.3 Implications of Possible Future Developments

Sometimes it is said that any precise delimitation of outer space agreed upon at present might become obsolete in the future as a result of new technological developments permitting, *e.g.*, vehicles to move freely both in air space and in outer space.

It is certainly true that quite a number of revolutionary technological developments have taken place in the past, and space technology itself is a good example of this. Therefore, it would seem preposterous to claim that no such developments will occur in the future. All over the world studies are carried out involving the development of new propulsion systems for space vehicles. It is quite possible that at some stage in the future spacecraft will be provided with new types of motors which will greatly facilitate the ascent to and descent from orbits around the Earth. However, it is very difficult to anticipate exactly what would be the consequences of such developments for the present delimitation problem.

So, for the time being it seems better to proceed from the present situation and its expected changes in the near future (as, for example, discussed in secs. 3.3.2.2 and 3.3.2.3) and to base any legal considerations on these.

3.3.4 The Passage of Spacecraft through Foreign Air Space[24]

We have already pointed out in the previous section that in case of an agreement on spatial delimitation we might be confronted with the problem of rights of passage through foreign air space for space objects.
In favour of such passage rights it has been argued that the freedom of outer space also includes free *access* to outer space. Otherwise, only a limited number of States would be in the privileged position to profit from the freedom of outer space, while other 'space locked' States (*i.e.* States whose territorial conditions preclude the ascent or descent of spacecraft solely through their own air space; see sec. 3.1.2) would be deprived of the right to explore and use outer space on an equal basis. It is also argued that the passage of space objects is by no means harmful to the State overflown, as in most cases it only takes a few minutes to complete such a passage.
On the other hand, it has to be taken into account that according to international law *no* such passage rights are acknowledged. Therefore, specific legal norms will be required, if a demand for passage rights is granted[25]. However, in case that legal rules are elaborated, *e.g.* by the UNCOPUOS Legal Sub-Committee, it will not suffice simply to codify the right of passage for space objects for the purpose of take-off or landing on the territory of the launching State; quite a number of practical aspects will have to be taken into consideration. They include, *e.g.*, the impact trajectories of spent stages of the launching

136 rocket, and the possible interference of landings on a widely used airfield in a crowded area with normal civil air traffic.

3.3.5 Summary: Present Situation and Future Aspects of Delimitation

Until the present time (mid 1984) no delimitation of outer space could be agreed upon within UNCOPUOS. A great number of States are in favour of a delimitation at a fixed altitude at or near 100 km above sea level (according to a proposal made by the USSR mentioned in sec. 3.2.1). Still, even the basic question which has to be discussed before a decision on this or any other delimitation proposal can be made, *i.e.* whether delimitation as such is necessary or whether it is preferable to continue the present situation without delimitation, has not been agreed upon.

As to the scientific and technical aspects of delimitation, it has been demonstrated in the previous sections that space around the Earth consists of two domains (air space and outer space) in which vehicles have to use fundamentally different propulsion techniques. These two domains are well separated by a transition region. From the scientific and technical point of view it is therefore quite feasible to select a suitable boundary between the two domains (see secs. 3.1.1 and 3.3.3.2 above).

However, any agreement on such a demarcation altitude has to be based not only on scientific and technical information, but also on *legal, political, economic, and military considerations.* In this respect, a delimitation at a fixed altitude has its advantages and disadvantages (see sec. 3.3.1 above).
The lack of an agreed delimitation has not resulted in any international conflict so far. Real or potential damage caused by spacecraft could until now be dealt with on the basis of existing international law, including space law. Furthermore, one has to bear in mind that even if an agreement should be achieved, *e.g.* based on a spatial delimitation at an altitude of 100/110 km, this will not put an end to problems arising from the passage of spacecraft through the (then newly defined) air space of foreign States: as has been pointed out in the summary of the present debate within UNCOPUOS (sec. 3.2 above), the question was raised that spacecraft be granted the right of 'innocent (peaceful)' passage through foreign air space for the purpose of take-off or landing on the territory of the launching State (as to details see secs. 3.2.1 and 3.3.4 above). This question not only points to legal problems arising from a spatial delimitation, but it also constitutes an intricate matter of political dispute - especially as to the determination of the 'peaceful'[22] and 'innocent' character of a space object's passage. In this connection we have to bear in mind that approximately 75% of all space activities which are carried out by the two major space powers are military[23], and that at present there is no direct way to verify the peaceful (or military) character of a spacecraft passing through air space.

A fixed delimitation based on valid scientific and technical criteria has the advantage that it is clear from the outset which regime of international law is applicable to a given space activity. Problems like the claims for sovereignty over parts of the geostationary orbit (see sec. 3.4 below) would not have arisen in the case of an agreed delimitation. On the other hand, in case of a delimitation agreement, problems might arise from future developments which might evoke the need for a revision of the agreement.

3.4 Questions Relating to the Geostationary Orbit[26]

3.4.1 Basic Facts about the Geostationary Orbit[27]

In the strict scientific sense of the word, the geostationary orbit is a circular orbit precisely above the equator in which a satellite moves from West to East with a sidereal orbital period equal to the sidereal rotation period of the Earth, *i.e.* 23h 56m 04s. A satellite moving in this orbit will be permanently positioned above the same point of the equator. The geostationary orbit has an altitude of 35,787 km above the equator and consequently a distance of 42,165 km from the Earth's centre of gravity.

In practice, the orbit of a geostationary satellite will deviate from the ideal one due to irregularities in the Earth's gravitational field (the equator is not a perfect circle) and disturbances from the Sun and the Moon. These perturbations lead to oscillations of the satellite's position about the ideal one with amplitudes up to 90 degrees and periods of up to several tens of years. Moreover, the orbit into which a geostationary satellite is brought differs from the ideal orbit right from the beginning due to non-ideal performance of the rocket motors. Such deviations usually result in a slow drift of the satellite's position to the East or to the West.

Still, all these non-ideal orbits can be considered geostationary orbits, since usually a satellite is equipped with small motors to correct drift motions. On the other hand, in order to separate geostationary orbits from non-geostationary ones, it is necessary to specify the amount of deviation from the ideal orbit which can be tolerated for an orbit to be called 'geostationary'.

It should be emphasized that the geostationary orbit, just like any other orbit in space, is not something tangible. In fact, as has been shown, a satellite moving in such an orbit is not 'stationary' at all, since it describes an orbit of a length of about 265,000 km with a speed of just over 3 km per second or 11,000 km per hour. It only seems 'stationary' for an observer on Earth, because the Earth rotates with the same angular speed. Actually, it is the spacecraft which rotates along with the Earth, not the orbit as such. Perhaps it were better not to refer to the 'geostationary orbit', only to 'geostationary satellites'.

3.4.2 Present State of the Legal Debate

Looking at the legal debate about the character and utilization of the geostationary orbit, we have to deal first of all with the Equatorial countries' claim for sovereignty over the part of the geostationary orbit which is located over their respective territories. This claim was laid down for the first time in the Bogotà Declaration 1976[5] and was confirmed recently by a working paper entitled 'Draft General Principles Governing the Geostationary Orbit', which was submitted to the UNCOPUOS Legal Sub-Committee by Colombia, Ecuador, Indonesia, and Kenya in 1984[28](see Annex to this chapter). According to Principle V of this proposal 'the placement of a space object in the segment of the geostationary orbit superjacent to an Equatorial State shall require prior authorization by that State'.

Furthermore, this set of principles contains an important claim concerning environmental aspects; namely 'States and/or international organizations operating their space objects in the geostationary orbit shall take actions to remove non-operational or unutilized space objects from the orbit' (Principle VIII).

The claims relating to sovereign rights in the geostationary orbit have been rejected by the technologically developed countries. They argue that the geostationary orbit is an integral part of outer space. Therefore, it is not subject to national appropriation or claim of sovereignty, by means of use or occupation or otherwise, as it is laid down in Art. II of the Outer Space Treaty.

However, there also is a second aspect to the debate on the geostationary orbit: a great number of technologically developing countries, which do not expressly share the Equatorial countries' claims for sovereign rights, are deeply concerned about the possibility that the geostationary orbit, which is a generally recognized *limited natural resource*[1,3], might be increasingly overcrowded as a result of the practice of the 'first come, first served'-concept. They criticize that wide sections of the geostationary orbit are already occupied by the technologically developed nations. In 1982, 171 satellites were stationed in the geostationary orbit, only a few of which belonged to the developing countries[29]. For this reason, these States claim that equitable access to the geostationary orbit should be ensured for all States - especially the developing countries. This demand, however, has already been taken into account at the Second United Nations Conference on the Exploration and Peaceful Uses of Outer Space (UNISPACE 1982) by including a text into the report providing that particular geographical concerns of certain countries should be considered when orbit positions are assigned[30]. This wording is also included in Art. X of the revised version of the International Telecommunication Convention[31]. Furthermore, the Scientific-Technical Sub-Committee of the United Nations Outer Space Committee entrusted a study group with the detailed investigation of the topic from the technical point of view[32]. This group shall examine in how far a closer spacing in the geostationary orbit is possible, taking into account technical and economic considerations, especially with regard to the interests of the developing countries.

3.4.3 Comments

As to the Equatorial countries' claim for sovereign rights over the geostationary orbit, one may observe a connection between the problems relating to the geostationary orbit and the delimitation question. Both topics centre around the question of State sovereignty and its limitations as formulated in the Outer Space Treaty.

On the one hand, it cannot be maintained that the Equatorial countries' claim is incompatible with the express wording of the Outer Space Treaty, since the Treaty does not deal with the delimitation question.

On the other hand, as we have seen, the geostationary orbit is not something tangible: it is a corridor in outer space with the property that satellites moving within it around the Earth corotate with the Earth, and consequently remain in a more or less fixed position in the sky as seen from the surface of the Earth. This - from the legal point of view - renders the claim for sovereign rights over the geostationary orbit impossible, as no 'territory' exists at an altitude of approx. 36,000 km to which such a claim could be attached.

The growing concern of the technologically developing countries, which initially led to the above-mentioned position, is more than understandable. However, it can adequately be dealt with by an agreement on equitable access to the geostationary orbit for *all* States, which is entirely in the spirit of the Outer Space Treaty. The elaboration of a corresponding legal instrument would have to be effected by UNCOPUOS as well as by the International Telecommunication Union (ITU), because the saturation of the geostationary orbit is not only a question of space but is essentially also determined by the number of communication channels available for satellite communications[33] according to agreements reached in the ITU (ITU established detailed procedures for the allocation of frequencies which in fact are being observed before a new satellite system is approved of).

As to Principle VIII of the above-mentioned proposal by Colombia, Ecuador, Indonesia, and Kenya concerning the removal of non-operational space objects from the geostationary orbit, this paragraph can be interpreted as a practical precondition to ensure the equitable access to and the shared use of orbital positions in the geostationary orbit. This proposal also corresponds to the recommendation made by the UNCOPUOS Secretariat in its Study about the Physical Nature and Technical Attributes of the Geostationary Orbit in 1983[34].

The practical importance of such a proposal has already been pointed out by Smith, a specialist in aerospace and energy systems, who reported about a study prepared by the Aerospace Corporation in 1979 which dealt *i.a.* with the probability of collisions in outer space in general, *i.e.* mainly in orbits below a few thousand km: in the year when the study was prepared there were about 4,000 items in space, and the authors estimated that this would increase to 10,000 trackable items by 1985. They concluded that 'the probability of collision could be as high as 10% by 1985, and 20,000 trackable items could exist in space by 1995, increasing the probability of collision to 20%[35].' As concerns the probability of collision in the geostationary orbit, we do not have any precise estimates. Yet - high or low as it may be - as to the possible consequences of such collisions, we can read in the above- mentioned study by the UNCOPUOS Secretariat[36]:

In addition to the issue of congestion of the geostationary orbit, it is very important to realize that serious difficulties could arise from collisions between spacecraft in this orbit... Satellites which are used for verification of arms control agreements or for continuously monitoring the earth's surface to detect the launches of intercontinental ballistic missiles, and would thus give an early warning of a surprise attack by such missiles, form the basis for feelings of confidence and stable relationships between States. Their status is, therefore, an extremely sensitive one. A collision with such a satellite, or even with a military communications satellite, could arouse fears that an anti-satellite weapon had been used. In fact such fears have been aroused already on several occasions. This has to be viewed in the context of the development and even deployment of such systems. Moreover, as time goes on the probability of collision will increase because we can expect that there will be many more nations orbiting spacecraft in the GSO and because future satellites may be even larger than those currently deployed.

This shows that Art. IX of the above-mentioned 1984 proposal might not only be relevant for the safety of space operations as well as for the protection of the environment, but also for the maintenance of international security and peace on Earth.
In this connection it has to be pointed out that in 1983 for the first time a satellite was removed from the geostationary orbit after its active lifetime: in the framework of the Symphonie-Programme (a joint programme of the Federal Republic of Germany and France) a satellite was boosted into a higher orbit with its remaining fuel after nine years of active lifetime[37]. The same procedure was applied in January, 1984 by ESA with GEOS-2[38] and will be performed with OTS-2 later in 1985 [39].

Furthermore, Art. IX offers a solution to the problem which is caused by the pollution of the electromagnetic radiation spectrum. As was already pointed out by Dr. Reijnen in 1977[40], so-called 'dead' satellites and rocket remnants may disturb the receiving frequency bands in which sensitive instruments for scientific research are operating, such as radio telescopes. In this context, reference was made to an interview which had already been given in 1974 by F. Kerr, radio astronomer at the University of Maryland, who stated (referring to the Applications Technology Satellite-6) that satellites of that type were creating so much electronic interference that radio astronomers sometimes virtually were unable to distinguish the celestial radio signals so crucial to that type of work. Dr. Reijnen furthermore reported Kerr's statement that the satellites used a portion of the radio spectrum especially important to radio astronomy, and that ATS-6 broadcasts approached an even more important frequency, i.e. the 11 cm band, which had especially been set aside by the ITU for the use of radio astronomers in their explorations of quasars, pulsars, distant galaxies, and the Sun. Kerr observed that the signals from those celestial sources were often so faint that they could easily be overwhelmed by signal spill-over from the satellites' powerful radio transmissions, even when the complex crafts were in a different part of the sky, and concluded that we could perhaps live with one or two of such satellites, but if 20 or 100 satellites were put up that interfered in that way it would be catastrophic.

This shows that if the claim for equitable access to the geostationary orbit is to be taken seriously, also a solution to the problems which have been raised by Art. IX of the above-mentioned 1984-proposal relating to the character and utilization of the geostationary orbit will have to be found.

1. As to the debates between 1959 and 1982 we should like to refer to the excellent survey given by Christol, Carl Q., *The Modern International Law of Outer Space*, New York 1982, p. 435 ff, including additional reference; see also Kopal, Vladimir, *The Question of Defining Outer Space, Journal of Space Law* 1981, 154 ff.
   The reports of the UNCOPUOS Legal Sub-Committee of 1983 and 1984 are contained in UN Doc. A/AC.105/320 of April 13, 1983 and A/AC.105/305 of February 24, 1984
2. General Assembly Resolution 38/80 of December 15, 1983, sec. 4(c)
3. *The Question of the Definition/Delimitation of Outer Space*, Background paper prepared by the Secretariat, UN Doc. A/AC.105/C.2/7 of May 7, 1970 and Addendum A/AC.105/C.2/7/Add.1 of January 21, 1977
4. UN Doc. A/AC.105/39 of September 6, 1967, p. 7
5. International Telecommunication Union (ITU) Document WARC-BS (1977) 81-E of January 17, 1977. The text is also reprinted in Jasentuliyana, Nandasiri/Lee, Roy, (eds.), *Manual on Space Law*, Vol. II, New York/Alphen aan den Rijn 1979, p. 383
6. See Christol, *op. cit. supra* note 1, p. 451 ff.
7. Perek, L., *Remarks on Scientific Criteria for Definition of Outer Space, Proceedings of the 19th Colloquium of the International Institute of Space Law*, University of California School of Law, California, 1977, p. 185
8. UN Doc. A/AC.105/164 of January 1976
9. Robinson Jr., Clarence A., *USAF Spurs Spaceplane Research, Aviation Week and Space Technology*, March 26, 1984, p. 16 ff. Covault, Craig, *Spaceplane Called a Weapons Platform, Aviation Week and Space Technology*, July 23, 1984, pp 70-75. As to the development of a spaceplane in the Soviet Union see *Aviation Week and Space Technology*, June 6, 1983, p. 27
10. In case of a possible emergency landing of the space shuttle on Cologne/Wahn Airport such co-operation was ensured by the following bilateral agreement:

    Federal Republic of Germany, Auswärtiges Amt (Foreign Office), Doc. No. 423-455.000 USA of September 22, 1983

    Betr.: *Notlandemöglichkeit der amerikanischen Raumfähre 'Space Shuttle' in der Bundesrepublik Deutschland.*

    Unter Bezugnahme auf die bisher geführten Gespräche bestätigt die Bundesregierung, dass sie unter Berücksichtigung der vorgetragenen Wünsche dazu beitragen wird, eine eventuelle Notlandung der Raumfähre 'Space Shuttle' auf dem Flughafen Köln/Bonn zu ermöglichen. Notwendige Erleichterungen, die mit der Notlandung und späteren Bergung der Raumfähre im Zusammenhang stehen, werden gewährt.Die Bundesregierung geht davon aus, dass die Regierung der Vereinigten Staaten von Amerika für alle mit der Notlandung und dem Abtransport der Raumfähre verbundenen Kosten aufkommt sowie die umfassende Haftung für die aus einer solchen Notlandung eventuell entstehenden Schäden übernimmt.

    Inofficial Translation by the Authors:

    Ref.: *Emergency Landing of the US Space Transportation System 'Space Shuttle' in the Federal Republic of Germany.*

    With reference to the talks had up to present, the Federal Government confirms that in consideration of the requests put forward it will help to provide for a possible emergency landing of the space shuttle on Cologne/Bonn Airport. All necessary facilities connected with the emergency landing and the subsequent recovery of the space shuttle shall be granted. The Federal Government proceeds on the assumption that the Government of the United States of America will compensate for all expenses connected with the emergency landing and the recovery of the space shuttle as well as accept complete liability for all damages possibly resulting from such an emergency landing.

    See also *Aviation Week and Space Technology*, October 10, 1983, p. 55
11. As to the re-entry path of satellites in general see Stanek, Bruno, *Lexikon der Raumfahrt*, Bern 1983, p. 344; the re-entry path of the space shuttle is described on p. 286
12. UN Doc. A/AC.105/C.2/L.139 of April 4, 1983

13. See statement given by the USSR Delegate B. Maiorski during the 1983 session of the UN-
COPUOS Legal Sub-Committee as recorded in UN Doc. A/AC.105/C.2/SR.392 of
April 7, 1983, para. 16, p. 5
14. See UNCOPUOS Background paper of 1970 and 1977, *op. cit. supra* note 3; and the Reports of the UNCOPUOS Legal Sub-Committee of 1983 and 1984, *op. cit. supra* note 1
15. UNCOPUOS Background paper of 1970, *op. cit. supra* note 3, para. 31, p. 13; Christol,
op. cit. supra note 1, p. 435
16. As to a comprehensive description of space centres and their location see Gatland,
Kenneth, (ed.), *The Illustrated Encyclopedia of Space Technology*, New York 1980, p. 32
ff.
17. See sec. 3.2.1 above
18. As to a comprehensive description of the space shuttle see Gatland, *op. cit. supra* note 16,
p. 198 ff; and Stanek, Bruno, *op. cit. supra* note 11
19. *Aviation Week and Space Technology*, June 6, 1983, p. 26
20. See introduction to chapter 4, below
21. Rex, Dietrich, *Der Wiedereintritt grosser Satelliten in die Erdatmosphäre - Risiko und Vorausberechnung (Re-entry of large satellites into the Earth's atmosphere - risk and precalculation), Zeitschrift für Flugwissenschaft und Weltraumforschung* 1980, pp. 354, 356
22. As to the interpretation of the term 'peaceful' see chapter 4, sec. 4.3.1.1, below; and Christol, *op. cit. supra* note 1, p. 25 ff.
23. See chapter 4, sec. 4.1, below
24. As to the question of passage rights in general see Lachs, Manfred, *The Law of Outer
Space*, Leyden 1972, p. 59 ff; Zhukov, Gennadij, *Weltraumrecht*, Berlin 1968, p. 340;
Gál, Gyula, *Fundamental Links and Conflicts Between Legal Rules of Air and Space
Flight*, Presentation made during the 26th Colloquium on the Law of Outer Space, Budapest, October 10-15, 1983; the Proceedings of this colloquium will be published by the American Institute of Aeronautics and Astronautics, New York; Sontag, Peter Michael, *Der
Weltraum in der Raumordnung des Völkerrechts*, Köln 1966, p. 104 ff.; Schwenk, Walter,
*Der Durchflug von Weltraumfahrzeugen durch den nationalen Luftraum, Zeitschrift für
Luft- und Weltraumrecht* 1982, p. 3 ff.; Christol, *op. cit. supra* note 1, pp. 437, 444, 451
25. See Zhukov, Sontag, Schwenk, Gál, *op. cit. supra* note 24. As to the possibilities of co-ordination by the International Civil Aviation Organization concerning interferences between civil aviation and outer space objects traversing the navigable air space see ICAO
Background paper on the Civil Aviation Interests in the Use of Outer Space, as submitted
to the 2nd UN Conference on the Exploration and the Peaceful Uses of Outer Space
A/CONF.101/BP/160/1 of June 1, 1981, pp. 5-6
26. As to the history of the debates see Christol, *op. cit. supra* note 1, p. 451; and the reports
from the UNCOPUOS Legal Sub-Committee of 1983 and 1984, *op. cit. supra* note 1
27. As to the physical nature and technical attributes of the geostationary orbit see Study of the
UNCOPUOS Secretariat A/AC.105/203 of August 29, 1977; Addendum 1 to this paper
of December 11, 1978; Addendum 2 of January 17, 1979; Addendum 3 of May 22, 1979;
and Addendum 4 of May 18, 1983
28. UN Doc. A/AC.105/C.2/L.147 of March 29, 1984
29. See Study of the UNCOPUOS Secretariat, Add. 4, Annex, *op. cit. supra* note 27
30. Report on the 2nd United Nations Conference on the Exploration and the Peaceful Uses
of Outer Space, Vienna, August 9-21, 1982, UN Doc. A/CONF.101/10, paras. 277-288
31. Art. 10, as amended by the Plenipotentiary Conference of ITU, Nairobi 1980: '...taking
into account the needs of Members requiring assistance, the specific needs of developing
countries, as well as the special geographical situation of particular countries'
32. 1983 report of the UNCOPUOS Scientific and Technical Sub-Committee, UN Doc.
A/AC.105/318 of February 24, 1983, p. 10 (c)
33. See Study of the UNCOPUOS Secretariat of August 29, 1977, *op. cit. supra* note 27, pp. 1,
7, 8
34. See Study of the UNCOPUOS Secretariat of May 18, 1983, *op. cit. supra* note 27, pp. 8, 9
35. Smith, Marcia, *Protecting the Earth and Outer Space Environment: Problems of on-orbit
space debris*, Proceedings of the 25th Colloquium on the Law of Outer Space, International Institute of Space Law, New York 1983, p. 47. In her article Ms. Smith refers to Wolfe,
M.G., *Mission Requirements for Orbit Transfer Operations: Final Report*, Vol. I: Executive Summary, El Segundo, California, Aerospace Corporation, February 1979, Aerospace Report No. ATR-79 (7723)-1, Vol. I. As to the problem of space debris in general
see articles by Szilágyi, van Traa-Engelman, and Gordon, also in the Proceedings of the
25th Colloquium on the Law of Outer Space, pp. 53, 55, 63
36. See Study of the UNCOPUOS Secretariat of May 18, 1983, *op. cit. supra* note 27, p. 9
37. See statement delivered by the delegate of the Federal Republic of Germany, K. Damian,

144   on June 18, 1984 during the 27th Session of the UNCOPUOS Main Committee as recorded in UN Doc. A/AC.105/PV.263 of July 18, 1984, p. 20

38.   *Spaceflight*, Vol. 26, No. 6, June 1984, p. 256; Beech, P. et al., *The De-orbiting of GEOS-2, ESA Bulletin* 38, May 1984, pp. 86-89
39.   Ashford, E.W., *OTS Enters Sixth Year of Service, ESA Bulletin* 37, February 1984, pp. 72-76
40.   Reijnen, G.C.M., *Legal Aspects of Outer Space*, Utrecht 1977, p. 69.

COLOMBIA, ECUADOR, INDONESIA, KENYA: WORK-
ING PAPER DRAFT GENERAL PRINCIPLES GOVERN-
ING THE GEOSTATIONARY ORBIT

(UN Doc. A/AC.105/C.2/L.147 of March 29, 1984)

Preamble

Affirming that the Geostationary Orbit which lies on the equatorial plane and the existence of which mainly depends on its relation to gravitational phenomena generated by the earth is a limited natural resource, and therefore its utilization should be rational and equitable and exclusively for the benefit of all mankind;

Bearing in mind that the application of space science and technology relating to the Geostationary Orbit are of fundamental importance for the economic, social and cultural development of the peoples of all States, in particular those of the developing countries, including the equatorial countries;

Recognizing that the Geostationary Orbit shall be used exclusively for peaceful purposes and for the benefit of all mankind;

Noting the urgency of narrowing the gap in the field of space science and technology between the developed and the developing countries;

Recognizing the need to establish a specific legal regime applicable to the Geostationary Orbit which derives from its special physical nature and technical attributes, taking into account the existing legal regimes governing air space and outer space.

Principle I

The Geostationary Orbit shall be used exclusively for peaceful purposes and for the benefit of all mankind.

Principle II

The Geostationary Orbit is a limited natural resource which shall be preserved in the interests of all States, taking into account the needs of the developing countries and the rights of the equatorial States. For that purpose it shall be governed by a specific legal regime.

Principle III

The equatorial States shall preserve the corresponding segments of the Geostationary Orbit superjacent to their territories for the opportune and appropriate utilization of the Orbit by all States, particularly the developing countries.

Principle IV

The equatorial States shall have preferential right to the segment of the Geostationary Orbit superjacent to the territory under their jurisdiction.

Principle V

The placement of a space object in the segment of the Geostationary Orbit superjacent to an equatorial State shall require prior authorization by that State. Transit for peaceful purposes of any space object through this segment shall be allowed.

Principle VI

All States shall endeavour to co-operate in the efficient and economic utilization of the Geostationary Orbit on regional and on global basis, directly or through the United Nations and its specialized agencies and other competent international organizations.

Principle VII

The developed countries, international organizations as well as the developing countries which have already acquired capabilities in space technology should take necessary steps to facilitate and accelerate space science and technology transfers to other developing countries to achieve capabilities in the use of the Geostationary Orbit to serve their national development objectives.

Principle VIII

States and/or international organizations operating their space objects in the Geostationary Orbit shall take necessary actions to remove non-operational or unutilized space objects from the Orbit.

THE PREVENTION OF AN ARMS RACE IN OUTER SPACE

by G.C.M. Reijnen

Introduction

A growing and global concern regarding the militarization of outer space can be noticed. In every newspaper, scientific magazine, radio and television, society is warned against the dangers for the Earth coming from outer space military systems, for example in the form of nuclear blasts as a consequence of warring satellites. To us, it seems that this concern, though justified, is coming somewhat late. When reading material on the history of space research one cannot possibly overlook the indications that space research was a/ a follow-up of military aviation, and b/ a new tool in the pursuing of the balance of power, this time in space. The balance of power was seriously unbalanced in August 1945 by the decision to throw the first atomic bomb ever constructed in human history on the Japanese cities of Hiroshima and Nagasaki. This bomb ended World War II. The research underlying the construction of this bomb was the starting point for accelerated scientific investigation as to the continuation of this type of bomb, or other types such as the hydrogen bomb, or more recently, bombing systems in outer space.

It is perhaps instructive to cite here from the scientific report released in October 1945, six weeks after the first bomb fell, because it shows that forty years later no essential changes took place either in strategic tactics - as the rest of this chapter shows - or in the endeavours to use scientific data for destructive aims:

'Mankind's successful transition to a new age, the Atomic Age, was ushered in July 16, 1945, before the eyes of a tense group of renowned scientists and military men gathered in the desertlands of New Mexico to witness the first end results of their $ 2.000.000.000 effort. Here in a remote section of the Alamogordo Air Base 120 miles southeast of Albuquerque the first manmade atomic explosion, the outstanding achievement of nuclear science, was achieved at 5.30 am of that day.

'Mounted on a steel tower, a revolutionary weapon destined to change war as we know it, or which may even be the instrumentality to end all wars, was set off with an impact which signalized man's entrance into a new physical world. Success was greater than the most ambitious estimates. A small amount of matter, the product of a chain of huge specially constructed industrial plants, was made to release the energy of the universe locked up within the atom from the beginning of time. A fabulous achievement had been reached. Speculative theory, barely established in pre-war laboratories, had been projected into practicality.

'At the appointed time there was a blinding flash lighting up the whole area brighter than the brightest daylight. A mountain range three miles from the observation point stood out in bold relief. Then came a tremendous sustained roar and a heavy pressure wave which knocked down two men outside the control center. Immediately thereafter, a huge multicoloured surging cloud boiled to an altitude of over 40.000 feet. Clouds in its path disappeared. Soon the shifting substratosphere winds dispersed the now grey mass. The test was over, the project a success. The steel tower had been entirely vapourized. Where the tower had stood, there was a huge sloping crater. Dazed but relieved at the success of their tests, the scientists promptly marshalled their forces to estimate the strength of America's new weapon. To examine the nature of the crater, especially equipped tanks were wheeled into the area, one of which carried Dr. Enrico Fermi, noted nuclear scientist. Answer to their findings rests in the destruction effected in Japan today in the first military use of the atomic bomb'

(taken from Appendix 6. War Department Release on New Mexico test, July 16, 1945, as cited in 'Atomic Energy for Military Purposes', in: Review of Modern Physics, vol. 17 no. 4, October 1945).

It was in 1958, thirteen years after the above event and one year after the successful launching of the first artificial satellite, that Eugen Sänger, one of the fathers of space research, remarked (translation GCMR)[1]: 'the strategic position of Europe during the past ten years and in regard to these (spaceflight) technological developments is such that any point in Europe is within scope of middle term ballistic missiles, which type of missiles is today already in the hands of the troops, especially the navy'. Also, Sänger indicated in detail the way in which 'pure energy rays can be used to follow and destroy every material body' (p. 90). He predicted, in two years from 1958, the development by the air force of slightly altered versions of intercontinental war satellites, to be sent to outer space (p. 91).

All of his rather nerve-shattering predictions came true, and worse than that, as we shall see further in this chapter.

However, space research has, from its early beginnings up to now, a double function. The first function is to develop and build instruments able to derive scientific information in regard to the universe, and to use this information so as to continue developing new, more refined scientific instruments and further knowledge of the universe.

This is the civilian part of space research. The second function is to apply the scientific instruments themselves and the outcome of their investigations to political purposes, such as to maintain the balance of power in the world.

This is the military part of space research.

These two parts nowadays do increasingly intermingle.

As to the balance of power, it is interesting to note that the United States is superior or equal to the Soviet Union in 19 of 20 basic technologies that will influence the balance of power during the next 10 to 30 years. The quality of US weapons is equal or superior to the quality of Soviet weapons in 27 of 32 separate categories, including land-based nuclear missiles, submarines and bombers[2].

Space research, essentially, can be used either for civilian or for military purposes as we said. We read, though, that[3] military activities account for about three-quarters of the expenditure on space projects by both the USA and the USSR. So, for example, in 1981 the USSR launched 858 military and 392 civilian missions, while the US launched 420 military and 327 civilian payloads.

As space research was up to the early eighties a strictly governmental affair in set-up and financing, it is not unnatural that a strong interrelation existed and still exists between the civilian and the military part of space research. This interrelation is particularly clear in the US space shuttle which, in the early phases of its development, was said to concentrate on civilian purposes whereas at the fourth flight of the shuttle in 1982 it was officially announced that no particulars of this flight could be given, as the majority of its payloads were of a military nature[4].

In 1983 we read[5] that a national space transportation system budget that would combine several billion dollars of both Defense Department and NASA shuttle facility and operations costs into a separate entity is under initial evaluation at NASA. This means that the difference between civilian and military operations of the shuttle is becoming increasingly smaller and that no more specification of the exact purposes of the shuttle flight shall be given or needed.

Also, the space shuttle policy calls for the development and operation of the shuttle by NASA in co-operation with the Department of Defense, but while referring to the shuttle as the primary launch system for both military and civilian missions, it gives priority to national-security missions[6].

It should be noted here that civilian missions are viewed as being of a peaceful nature, whereas military missions are not. However, military purposes can, in the USA point of view, also be peaceful, since peaceful purposes include activities in pursuit of national security goals (also note 6).

Let us see, then, what the shuttle will transport into space in order to secure national security:

— defense satellite communications systems - a series of satellites for the geostationary orbit
— defense support programme - early warning satellites
— Navstar global positioning systems - four craft each in three separate orbits 16.000 km above the Earth to be launched in 1986-1987
— a classified payload described in Congressional testimony as having orbital characteristics similar to a satellite interceptor
— defense meteorological satellite programme. The craft are similar to the weather satellites that the civilian National Oceanic and Atmospheric Administration operates
— advanced follow on to the Big Bird (officially entitled: Program 467) and Keyhole 11 spy satellites, in polar orbit.

Big Bird is a reconnaissance type of satellite. It transmits medium resolution images by radio and sends high resolution images back to Earth by means of one of the five containers with which it is equipped.

Keyhole also is a reconnaissance satellite, first launched in 1976. It has a medium resolution.

Furthermore, in the near future the military may be driving its own version of the shuttle. The Air Force has studied a small space plane that a Boeing 747 would launch piggyback fashion. It would go into space at short notice, for example to replace satellites or take a quick look at troop movements and then land on a runway like an ordinary aeroplane[7].

Also, both NASA and the Defense Department are becoming increasingly convinced that the USA should develop a new unmanned heavy launch vehicle to supplement the space shuttle. The Defense Department remains concerned about placing too much emphasis on the complex shuttle system with only a few orbiters for its military space launch needs. A heavy unmanned launcher development using shuttle Thiokol solid-rocket motors as the primary element would cost about 1.5 - 2 billion and be capable of placing a 34.000 - 61.000 lb payload in orbit depending on the configuration selected. Whereas the US assesses a new heavy unmanned launcher, the USSR are approaching their first launch attempt with a much larger Saturn 5-class vehicle capabel of placing about 300.000 lb in orbit (AW&ST, October 31, 1983, p. 17).

As said before, from the beginning space research has intended to serve defense purposes. In this respect, space research in 1985 differs from that in 1945 not so much in a qualitative sense, but rather in a quantitative sense, which leads to an increase in concern as regards militarization of space: with the refinement and development of space science techniques outer space offered increasing opportunities to fundamentally change the balance of power on Earth. So, for example, the USSR launched spacecraft to monitor Israel's incursion into Lebanon and the war between Great Britain and Argentina over the Falkland Islands[8]. It is not only in quotations as those given herefore, but also in the preliminary discussions to international agreements in the United Nations that we find proof for the essentially military impact of space research. In the official analysis of article IV of the UN Outer Space Treaty 1967 we read[9]: 'majority military opinion holds that orbital bombardment is not an effective weapon as compared to land-based ballistic missiles. An effort to use space based nuclear weapons would have the effect of a strategic warning, thus placing an aggressor in the position of being open to retaliation by strategic weapons. It is generally believed to be in the interest of long-range peace and arms control to try to ensure that the Moon and other celestial bodies will be non-nuclear, non-military zones'.

We shall return to the United Nations negotiations and treaty activities as regards military activities in outer space in part 2 of this chapter. Suffice it to say at this point that when initial international negotiations started in the United Nations in 1958, it was a priority item on the agenda. In 1984 it will be likewise - which can be considered an indication of the importance of the subject in present international relations and co-operation.

In order to get a clear view on this rather many-sided topic of immediate concern to humanity we shall deal with it as follows:

1. existing or planned military systems for outer space
2. history of counteracting measures of a political nature
3. legal aspects as regards the militarization of outer space
4. conclusion
5. notes
6. annexes.

We start, after this general introduction, with

4.1 Existing or Planned Military Systems for Outer Space

It is difficult to give a complete survey of all space systems performing military
tasks in outer space.
One reason is that no exact numbers and types of such systems are available,
since satellites, intended for civilian purposes, can very well be programmed
for military purposes too.
The *reconnaissance* technique, for example, can be used for the discovery of
typhoon births as well as for the monitoring of naval and troop movements, as
was done in the war between Great-Britain and the Falkland Islands[8]. The
technique is, in itself, a neutral one - it depends upon the use man wishes to
make of it whether any type of satellite system is used for civilian or for military
purposes.

A second reason is that most of the satellite systems in space with a military
character is not published, or published in such a general way that only insiders
can guess what is hidden behind the often disguising descriptions.
Examples of such information can be found in Annex I and II to this chapter.

It is, however, possible to enumerate many multi-purpose space systems such
as to give the reader at least an idea of what is actually going on in space as regards militarization. It should, once again, be noted that *all* types of satellites
essentially can have a military aspect: meteorological satellites; direct broadcasting satellites; remote sensing satellites; oceanographic satellites; geodetic
satellites, etc.

As it stands, some 75% of all satellites are launched for military purposes - a
number of scientific satellites being excluded from this percentage, though
strictly speaking any amount of them might be of indirect military nature, *e.g.*
as regards the data collected by them.

An important category of satellites which is increasingly used for (indirect)
militarization is that of the *communication* satellites. Apart from doing what
their name implies viz. to take care of communication by means of transatlan-
tic telephone and telex connections and by relaying television programmes,

the task of this category of satellites now mainly is to back defense purposes such as improved communications with the nuclear forces.

Though of a military nature, this type of satellite is, in itself, not of an attacking or destroying nature. It is not difficult, however, to see that this latter type of communication can be of vital importance for strategic reasons, as a consequence of which much is being done to develop methods of destroying the potential or real enemy's spacecraft.

The solution was, on the USSR side, found in the family of interceptor satellites which has operated in space since 1981[10], after initial tests since 1963. The USA began operational testing of its ASAT (= anti-satellite) system in 1976 and intends to achieve operational status by 1985, though the actual research for this system goes back to the early sixties.

Up to now we spoke, by way of introduction, of what the two main space powers on Earth are planning in regard to the defense of their national interests. But there are a great many of other countries aiming at the same goal of self-defense. These can be individual states like India, China, Japan, some African and Latin American countries like Lybia and Brazil, or conglomerates of states united for example in the North Atlantic Treaty Organization (NATO), which latter organization has some 7000 tactical nuclear weapons in Europe[11].

Nevertheless, apart from the many States mentioned here which are capable of developing military space systems, our investigations will concentrate on the two major States struggling for the maintenance of peace on Earth: the USA and the USSR. It is important to note that though on USA-side many space projects remain classified - that is, not accessible but for a small category of insiders -, a wealth of information is given and published as regards the USA space projects, civilian as well as military. The same cannot be said in regard to this type of publications on the USSR side, though an increasing tendency to come into the open in this respect is apparent.

4.1.1 The USSR and its Military Space Programme

Given the fact that space research was an aftermath of the technological developments during World War II, it is interesting to note that it was only in the early seventies that the route which the Soviet space research took for military purposes became clear.

A second point is that contrary to American military space endeavours, the Soviet space research was, in those years, concentrated on manned flights. The flights of many Salyuts and Soyuz clearly were of a military nature. So, for example, Salyut 3 and 5 contained, in all probability (at that time information was still scarce) a ground reconnaissance system. Also, Salyut 5 had as an objective to test the long-duration role of military man in space, as well as his ability to work and select targets for reconnaissance and surveillance.

The crew of this Salyut 5 was to observe, *e.g.*, Soviet war games in Siberia[12]. This is an early example of reconnaissance on the Soviet side; actually, the first well-known reconnaissance type of satellite is the (American) Landsat-1, launched on July 23, 1972.

Since those early seventies quite a few things have happened in space research. As an example, the SIPRI Yearbook 1982 lists approximately a hundred satellites, mainly in the Cosmos series which are assumed to be of a military character. Of these, 54 are reconnaissance satellites of various types and 39 are communication satellites[10].

Furthermore, there are indications that in 1982 the USSR launched three navigation spacecraft to form a global positioning system similar to the USA Navstar programme: the Cosmos 1413, 1414 and 1415[13].
Also, the USSR is said to have launched some Cosmos satellites in pairs since 1967, one of the pair to be the target, and the other the interceptor. In communication satellites the USSR is supposed to have used their Raduga geostationary satellites as well as the Molniya space systems at least partially for military purposes[14].

A relatively new development in space militarization is the refinement of laser beam experiments, intending to damage or destroy the enemy's spacecraft. There are indications that also the USSR is experimentally working on high energy laser beams, though exact information in this regard still is very scanty[15].

4.1.2 The USA and Its Military Space Programme

In the early sixties the USA had two anti-satellite-weapon programmes that involved substantial launch activity and some successful space intercepts. The two programmes were the projects *Mudflap* and *437 Thor.*
Under project Mudflap at least eight Army Nike Zeus ground-launched missiles were fired from Kwajalein Island in the Pacific on anti-satellite tests between May 23, 1963 and January 13, 1966. The first successful US anti-satellite intercept using a ground-launched system occurred on May 23, 1963, when one of the rockets under the Mudflap programme intercepted a Lockheed Agena D in orbit.

Under project 437 Thor, sixteen large MacDonnell Douglas Thor boosters were launched from Johnston Island in the Pacific on US anti-satellite-weapon tests between February 1964 and September 1970. In addition to the spacecraft attack role practiced by this group, the project was established to enable close-up photography of Soviet spacecraft in orbit by a vehicle launched by the Thor, which then returned the film to Earth in a re-entry vehicle. Both projects would have utilized small nuclear warheads in wartime to destroy Soviet spacecraft (communication in AW&ST, August 29, 1983).

Since 1976 the USA has had a small-sized anti-satellite weapon of 30 cm in diameter and 32 cm in length, a missile shot like a bullet by a rocket with 50 cm diameter and a length of 6 m; its weight is about 1500 kg. The rocket is launched from an aeroplane in flight, the F-15.
This is a relatively simple anti-satellite in comparison with projects such as Talon Gold, LODE (Large Optics Demonstration Experiment) or Alpha, a laser-type destructor, which projects will be discussed on p. 156 of this chapter.

154 In the reconnaissance-type of satellites the USA has deployed a rich variety in systems. In the seventies there were three main types: the Big Bird, the Discoverers and the Keyhole 11. In the eighties there is an acceleration in defense systems. So, for example, we know about

1. the 647 Early Warning Satellite system, which is in the geostationary orbit at 36.000 km about the Earth, and which permanently monitors missile launchings. There are two of these EWS above the Western hemisphere, and one above the Eastern hemisphere
2. the Navy Ocean Surveillance Satellite, a few hundreds of kilometers above the Earth. It records radio and radar signals
3. the Defense Satellite Communication System, placed in the geostationary orbit, consisting of six satellites with the task to ensure long-range liaison between American bases all over the world. This is an Air Force system, but the Navy has a corresponding system called: FleetSatCom
4. the FleetSatCom system comprises four huge geostationary satellites which have to ensure communication between ships, submarines, aircraft and troops
5. Satellite Data System, consisting of three satellites over the Northpole. The SDS is part of the AfSatCom satellite communication system serving USA strategical force of B52 and FBIII bombers, flying command centres, nuclear arms bases, etc.
6. Navstar satellites, also called GPS (Global Positioning System). It consists of six satellites, plus five in the launching phase (1983) and 18 more scheduled for 1985[16].

The above mentioned six systems are *space* defense systems; there are also the more conventional Earth-based new nuclear weapons such as the cruise missiles, neutron warheads and the Polaris missiles in the USA submarines[17]. Since our investigation concentrates on *space* defense systems we shall not go into more detail as regards terrestrial militarization.

Apart from the above six systems the latest development in space militarization is that of *laser beam experiments*. In view of their importance we shall discuss them here in some detail.

Both the USSR and the USA are experimenting with lasers for military purposes in their laboratories. As to the *USSR*: the information officially (published in the west) indicates Soviet laser beam experiments to be undertaken in order to destroy or damage the enemy's spacecraft[18] - without much more details being given. However, the USSR high-energy laser programme is said to be three to five times larger than the USA efforts, including research development, test and evaluation of a space-based laser weapon. The USSR could achieve an initial operational capability with a space based laser about 1983[19].

As to *USA* plans in this respect we have been informed that laser weapons development for ballistic missile defense centered on talks at the White House, Defense Department and US Senate, and that in the fall of 1982 the US President met with Edward Teller, the nuclear physicist instrumental in developing the hydrogen warhead, and Lowell L. Wood, an expert in development of

X-ray lasers at Lawrence Livermore and Los Alamos Laboratories. Teller has
been critical of the Administration, claiming that the White House is ignoring
technology advances in short-wave-lengths lasers, especially the X-ray laser
pumped by a small nuclear device. The USA is conducting (1982) X-ray laser
tests at the Nevada underground nuclear test site. Teller is urging that funding
be increased for this effort by approximately $ 200 million a year over the next
several years. Teller and Wood also talked to Senator Ted Stevens (Alaska),
chairman of the Appropriations defense subcommittee, telling him they support the congressional expense of the US Air Force management plan for
space-based, long-wave-length chemical lasers[20].

Furthermore, as regards the *funding* of laser experiments, we learn[21] that Air
Force space laser research will receive more than a twelvefold increase in funding from fiscal year 1987 to 1988 under a plan prepared by the Department of
Defense. The funding would apply to anti-satellite weapons rather than anti-
ballistic missiles defense mentioned by the President of the USA. The Air Force anti-satellite space laser programme, currently (1983) at a proposed $ 36
million for 1984, would reach $ 40.9 million in 1987 and then increase to
$ 518.4 million in fiscal year 1988.
Air Force space surveillance research also will receive a large funding increase
from $ 38 million in fiscal year 1985 to $ 106 million in fiscal year 1986, according to the Defense Department's five year development plan. The figures
will change many times in future planning. The Army's high-energy laser components research programme jumps from $ 42.4 million in fiscal year 1985 to
$ 204.8 million in fiscal year 1986.
Ballistic missile defense system technology research, another Army project,
shows an increase from $ 538 million requested for fiscal year 1984 to $ 1.6
billion anticipated for fiscal year 1988.
Particle-beam research by Defense agencies, excluding the military services,
was requested at $ 33 million in fiscal year 1984 and will increase to $ 54.6
million in 1988 - a small change when compared with the anticipated activities
in laser technology.

Laser beam experiments are those hinted at by Eugen Sänger in 1958 (see introduction to this chapter). They are directed-energy weapons which can destroy targets rapidly by means of intense electromagnetic radiation or particle
fluxes[22].
A report to the USA Congress, prepared by the USA General Accounting Office[23], centers on the concept of a constellation of laser battle stations in space
with the potential for credible air and ballistic missile defense of the USA. The
joint DARPA/USAF (= Defense Advanced Research Project Agency/US
Air Force) space based laser programme for fiscal year 1983 through fiscal year 1987 is continuing, however, as a funding-limited effort, which means that
the programme is to be developed at a relatively slow pace.
There are three main laser projects under investigation at present[24]:
— the *Alpha* programme; the idea is to build a cylindrical 2-3 megawatt hydrogen fluoride chemical laser device to demonstrate the feasibility of directly extrapolating chemical laser technology to 5-10 megawatt levels.
   Ground tests are planned for the mid eighties

— the Large Optics Demonstration Experiment *LODE* - intending to demonstrate a 4-meter diameter primary mirror and associated beam control system for experimental use. The programme foresees in a ground-based feasibility test with low power in the mid eighties

— *Talon* Gold, a space-based demonstration system for advanced acquisition, tracking and precision pointing system, scheduled for testing with the space shuttle in 1987 to track targets at ranges up to 1500 km with an accuracy of 0.2 microradians (a microradian is the angle subtended by a sphere from a distance which is one million times its diameter. At a distance of 1500 km, an angular accuracy of 0.2 microradians corresponds to a linear accuracy of 30 cm).

Space-based lasers function best in mixed forces with other more conventional ballistic missile alternatives, because of the stress involved in a damaging limited mission.

Laser beam technology is now rapidly developing so as to improve beam quality. A breakthrough was reached in 1983[25] with the *Raman* technology, which is expected to permit ways to process the beam that enables construction of relatively small, inexpensive, so-called excimer laser devices coupled in banks or arrays that could be ground-based for direct target engagement (an excimer is a molecule consisting of a noble-gas atom and a halide atom, *e.g.* xenonfluoride, which has the property that after formation it is in an excited state, and after returning to the ground state and emitting microwave radiaton, it dissociates. This property strongly facilitates the laser operation).

Though laser beam experiments are regarded by many to offer the best possibility at present for securing the balance of power, they have, according to some[26], a critical flaw that most Pentagon planners seem to have ignored; the exotic weapons and other military satellites could easily be destroyed by *a single nuclear blast* in outer space. Such a blast would instantly set up an electric pulse of up to a million volts per meter in hundreds of satellites and battle stations, and disable them.

Nevertheless, officials at the USA Defense Advanced Research Project Agency (DARPA) and the USA Air Force seem to continue ignoring the possibilities of nuclear blasts in outer space, because of the magnitude of the problem at present. Chapter 2 of this book offers an in-depth study of the dangers for the Earth and humanity as a consequence of the use of nuclear power sources in outer space. Full information on the said subject is to be found there, though the emphasis in chapter 2 is on the use of nuclear power sources for peaceful purposes, for example as a source of energy, and not as a potential weapon.

Not only could, according to some[26] scientists, a single nuclear blast destroy military satellites, it is also highly questionable whether lasers (and charged particles) could possibly serve at all military purposes in space.
During the 1983 33rd Pugwash Conference in Venice/Italy Prof. K. Tsipis (MIT) of the USA came to the conclusion that

a the current state of high energy long wavelength-infrared-lasers cannot support an operational space-borne ballistic missile defense system

b research into short wavelength lasers may in the future, that is in a period

of 10 to 20 years from now, provide prototype lasers with the requisite
characteristics for such a weapon system
c   numerous other technical and operational problems have to be solved before one can even begin to imagine how such a system could be made operational.

Additionally, Prof. Tsipis stated that
a   X-ray lasers powered by the detonation of a nuclear warhead that have
been bruited about, are operationally impractical for a number of reasons,
even if they were made to work, and
b   there exists a variety of countermeasures that can degrade the performance of a laser BMD system very severely at a fraction of the cost of a laser-
powered BMD system
(taken from 'Technical overview of directed energy weapons': background paper nr. XXXIII-26 of the said Conference).

On the other hand, tests regarding the applicability of lasers in space still continue. As an example we quote that the US Air Force has finally succeeded in
shooting down anti-aircraft missiles with laser beams after attempts, made two
years ago, went wrong. The latest tests, carried out in May 1983, but only just
disclosed, took place over the China Naval Weapons Test range in California.
They were carried out by the Airborne Laser Laboratory. The Americans used
a carbon-dioxide laser which emits a continuous beam of 400.000 watts at an
infrared length of 10 micrometers. The laser was mounted in a military Boeing
707 and shot down five missiles out of a total of 13. The first eight shots were
used to sight the equipment. The 13 AIM-9 air-to-air missiles were launched
from A-7 attack planes and are capable of reaching speeds of 3200 km/h. The
successful tests were undoubtedly a relief to the airforce, because the Airborne
Laser Laboratory is under attack from critics in Congress who want to chop the
programme (New Scientist, August 18, 1983, p. 457).

Also, an anti-satellite system *not*launched into outer space by rockets or other
launching systems but from an airplane, the F-15, is under development, as we
see from the following (in AW&ST, August 29, 1983, p. 22) in which we read
that upcoming tests with the F-15 anti-satellite-weapon system will build on
24 year old flight test data, acquired in 1959, when a Martin Marietta Bold Or-
ion rocket, launched from a Boeing B47 bomber, intercepted the Explorer 6
spacecraft over Cape Canaveral. That test was the first successful US anti-satellite intercept and demonstrated that the concepts used in the current F-15
air-to-space system was feasible shortly after the US and the USSR began
competing in space. Since then 24 more US anti-satellite missions and at least
20 Soviet anti-satellite tests have been flown.
The first F-15 Asat system test is expected by October 1983 and will involve
the booster system only going into space. The system consists of a miniature
non-explosive homing vehicle carried into space by a two-stage rocket. The
vehicle would locate its target with infrared sensors and destroy it by collision.

When discussing military systems to be used in outer space, some serious drawbacks of weapons of mass destruction placed in orbit around the Earth should be mentioned. Hitting a predetermined target on the Earth's surface with a warhead launched from a satellite which is orbiting the Earth is only feasible during certain hours of the day, when the target will be sufficiently close to the ground track of the satellite's orbit on the surface. Hitting a target which is far from the ground track at the moment of launch is not impossible, but it would require a far more powerful rocket motor (see also chapter 2, sec. 2.2 of this book).

Furthermore, there would be problems of maintenance, command and control. A satellite-based weapon could relatively easily be intercepted or at least rendered inoperative. Storing the weapons in question in manned orbital stations would hardly relieve these operational inconveniences. Altogether, the disadvantages of placing nuclear or other weapons of mass destruction in outer space outweigh their military usefulness. Therefore, in agreeing to ban them, the USA and the USSR have sacrificed little, if anything. Both powers continue to rely on groundbased and sea-based nuclear weapons which can both be better maintained and controlled, and be launched with greater precision[34].

In concluding this rather general survey of military systems operating in space or under development for future operational service in space, we refer to a statement made in 1954 before the MacCarthy Commission by Prof. R. Oppenheimer, managing director and principal investigator of the Los Alamos Laboratory in New Mexico, under whose supervision the first atomic bomb was constructed, tested and applied on Hiroshima and Nagasaki on August 6, 1945. Prof. Oppenheimer remarked among other things:

> 'I wonder whether we have not betrayed the spirit of science when we left our discoveries to the military, without thinking of the consequences. And so we live now in a world in which people follow the discoveries of scientists with fright. Every new discovery evokes new fears in them.
> We physicists experience that we never were more important and never more powerless. In evaluating here my life it became clear to me that my movements that show my guilt, according to your Commission, are nearer to the idea of science than my qualifications. We gave the best years of our life to the investigation of the most perfect means of annihilation. We took the work off the hands of the military, and I strongly feel now that this was wrong. We did the devil's work and now return to our real task'.

4.2   History of Counteracting Measures of a Political Nature

The conclusion of the foregoing must be that at present as well as in the past militarization of space was seen as a means to secure peace on Earth. But militarization was and is not the only possible means to do so. Actually, the application of warring military systems in space has so far successfully been pre-

vented by means of negotiations of many kinds. We name a few of the most important.

4.2.1   *International and National Activities Outside and Inside the United Nations*

On the *international* (bi-lateral) level, for example, we mention
— the 1972 Anti-Ballistic Missiles Treaty (ABM), which treaty intends to limit the use and capabilities of such missiles
— the Strategic Arms Limitation Talks Agreement (SALT) - of 1973 and
  1979, intending to limit the use of certain strategic weapons (see Annex III
  to this chapter)
— the Anti-Satellite Programmes (ASATS) - attempts by the USSR and the
  USA to discuss the control of their anti-satellite (which means: intercep-
  tor/destructor satellites) programmes.

On the *multi*-lateral level we mention
— a very important French proposal from 1978 to set up an International Satellite Monitoring Agency (ISMA), brought before the UN General Assembly. The General Assembly requested the Secretary-General to undertake, with the assistance of qualified government experts, a study on the
  technical, legal and financial implications of establishing an ISMA. The results have been published[27].
  The main conclusions of the report are that
  1. space technology would allow observations from satellites for the veri-
      fication of compliance with arms control and disarmament treaties
      and for monitoring crises areas on Earth
  2. there is no provision in international law that would entail a prohibi-
      tion for an international governmental organization such as ISMA to
      monitoring activities by satellite
  3. the financial burden of the agency in its final phase, when it launches
      and operates its own satellites and carries out data processing and an-
      alysis, is expected to be about $ 1500 million for one satellite spread
      over a ten year period. In any case the annual cost of an ISMA to the
      international community would be very much less than one percent of
      the total yearly expenditure on armaments[28]
— the United Nations Committee on Disarmament
— the United Nations Special Political Committee
— the ENMOD Convention of 1977, the signatory parties to which undertake not to engage in military or any other hostile use of environmental
  modification techniques, defined as techniques for changing the dynamics,
  composition or structure of the Earth or of outer space
— the establishment of a Special United Nations Ad Hoc Working Group -
  for 1983 - (see UN Document A/37/669 of 6.12.82), with the aim to find
  ways and means for the control of space militarization
— the Resolution nr. 145 adopted by the North Atlantic Assembly during its
  29th annual session (The Hague/Netherlands, October 2 - 7, 1983), on
  Ballistic Missile Defence; the Assembly urges member governments of the

North Atlantic Alliance:

1. to continue to determine as accurately as possible the nature and scale of Soviet ballistic missile defence programmes in order to ensure that there will be no profound disparity in Soviet and United States' ballistic missile defence capabilities
2. to continue, with the Soviet Union, to observe arms control agreements governing deployment of ballistic missile defence systems, and to seek to improve upon such agreements under appropriate conditions
3. to seek vigorously a verifiable arms control agreement with the Soviet Union governing anti-satellite weapons
4. to take all possible steps to avoid an arms race in weapons for use in space and to forgo deployment of such systems if the Soviet Union formally agrees to a parallel commitment
5. to assess carefully the degree of protection that different prospective ballistic missile defence systems would afford the Alliance as a whole, to take account of these aspects should deployment of such systems be unavoidable under the terms of ballistic missile defence agreements, and to consider carefully ways of ensuring joint participation in the research and development necessary for the creation of ballistic missile defences.

The full text of this Resolution 145 is to be found in Annex IV to this chapter.

On the *national* level we know of
— the USSR initiative of August 10, 1981, to propose to the United Nations a new treaty banning the placement of any kind of weapons into an orbit around of the Earth[29], to which we return on p. 167 of this chapter, and
— of the establishment, in the USA, of a Senior Interagency Group (SIG) that will advise the President on space issues. The Chairman of SIG is assistant to the President for national security affairs. Of the seven members of the group four are military
— also in the USA, a Space Command has been set up per 1.9.82 to further consolidate USA Air Force operational space activities, to link the Research and Development group and users, as well as to run the North American Air Defense Command[30]
— the USSR initiative of August 19, 1983, to propose to the United Nations another treaty on the prohibition of the use of force in outer space and from space against the Earth. The text of the proposal is given in Annex V to this chapter.

The acceleration in space militarization is only parallelled by the concern of many nations regarding the security of their territory. This concern is voiced in many places, both national and international. With a view to the international character of space militarization the majority of States prefers to voice their concern in the United Nations, or in bi- and multi-lateral negotiations, as stated above.

Let us now turn to what has been achieved so far in the *United Nations*. To that end, we need some historical background, because it is very difficult to understand present developments without having a view on the past.

Before the launching of the first artificial satellite in 1957 neither direct nor strong needs were felt for close international co-operation in space affairs. At that time space research was limited to experiments with sounding rockets, of rather short range, and was thus a national affair of the country involved. In this field no direct need for intense technical co-operation existed, although scientific results were exchanged internationally in many cases.

In international co-operation the launching of Sputnik 1 had far-reaching effects, stimulated by the feeling of the large public that the relative balance of power had changed. The USA sought to establish an instrument for international co-ordination in space affairs. In the attempts to achieve such a co-ordination the most appropriate medium seemed to be the United Nations.

It was also understandable that the USSR, with the remarkable event of being the first launching nation in their files, although certainly not opposed to a form of international co-ordination of space affairs, did not feel inclined toward the kind of co-operation sought by the USA.

The US representative to the United Nations, Henry Cabot Lodge, asked by letter on September 2, 1958, from the Secretary-General of the United Nations inclusion in the agenda for the forthcoming session of the United Nations General Assembly of the item: 'Programme for international co-operation in the field of outer space'. In this session of the General Assembly the United States and 19 other nations sponsored a Resolution on the establishment of an Ad Hoc Committee, which became the Permanent Committee by General Assembly Resolution 1472 of December 12, 1959, after a vote. The responsibilities for the Permanent Committee were different from the responsibilities proposed for the Ad Hoc Committee in that the disarmament aspect of the use of outer space was *not* included in the set of tasks for the Ad Hoc Committee.

It is in this United Nations Permanent Committee for the Peaceful Uses of Outer Space (UNCOPUOS) that until recently all matters pertaining to the use of outer space were discussed, negotiated and formulated in treaties. In view of the seriousness of the militarization of outer space other UN Committees also deal with this subject, *e.g.* the Special Political Committee and the Committee on Disarmament.

The space treaties formulated so far under United Nations auspices are:
— the 'Treaty on Principles Governing the Activities of States in the Exploration and Use of Outer Space, including the Moon and Other Celestial Bodies', commonly called the Outer Space Treaty, of 1967
— the 'Agreement on the Rescue of Astronauts, the Return of Astronauts and the Return of Objects Launched into Outer Space', called the Rescue Agreement, of 1968
— the 'Convention on International Liability for Damage Caused by the Launching of Objects into Outer Space', called the Liability Convention of 1972
— the 'Convention on Registration of Objects Launched into Outer Space',

called the Registration Convention, of 1976
— the 'Agreement Governing the Activities of States on the Moon and Other Celestial Bodies', called the Moon Agreement, of 1979.

Also under UN auspices were formulated the 'Principles Governing the Use by States of Artificial Earth Satellites for International Direct Television Broadcasting', colloquially called the Code of Good Conduct, 1982. Proposals do exist to establish, on the basis of the said Code, a treaty text.

4.2.2   The Outer Space Treaty of 1967, in particular Article IV

The Outer Space Treaty is the basic treaty out of which all other space agreements developed.

We shall restrict ourselves here to a discussion as to the relevant part(s) of this Treaty regarding arms control. In fact, only one clause of this Treaty, *viz. Article IV*, is strictly applicable to this subject.

At the basis of the Outer Space Treaty, and consequently of Article IV, are three unanimously adopted UN General Assembly Resolutions: the numbers 1962 (XVIII) of December 13, 1963; 1963 (XVIII) of the same date, and 1884 (XVIII) of October 17, 1963[31]. It is this latter Resolution that is of special importance to us, because this Resolution deals with the 'Question of General and Complete Disarmament'.

The spirit of this Resolution is to be found in Article IV, which reads:
'States Parties to the Treaty undertake not to place in orbit around the Earth any object carrying nuclear weapons or any other kinds of weapons of mass destruction, install such weapons on celestial bodies, or station such weapons in outer space in any other manner.
The Moon and other celestial bodies shall be used by all States Parties to the Treaty exclusively for peaceful purposes. The establishment of military bases, installations and fortifications, the testing of any type of weapons and conduct of military personnel for scientific research or for any other peaceful purposes shall not be prohibited. The use of any equipment or facility necessary for peaceful exploration of the Moon and other celestial bodies shall also not be prohibited'.

In Article IV we find the clearest indication of the striving for peace in outer space. The crux of the text of this Article is, we think, to be found in the term 'peaceful'. As to the various interpretations of this term see sec. 4.3.1 below. Though attempts were made to *negatively* define in Article IV certain categories of activities which certainly are *non*-peaceful, it is, years after the establishment of the Treaty, only all too clear that a *positive* definition of the term 'peaceful' would have prevented much of the present series of interpretations of the term 'peaceful'.

Why this lack of clarity in a legal text of so far reaching importance for the maintenance of peace on Earth and in the rest of outer space?

It has been stated[35] that the text of Article IV is not a legal one in the strict sense of that word, but rather a political one. Consequently, the text of Article IV is indicating intentions, or, at best, the political reality at the time of the conclusion of the Treaty in 1967. The political reality at that time was, as it is at present, that sovereign States desired to maintain by all means their influence on Earth as well as in the rest of space. The aim of the Treaty is that outer space shall be used by all States, in international co-operation. Nationalistic tendencies of individual States were not at the basis of the Treaty. Nevertheless, the recent past showed us an increase in nationalistic endeavours in space.

The primary aim of the text of Article IV thus being clear, we now come to another equally important reason why Article IV is giving so much difficulty: the matter of interpretation of the term 'peaceful'.
There are many legal systems in the world, each based on national peculiarities. Behind these peculiarities we often find different schools of thought on the same matter. In our opinion this is also the case with the interpretation of the term 'peaceful'.
In matters of interpretation the Vienna Convention on Treaties gives, in article 31[36], the general outline applied by international law, namely that of the textual approach: 'a treaty shall be interpreted in good faith in accordance with the ordinary meaning to be given to the terms of the treaty in their context and in the light of its object and purpose'. But as we saw in the foregoing no *communis opinio* exists as to what the ordinary meaning to be given to the term 'peaceful' in general is.

Let us now see how the term 'peaceful' in Article IV of the Space Treaty is to be interpreted. Before doing so it is of importance to note that the majority of authors[52] on the interpretation of the term 'peaceful' in space law agree that, generally speaking, the preparatory work and the negotiations leading to the Space Treaty clearly do *not* indicate the intention to impose the demand that outer space must be used exclusively for peaceful purposes. This means, in itself, that Article IV of the Space Treaty suffers from this interpretation in such a way that apart from the inner divergences in the text of that article, the article in itself is of considerably less importance than is generally attributed to it.

It is not only the preparatory work and the negotiations that give such an indication: from the official (USA) analysis of Article IV of the Space Treaty[37] we quote:
> 'majority military opinion holds that orbital bombardment is not an effective strategic weapon as compared to land-based ballistic missiles. An effort to use space based nuclear weapons would have the effect of a strategic warning, thus placing an agressor in the position of being open to retaliation by strategic weapons. It is generally believed to be in the interest of long-range peace plans and arms control to try to ensure that the Moon and other celestial bodies will be non-nuclear, non-military zones'.

The above text leaves no doubt that the reason why Article IV is said to refer to 'peaceful' activities in outer space is that from the strategic point of view space-based nuclear weapons *are strategically not as effective as the land-based missiles.*

Mind: this was written at the time of the conclusion of the Outer Space Treaty, that is in 1967. Meanwhile, seventeen years have passed and space research developed techniques which may at present be strategically more effective than land-based missiles. But there is, as yet, no formal proof by the signatories to the Treaty - especially the major space powers - that Article IV might possibly need adaptation - which would permit the conclusion that the signatories do not really intend to use space exclusively for peaceful purposes. We make an exception for Italy, which put forward already in 1968 a proposal for the review of Article IV (see also p. 166 hereinafter), as well as Brazil and Chile (p. 166).

Close analysis of Article IV of the Space Treaty only supports the view that a great number of the signatory parties to the Treaty do *not* seem to have the intention to keep space a peaceful region, as will be discussed hereinafter.

And the signatory parties could not possibly foster such intention as the Legal Sub-Committee of the UNCOPUOS is not authorized to decide in matters of peace and war. As its name indicates it is held to deal with the peaceful use of outer space. As to matters of war: these are under the jurisdiction of the Committee on Disarmament, the Security Council and the General Assembly, to name only a few of the most important UN-bodies in regard to non-peaceful use of space. Apart from that, we now proceed on discussing the text of Article IV in detail. That article reads as follows: 'States Parties to the Treaty undertake not to place in orbit around the Earth any objects carrying nuclear weapons or any kinds of weapons of mass destruction, install such weapons on celestial bodies, or station such weaons in outer space in any other manner. The Moon and other celestial bodies shall be used by all States Parties to the Treaty exclusively for peaceful purposes. The establishment of military bases, installations and fortifications, the testing of any type of weapons and the conduct of military maneuvers on celestial bodies shall be forbidden. The use of military personnel for scientific research or for any equipment or facility necessary for peaceful exploration of the Moon and other celestial bodies shall also not be prohibited'.

Analysis of Article IV, paragraph 1

a.   the first striking feature of the first paragraph of Article IV is that it is formulated in the negative: '.... *not* to place ....' - follows a list of items prohibited to be placed in outer space.
May we infer that any category not mentioned in this negative list is permitted? Legally seen this is jumping to a conclusion too early drawn - but present military practice shows that, indeed, any category not forbidden is carried into orbit, for example spy satellites, interceptor satellites, laser beam experimental satellites

b.   next, we see the narrow limitation of the placement of certain categories of objects in space *in orbit around the Earth.*
Given the negative formulation in the first complete sentence of the first paragraph we infer from the formulation 'in orbit around the Earth' that as soon as technology permits other orbits, around other planets, and be-

tween those, and in deep space, those are *not* prohibited.
In 1967, when the Space Treaty entered into force, space technology was hardly in the position it is in at present, namely to bring missiles in, *e.g.*, orbits around the Moon with the purpose of maintaining the balance of power in space and, hopefully, thereby preserving peace on Earth

c. the text speaks of 'objects carrying to or stationing nuclear *weapons* in outer space, or on celestial bodies'. Is the mere mentioning of this category of objects to be taken as an indication that the formulation of this paragraph was *to stop* such carrying or stationing?
    In any case: the years after 1967 have shown an increase in carrying satellites with military aims and nuclear payloads - as far as known no nuclear weapons as yet - into orbits in outer space

d. — the text speaks of weapons of *mass* destruction - which leaves open the possibility of the use of weapons of destruction in general, not for mass destruction but for example for the destruction of single satellites, such as geostationary satellites or telecommunication satellites.
    It has been argued[38] that for certain types of space research nuclear sources (not: weapons) are of primordial importance. Here, the difficulty is: where does scientific space research end and the application of that same space research for non-peaceful ends begin? In our opinion it is doubtful whether the common interest of all mankind (Article I, Space Treaty) is served by the application of nuclear power sources in space, as long as it cannot be guaranteed that those sources do not inflict any hazard resulting from the failure of a satellite subsystem;

Article IV, paragraph 2

a. 'exclusively for peaceful purposes'.
    The adverb 'exclusively' in our opinion only figures here to emphasize the intention of 'peaceful'.
    But why was it necessary to use that adverb when 'peaceful' in itself was sufficiently expressing the intention to maintain space a peaceful region? Several explanations are possible. The first is, as we said, to emphasize the meaning of 'peaceful'.
    Others are that this part of Article IV is a repetition of the texts of other treaties on international regions, such as the Antarctic Treaty of 1959 (article I) and the provisions of the proposed legal rules for the use of the seabed and the ocean floor. It is also possible, however, that this first complete sentence of paragraph 2 of Article IV is giving a general rule whereas the second sentence is more specific. This would mean that, within one article, we find two different interpretations: one indicating the exclusive peaceful use, the other (only) peaceful use.
    The implication of this way of thinking is that we have to infer from complete sentence 3 of Article IV that military (!) personnel doing scientific research has to do that research peacefully but not exclusively peacefully

b. the second complete sentence of paragraph 2 of Article IV gives a list of prohibited activities - we are not sure whether this list is a limitative or an explanatory one. Given the fact that Article IV is rather a political than a legal text we are, however, inclined to see it as explanatory. But even so, present practice shows that - albeit for scientific research - military activities are carried out in outer space

c. according to the last complete sentence of Article IV peaceful exploration of the Moon and other celestial bodies is *not* prohibited. The term 'exploration' dates back to the early times of space research, that is in the sixties when all activities in outer space were of an exploratory nature. In the eighties space technological achievements such as the space shuttle no longer intend, however, to explore but to exploit. In that connection one can wonder whether the term 'peaceful ex*ploitation*' would not be more in agreement with reality. One can wonder also whether the international co-operation promoted by so many explicit and implicit space law provisions will be able to bear, in peace, the weight of the huge economic benefits to be gathered from space.

In resuming our analysis of Article IV we think that the present text of Article IV of the Space Treaty leaves open too many important questions regarding the peaceful use of outer space than that it may be called a legal rule representing the real proportions of power and co-operation on Earth. In the foregoing we indicated its shortcomings - which may possibly serve as a *stimulus* for adaptation to a treaty text more in conformity with present space exploitation reality.

Suggestions for such adaptation are not new - in fact one year after the entering into force of the Outer Space Treaty Italy put forward, on September 9, 1968, a proposal for the review of Article IV of the 1967 Treaty (A/7221). On February 1, 1978, both in New York and Geneva, Italy suggested the adoption of further measures to prevent the extension of the arms race to outer space (Working Paper A/AC.187/97). That suggestion is reflected in paragraph 80 of the Programme of Action of the Final Act of the first special session on disarmament. Lastly, on March 26, 1979, Italy submitted to the Committee on Disarmament for consideration a memorandum and attached draft protocol with a view to supplementing the rules of the 1967 Treaty[39]. To this end, the prohibition contained in Article IV of the Treaty should be extended. In particular, the parties to the protocol would undertake to refrain from engaging in, encouraging, or authorizing or participating in 'any measure of a military or other hostile nature' in outer space, such as the establishment of military bases, installations and fortifications, the stationing of devices having the same effect, the launching into Earth orbit or beyond of objects carrying weapons of mass destruction or any other types of devices designed for offensive purposes, the conduct of military manoeuvres, as well as the testing of any types of weapons.

The main objective pursued by Italy was to prohibit the development and use of Earth-based and space-based systems designed to damage, destroy or interfere with the operations of other States' satellites[40].

Also, Brazil and Chile proposed (see UN Document A/SPC/37/SR.16, of

November 2, 1982) to the United Nations General Assembly an additional protocol to the Outer Space Treaty, with a view to preventing the indiscriminate militarization of outer space.

Apart from the space treaties concluded so far in the United Nations, quite a number of other United Nations documents express their concern about militarization of space.
We shall discuss a selection of them, and present the opinion of a few specialists in international law as regards the proposals put forward in these documents.

4.2.3 Major Proposals Regarding Demilitarization brought before the United Nations

4.2.3.1 Proposals by the USSR of August 20, 1981, and August 19, 1983

A very important request, done by the USSR by its letter of August 20, 1981, was the one proposing the 'Conclusion of a treaty on the prohibition of the stationing of weapons of any kind in outer space' (see Annex VI to this chapter). This USSR proposal contained in fact a treaty of unlimited duration which would prohibit the stationing of weapons of any kind in outer space, including stationing on 'reusable' manned space vehicles (a clear reference to the US space shuttle programme). Moreover, the parties to the treaty would undertake not to destroy, damage, or disturb the normal functioning or change the flight trajectory of space objects of other states if such objects were placed in orbit in 'strict accordance' with the above-mentioned provision. Compliance with the treaty would be assured with the national technical means of verification at the disposal of the parties and, when necessary, the parties would consult each other, make inquiries and provide relevant information[41]. The USSR proposal does not specify whether the development and testing of anti-satellite systems would be prohibited, and whether states would be obliged to dismantle those systems which they have already developed and tested. As a matter of fact, the draft treaty does not seem to prohibit anti-satellite weapons as such; only their deployment in space and use would be banned. One clause implies that these weapons may even be resorted to in case of violation of the agreement. In this context it is not at all clear who would make the judgement as to whether or not objects were placed in orbit in accordance with the provisions of the treaty and, consequently, under what circumstances parties would be relieved from their undertaking not to interfere with space objects of other states. Moreover, whatever national means may be used to verify compliance, for the majority of nations lacking such means the treaty right to verify would be meaningless. Notwithstanding the apparent deficiencies of the Soviet text, the envisaged ban would be of significant importance as an arms control measure, were it to cover not only weapons placed in orbit but also weapons that could strike space objects from the ground and from the atmosphere[52].
The request of the USSR was granted. UN Document A/36 A/37/669 of December 6, 1982 contains the official text and proposals. They are to be found in Annex VII to this chapter.

168   In a statement on outer space at the First Committee Meetings of the 36th regular session of the General Assembly in 1981, the Byelorussian SSR delegation supported (see PV, 18, p. 10) the USSR proposal as follows:

'The draft treaty submitted by the Soviet Union contained in document A/26/192 contains in addition to those provisions another provision that States parties to the treaty should undertake not to destroy, damage or disturb the normal functioning or change the flight trajectory of space objects of other States parties, if such objects were placed in orbit in strict accordance with the provisions of the treaty. That provision of the treaty takes account of the desire expressed during this debate relating to the need to ensure the inviolability of space objects of all States placed in space for peaceful purposes. The draft treaty also contains a necessary and adequate system for ensuring compliance with provisions of the treaty; this is contained in article 4 of the draft treaty. As can be clearly seen from the content of the proposed treaty relating to the obligation of States parties such an international legal instrument would require, under equal conditions, all present and future owners of technology for the production and stationing in outer space of weapons of any kind not to put such weapons into outer space. No single country would have any unilateral advantage and the human race as a whole would breathe more easily. Considerable resources could thus be released for the civilian sector of the economy'.

The USSR proposal of 1981 was discussed during the 1983 38th session of the UN General Assembly.

It is important to note that following this treaty proposal, another treaty proposal in regard to the demilitarization of outer space was submitted by the USSR to the United Nations on August 19, 1983, on the Prohibition of the Use of Force in Outer Space and From Space Against the Earth (Pravda, August 22, 1983, as well as UN Document A/38/194, August 23, 1983). The text of the proposal can be found in Annex V to this chapter.

4.2.3.2   Proposal by France of Spring 1978

The proposal of France to the United Nations General Assembly for the establishment of an International Satellite Monitoring Agency (ISMA) has already been described in general in section 4.2.1 of this chapter. We elaborate on it somewhat further here. The French proposal, submitted to the UN General Assembly in the form of a Memorandum in spring 1978, intends to assure the global community that compliance with arms control agreements is taking place. According to the proposal observation satellites would be used for such control within the framework of disarmament and be placed at the service of the international community.

The proposal is identified as A/S-10/AC. 1/7, and is entitled 'Memorandum from the French Government Concerning an International Satellite Monitoring Agency', of June 1, 1978.

Not only would observation satellites under the ISMA proposal be used to control activities in space within the framework of disarmament. It also has been discussed that ISMA should attribute additional functions in the fields of resource management and environmental monitoring (see 'Letter to the Editor' by C. Voûte; International Journal of Remote Sensing, Fall 1983).
In the context of this chapter we restrict ourselves to the main aims of ISMA.

The main aims of ISMA would be that, as part of the United Nations system[43],
— it should have access to and be able to use data collected by the satellites of the States that possess them until it can acquire its own, but should have for itself the technical capacity to interpret the data so received
— it would become an essential adjunct to disarmament agreements and to measures to increase international confidence and security by providing interested parties with information that they were entitled to demand.

The study following the ISMA proposal (called 'Study on the implications of establishing an international satellite monitoring agency' - Report of the Secretary-General of the United Nations, dated August 6, 1981) seems to favour the establishment of an ISMA as a parallel to the International Atomic Energy Agency (IAEA, Vienna/Austria).

Though the ISMA proposal sounds as one of the most positive as to effective disarmament control it presupposes an at present non-existent maturity in States, namely the one which does *not* seek first and foremost the exclusivity associated with their own security and defense needs and policies. As soon as States would overcome their desire to secure international peace by means of establishing their own security first, instead of *first* striving for international peace, disarmament might become effective, at least in principle. But neither of the space powers is favourable to the establishment of an ISMA: the USSR because the acceptance of such an establishment would mean that an *international* agency would acquire data of a military or strategic nature, whereas the USSR strongly supports the fundamental principle of (national) *State* sovereignty which implies prior consent; the USA because an ISMA would enable states to engage in espionage or activities that are at present inconsistent with national security or national policies[44].

Notwithstanding views opposing the French ISMA proposal of 1978, it has served and continues to serve as a stimulus for many nations to study the essential questions as regards global order and the security of that order. Those essential questions concern the fear that nations foster against hypothetically or effectively possible threats of otherwise friendly or even adverse States.
Sprouting from that fear are misunderstandings and malcommunication which hamper a continuous and constant endeavour to secure peace on Earth and in the rest of outer space.

As to the legal implications of the functions of an ISMA, the Report of the UN Secretary General (UN Doc. A/AC.206/14, of August 6, 1981) emphasizes the fact that during the past two decades, verification has probably represented one of the most serious obstacles to progress in negotiations of disarmament and arms limitation agreements. Solutions to that problem have differed from agreement to agreement, depending upon the nature and the scope of obligations contained therein. Also, according to the said Report, a number of disarmament proposals have failed to attract support because they lacked adequate monitoring provisions that would afford acceptable risks to the participants. On the other hand, the conclusion of certain arms limitation treaties has been significantly facilitated due to the fact that modern Earth observation technology including devices operating from outer space, provides the contracting parties with an effective instrument of monitoring mutual compliance. The SALT agreements concluded between the USA and the USSR are an illustration of such treaties.

Adequate verification has been a major issue in connection with the conclusion and ratification of the SALT I and II Agreements. Both have been largely shaped by verification considerations. Parties to these agreements rely for verification on 'national technical means', which is a general term encompassing a variety of technical collection methods for monitoring compliance and, in the context of SALT arrangements, include, in addition to reconnaissance satellites, ships, aircraft, radar ground stations and other technical devices. As regards verification of the SALT Agreements - which includes verification from space - the Parties have agreed to refrain from using concealment measures which would impede verification by national technical means of compliance with the Agreements. Furthermore, the Parties have undertaken not to interfere with each other's means of verification.

As to monitoring compliance with existing international arms regulation and disarmament agreements:
the Group of Experts on the ISMA proposal was aware that certain arms regulation and disarmament agreements at present in force might need to be modified or amended in order to provide for an ISMA's participation in their verification procedures. Existing bilateral and multi-lateral arms regulation and disarmament agreements, as well as the agreements currently under negotiation, may be divided, according to the verification measures provided for therein, into four categories: 1. agreements which contain no verification provisions, 2. agreements which provide for international verification measures, 3. agreements which only refer to 'national technical means' for verification, and 4. agreements which combine the characteristics of categories 2. and 3.

A detailed examination of the said categories of agreements is mainly to be found in Annex V of UN Doc. A/AC.206/14 of August 6, 1981.

The full text of the ISMA proposal is given as Annex VIII to this chapter. To end up our investigation into the various views on ISMA we cite here part of the address to the UN General Assembly First Committee Meeting in 1981, as an example showing the general tendency as regards the establishment of an ISMA:

> 'An interesting initiative might be to establish an international satellite monitoring agency, as proposed initially by France in the first special session of the General Assembly devoted to disarmament and subsequently considered by the General Assembly and by a group of experts who sub-

mitted a report to be considered at the second special session of the General Assembly devoted to disarmament, in 1982.

Such an initiative could contribute to verification of compliance with certain agreements on arms limitation and disarmament. On the other hand it could play an important role in the prevention or solution of international crises, thus helping to promote confidence among States.

In conclusion, we are in favour of the initiation of a study on the militarization of outer space in order to improve existing legislation on the subject'[45].

Also, during the Interregional Seminar of the ECA/ECWA regions (Addis Ababa, 4-8 July, 1983) a Draft Recommendation on ISMA was submitted by Egypt which runs as follows:

'In view of the increasing number of open reconnaissance satellites (high performance satellites) launched and planned to be launched in the near future by various states, and the continuous improvement of resolution for data collection by systems on such satellites, the participants at the Interregional ECA/ECWA Seminar recommend in the light of art. 515 of Unispace 82 that an International Satellite Monitoring Agency (ISMA) as a model for a world-wide system for earth observation be established within the UN. This includes earth observation, environmental monitoring, treaty compliance or other activity monitoring'.

In 1983, the Parliamentary Assembly of the Council of Europe recommended - in Recommendation 957 (1983), see Annex IX to this chapter - that the Committee of Ministers review the state of action on the ISMA proposal and examine the possibilities for renewed initiatives in this direction, either individually or collectively or in association with non-European industrialized or developing countries having a space capability.

It seems, therefore, that though still much opposition exists as regards an international satellite monitoring agency, in Europe at least opinions are favourable towards the establishment of such an agency.

4.2.3.3 Other Recent Negotiative Texts regarding the Demilitarization of Outer Space

We shall discuss in the following some of the negotiative texts as presented in the UN Committee on the Peaceful Uses of Outer Space Legal Sub-Committee, as well as those of the First Committee sessions, both of 1983 onward.

A note of concern can be derived from the fact that in the beginning of 1983 a political declaration was adopted by the Member States of the Warsaw Treaty making an appeal to all States to give fresh impetus to the work of the Committee on Disarmament, with a view, in particular, to starting negotiations as soon as possible on prohibiting the stationing of weapons of any kind in outer space. The declaration's further proposal for a treaty between Warsaw Treaty and NATO member states on the mutual renunciation of military force and the maintenance of peaceful relations would, according to the declaration, also contribute greatly to preserving peace in outer space[46].

Also, the report of the Legal Sub-Committee on the work of its 22nd session (March-April 1983) gives a declaration by the Latin American Countries, members of the said Sub-Committee, by way of a working paper as reprinted here:

Argentina, Brazil, Chile, Colombia, Ecuador,
Mexico, Uruguay and Venezuela: working paper
(A/AC.105/C.2/L.142 of 6 April 1983)

DECLARATION BY THE LATIN AMERICAN COUN-
TRIES MEMBERS OF THE LEGAL SUB-COMMITTEE
OF THE COMMITTEE OF THE PEACEFUL USES OF OU-
TER SPACE

The Group of Latin American countries, members of COPUOS, wish to place on record their views on some points relating to the utilization, exploration and exploitation of outer space, which should be based on the following basic principles:

a.   It should be regulated in accordance with the principles of the Charter of the United Nations, Resolution 2625 on friendship and co-operation among peoples, the 1967 Space Treaty and other relevant international instruments, taking into account that space law must be based on international co-operation

b.   The legal context referred to above is clearly indicative of the ob-ligation incumbent on all States to explore, exploit and utilize ou-ter space, the Moon and other celestial bodies exclusively for peaceful purposes. We consider it essential to avoid the continu-ation, in actual deeds or in planning, of an increasing militariza-tion and use for military purposes of outer space in flagrant viola-tion of the spirit of the 1967 Treaty, of agreed principles and of existing positive law. We advocate the early elaboration of an ap-propriate instrument additional to the 1967 Space Treaty (A/ AC.105/320).

The incitation to quote more of these statements is great; we restrict ourselves however to only a few more, such as the one made by the representative of the USA that the USA 'shares the concern expressed by many delegations that ou-ter space should be free from agressive activities' and that they 'are gratified that the Committee on Disarmament has agreed that this item (on disarma-ment; GCMR) be addressed as part of its agenda'.

Rather unequivocal ideas were also voiced by the German Democratic Re-public[49];

'Comprehensive obligations which would be binding under international
law, regarding the use of outer space for exclusively peaceful purposes
and a ban on all weapons in outer space, are therefore urgently necessary.
Only if the militarization of outer space can be halted will it be possible to
strengthen international peace and security and to resolve other global
problems of a social and economic, demographic and ecological nature.
Given the present level of the world's productive forces notably in science and technology, the required material and intellectual resources do
exist. Outer space must not become another source of threats to mankind.
Along these lines, the Warsaw Treaty member States, in their Political
Declaration adopted in Prague in January this year, called upon all
States, among other things, to give fresh impetus to talks in order to take
up immediately negotiations on the prohibition of the stationing of any
kind of weapons in outer space.
This appeal places the Warsaw Treaty member States in full agreement
with the non-aligned countries which, in their declaration at the close of
the seventh summit Conference in New Delhi, demanded that outer
space be used for exclusively peaceful purposes'.

To conclude this survey regarding demilitarization of outer space, as hoped for
and worked on by so many nations, we refer to several UN General Assembly
Resolutions of 1983 which are in one way or another emphasizing the peaceful
use of outer space and requesting for diplomatic action in this respect: the first
is called 'Prevention of an arms race in outer space', and the second 'General
and Complete Disarmament'.
As the titles of these Resolutions are self-evident we shall not elaborate on the
contents of both these Resolutions, but instead we refer to the complete texts
as given in Annexes X and XI to this chapter. Both Resolutions are part of the
much broader scope on work regarding disarmament where, in 1982 alone
and apart from the two Resolutions as given in our Annex, 15 other Resolution
texts have been negotiated, all containing detailed proposals as to the prevention of militarization of space, including of the Earth[50]. They are reprinted in
the Reports of the Committee on Disarmament. Such Reports are produced
annually and give important background information as to the proceedings on
the international diplomatic level as regards the general question of disarmament.

4.2.3.4 The UNISPACE 1982 Conference and Demilitarization

In August 1982 the majority of States represented in the United Nations met in
Vienna/Austria, where the second United Nations Conference on the Exploration and Peaceful Uses of Outer Space was convened. The first similar
conference was held in 1968, also in Vienna/Austria.
The aim of the Conference, called UNISPACE 1982, was to give all participants the opportunity to discuss, on a global scale, such subjects as 1/ state of
space science and technology; 2/ application of space science and technology,
and 3/ international co-operation and the role of the UN.

174   All these matters being of primordial interest for truly international co-operation in matters pertaining to the use of outer space it was felt, nevertheless, by
many States as a serious omission that the item of the increasing militarization
of space was left out of the official agenda of the Conference. The official statements made during and immediately after the Conference were judged to be of
too general a nature, whereas the concern, voiced *e.g.* by UN Secretary-General Perez de Cuellar, prevailed in almost all nations represented. From Conference paper A/Conf. 101/10 we take the following excerpt:
— the extension of an arms race into outer space is a matter of grave concern
    to the international community. It is detrimental to humanity as a whole
    and therefore should be prevented. All nations, in particular those with
    major space capabilities, are urged to contribute actively to the goal of pre-
    venting an arms race in outer space and to refrain from any action contrary
    to that aim
— the maintenance of peace and security in outer space is of great importance
    for international peace and security. The prevention of an arms race and
    hostilities in outer space is an essential condition for the promotion and
    continuation of international co-operation in the exploration and use of
    outer space for peaceful purposes. In this regard, the Conference urges all
    States to adhere to the Treaty on Principles Governing the Activities of
    States in the Exploration and Use of Outer Space, including the Moon and
    Other Celestial Bodies and strictly to observe its letter and spirit
— the Conference strongly recommends that the competent organs of the
    United Nations - in particular the General Assembly and also the Commit-
    tee on Disarmament - when dealing with measures aimed at a prevention of
    an arms race in outer space, in particular those mentioned in the relevant
    resolutions of the General Assembly, give appropriate attention and high
    priority to the grave concern here expressed.

A majority of States was not satisfied with the outcome of the Conference, as
the relevant paragraphs of the Final Report (as quoted hereabove) did not
adequately express the international community concern and fears regarding
the militarization of outer space.

A positive outcome of the Conference was, however, that it recommended to
the relevant UN bodies a number of studies to be undertaken, all aiming at the
preservation of outer space as a peaceful environment.
The years to come will prove whether this stimulating effect of UNISPACE
1982 will take shape.

After this survey of international diplomatic endeavours on the United
Nations level, we investigate hereinafter the opinions of some international legal specialists as to the present situation regarding the militarization of space.
Some of them proposed new, or adapted, legal rules in order to ameliorate the
present tense situation in international relations regarding the increasing militarization of outer space.

4.3.1   Interpretation of Relevant Terms in Space Law

To begin with, attention is drawn to the fact that the terminology regarding the maintenance of peace in outer space is rather diversified, both in general international law and in space law. We mention as the most widely used ones the terms peaceful, non-aggressive and non-military, whereas three other concepts are used to cover the maintenance of peace in outer space, namely
1.   the matter of disarmament
2.   the demilitarization of outer space, and
3.   the common interest principle of Article I of the Outer Space Treaty.

Are these terms just synonyms or other semantic peculiarities? Or do they cover different points of view? The difficulty in explaining these terms is that language in politics is not used to explain and to clarify facts and arguments but as a means to achieve a goal.
Should we take the terms in their semantic meaning, then *peaceful* means:
— disposed to peace; not contentious or quarrelsome
— marked by freedom from strife or disorder
— untroubled by conflict, agitation or commotion of or relating to a state or time of peace
— devoid of violence or force.
Non-aggressive indicates the absence of
— the tendency toward or the participation in aggression
— combative readiness.
Non-military is defined as follows:
— not of or relating to soldiers, arms, war, armed forces
— not performed or made by armed forces
— not supported by armed forces
— not of or relating to the army[51].

Demilitarization, on the other hand, presupposes the existence of militarization, which is the preparation for military activities both by persons and installations.

The common interest principle of Article I of the Space Treaty covers the interests of all countries *on Earth*, so only of a part of outer space(!).

So far for a linguistic approach. It is clear that all terms just described have to do with the maintenance of peace in space (including the Earth). That we have to speak on *maintenance* indicates that that same maintenance is endangered. Any danger to the maintenance of peace falls within the scope of the term 'aggression'. The United Nations (General Assembly Resolution 3314 (XXIX), contained in UN Document A/9631, December 14, 1974, 29 GAOR, Suppl. no.31, 142) understands by aggression: 'the use of armed force by a State against the sovereignty, territorial integrity or political independence of another State, or in any other manner inconsistent with the Charter of the United Nations as set out in this definition'.

Having thus led back our terms to their original meaning we now start with their political connotation.

4.3.1.1   The Terms 'Peaceful', 'Non-Military' and 'Non-Aggressive'

The vast literature on the subject shows, in space law, two major interpretations of 'peaceful': that of non-military and that of non-aggressive[53]. In international law 'non-military' is defined as the prohibition to use outer space for military activities in times of peace, whereas 'non-aggressiveness' refers to the permission to use at least *partial* military precautions. The term 'non-aggressiveness' includes the possibility to apply military activities in outer space *lawfully* as long as those activities do not aim at direct attack in the sense of the United Nations definition of 'aggression'.

The concept of non-aggressiveness is, from the political point of view, therefore a much broader one than the non-military one: it permits among other things almost all present activities in outer space such as those of 'spy' satellites, interceptor satellites, remote sensing satellites of a certain type as well as laser beam experiments and the use of nuclear power in outer space.
At this point it begins to be difficult for those among us who are in favour of peace on Earth as well as in the rest of outer space, because many outer space activities, scientific or not, have up to now been executed *by military personnel**; so that, if we had to get rid of the 'non-military', this would mean that space research as it stands would become impossible. But it would be difficult, if not impossible, to discontinue space research, the more so since international law, and, to a smaller degree space law, do not forbid the use of outer space for military purposes.

What, then, about the annual discussions in so many international bodies on the subject of the peaceful use of outer space? If we apply the outcome of our above investigations the conclusion has to be that no rule of international law, or space law, is opposing the military use of outer space. Neither do these discussions in so many international bodies seem to alter essentially the present tendency to use outer space as a scene where the newest technological devices of a military nature are probed.

We think we have to digest this conclusion slowly, in order to discriminate its deepest meaning, which is, as said before, that in spite of five space treaties promising mankind peace in outer space (including the Earth) humanity is endangered as it never was before; that it is *technology* as well as those who contribute to its development, and not law but *politics* of law that decide the future of space (including the Earth) - if there is any future.

---

*   As an example it may be mentioned that all six USA astronauts who actually flew in the Mercury programme were military officers (the only civilian member, O.K. Slayton, temporarily lost his active flight status on medical grounds). Similarly, of the six Vostok cosmonauts of the USSR only the pilot of Vostok-6, Valentina Tereshkova, was non-military.

4.3.1.2   The Terms 'Disarmament' and 'Demilitarization'

The terms 'disarmament' and 'demilitarization' are the *genus* to which the *species* peaceful, non-military and non-aggressive return; it is clear that the outcome of disarmament can lead to peace, as does demilitarization. We are to understand by them the striving for maintaining peace in outer space, by means of, among other things, political negotiations which lead to agreements to prevent outer space from becoming an arena in which the wars on Earth are continued, but by even much more sophisticated tools than are used at present on Earth.

One way to further disarmament of outer space is by arms control on Earth. Arms control in outer space is a terrestrial affair since it is the sovereign States on Earth that plan and effectuate, jointly or severally, launchings of spacecraft into outer space. As such, outer space merely is an extraterritorial extension of the Earth. Consequently it are the States Parties striving for arms control in outer space that can impose restraints by agreement on the type of launchings they wish to undertake.

The five space treaties are *one* means by which States Parties have tried, rather unsatisfactorily it must be admitted, to steer outer space disarmament policy. The use of outer space, either peaceful or not, is based on the important principle of the freedom for all States to use outer space, according to Article I of the Space Treaty[53]. What type of freedom is meant here? In examining Article I of the Space Treaty we find the terms

— (outer space ....) *free* for exploration ....
— *free* access (to all areas of celestial bodies)
— *freedom* of scientific investigation in outer space (parentheses GCMR).

The context of the three sentences of Article I of the Space Treaty indicates freedom *in* outer space - which differs essentially from freedom *of* outer space. In outer space, which is in itself an international region, it is, however, representatives of sovereign States which operate either peacefully or not peacefully.

Consequently, a particular State can found its national claims concerning military (or non-aggressive, or non-peaceful, etcetera) use of outer space upon that same principle of freedom and not on the older and much more adequate principle of sovereignty.

We have a Janus Bifrons here; very unsatifactory and dangerous as he was in ancient Rome, he is even more so at present.

Even when States come to establish agreements on disarmament and demilitarization, international law (and space law) show a sui generis defect: the agreements can be denounced by States Parties within a given time interval. It means that the agreements' effectiveness is doubtful.

The conclusion of the foregoing must be that the maintenance of peace is not and cannot be based on international agreements or other legal documents but on the co-operation, common sense and goodwill of governments.

4.3.1.3   The 'Common Interest Principle'

We return to a principle generally accepted to be worded in Article I of the Space Treaty: that of the common interest. Meant is the common interest of all mankind in the outcome of the use of outer space. It is clear that under present technological developments only the *peaceful* use of outer space can be a common interest for all mankind. As such, we judge disarmament of and in outer space to be an obligation under Article I of the Space Treaty in general and of the common interest clause in particular.

But what are, actually, and apart from the very general definition of 'common interest' as given hereabove, those common interests? To put it plainly: the economic benefits resulting from exploitation of outer space. Are the 'common interests' the same for all mankind?

One of the oldest principles of international law is that of State sovereignty. We hope to have made it sufficiently clear in the above that in spite of outer space being an international region, the principle of State sovereignty did not and does not loose one iota of its importance in the formulation of the moderately modern space law rules. That means that the space treaties, basically, serve to protect *national* interests, and to defend them, when need comes, against all intrusion. It means also that, common interests principle or not, competition in sharing the outcome of exploitation of space prevails, in spite of the many calls for international co-operation.

So far for the common interest principle as worded in Article I of the Space Treaty. It is judged to be a most important *general* principle of space law, as Article IV of the same Treaty is generally seen as the most *specific* article on the peaceful use of outer space. In Article IV we find the clearest indication of the States' opinions regarding the maintenance of peace in outer space. The crux of the text of this Article is, we think, to be found in the term 'peaceful'. Though attempts were made to *negatively* define in Article IV certain categories of activities which certainly are *non*-peaceful, it is, fifteen years after the establishment of the Treaty, only all too clear that a *positive* definition of the term 'peaceful' would have prevented much of the present series of interpretations of the term 'peaceful'.

4.3.2 Space Law as Part of International Law

This general explanation as to the terminology used to express concern on the increasing amount of satellites with military purposes launched into outer space is to serve as an introduction to the rather complicated discussions on the subject in legal circles.

To begin with, space law is part of international law, and as such subject to the rules set by international law. Space law is *ius speciale*, whereas international

law is *ius generale*. The Charter of the United Nations being part of international law, the Charter's rules also apply to all rules of space law. Every State,
Member of the United Nations and having adopted the rules of the Charter,
gives up the *ius belli,* that is: that part of its State sovereignty which before the
entering into force of the Charter enabled a State (or States) two wage war with
(an)other sovereign State(s). On the other hand, every State preserves, under
article 51 of the Charter, the right of self-defense. It should be noted that this
right of self-defense does *not* include the right of *preventive* self-defense.

Though the Charter abides by the concept of State sovereignty this is not so in
space law, where we read in Article II of the Space Treaty [55] that outer space is
not subject to national appropriation by claim of sovereignty, by means of use
of or occupation, or by any other means.

This indicates a very important divergence between two systems of law, or
rather: between the main system: international law, and one of its subsystems:
space law.
A consequence of this divergence is, as we may note in the present use of outer
space that, as the striving for national hegemony in space accelerates, space
law becomes less effective in favour of article 51 of the UN Charter (being international law) that provides States with the possibility to maintain national
sovereign rights, also in outer space.

The above being a matter of the relation between two basically unequal law
systems, we also have to deal with the matter of *interpretation* of the legal texts
pertaining to the use of outer space. In matters of interpretation, art. 31 of the
Vienna Convention on the Law of Treaties provides for the appropriate standard of interpreting international treaties:
    'A treaty shall be interpreted in good faith in accordance with the ordi-
    nary meaning to be given to the terms of the treaty in their context and in
    the light of its object and purpose ....'. Also, 'A special meaning shall be
    given to a term if it is established that the parties so intended'[56].

According to art. 32[56] of this Convention 'recourse may be had to supplementary means of interpretation, including the preparatory work of the treaty and
the circumstances of its conclusion' only in order to confirm the pure textual
analysis, or if 'the interpretation according to article 31: a/ leaves the meaning
ambiguous or obscure, or b/ leads to a result which is manifestly absurd or un-
reasonable'.

The remarks stated hereabove on the divergence between two law systems and
international rules should be kept in mind in reading the rest of this chapter.
Even a term so English as 'liability' may have different meanings in different
nations or under different law systems. The terms 'liability' and 'responsibility'
are, for example, in Russian covered by the same word: otvyetsvennost.
We make this remark as one out of many examples as to the importance of internationally accepted legal terms with the same semantic meaning, or not.

Let us now start our discussion as to the opinions of some legal specialists regarding demilitarization of space.

Actually, many meetings of many international entities take place in which the demilitarization of space is on the agenda. Apart from the - general - UNCOP-UOS Legal Sub-Committee meetings discussed earlier in the present chapter, meetings of *specialists* in international law and space law are convened.

Two of the most important of these meetings are those of the International Law Association (biennially), with its national subdivisions, and, on matters pertaining to space law, the International Institute of Space Law (annually). As the same subject of demilitarization is discussed in both organizations mainly by the same people, we restrict ourselves to the opinions as voiced in the discussions of the International Institute of Space Law (IISL).

In a session of the 1982 IISL meeting called 'Legal aspects of the peaceful use of outer space in the light of article IV of the 1967 Outer Space Treaty' Mrs. Eilene Galloway, Honorary Director of the above Institute, proposed the establishment of a working group of about fifteen experts in space science and technology, and international law, who would in her vision, 'assemble the basic facts, assumptions and objectives (of arms control and disarmament; GCMR) in a balanced, unemotional statement, capable of being translated into legal provisions designed to maintain outer space for peaceful, beneficial purposes while protecting it from all forms of danger. Discriminating thoughts should be given to the question of what we should permit and what we should forbid ....'[57].

Though the spirit of this proposal is to find ways and means to further demilitarization, we are of the opinion that the tasks set by this proposal and which are to be translated into legal provisions, have been worded previously in international law, as well as in space law and in other international agreements. In regard to demilitarization the problem is that in spite of these wordings, the parties concerned do not stick to what they formerly agreed upon in the form of conventions, agreements, sets of rules, etcetera.

If the existing legal provisions in regard to the peaceful use of outer space would be abided by, and if all parties concerned would really be intending to keep outer space a peaceful region, no such questions as 'what we should permit and what we should forbid' would ever be posed.

In addition, we are of the opinion - and paragraph 1 of this chapter gives evidence to it - that the matter of disarmament of outer space is of an order magnitudes higher than it is voiced in the above proposal.

For example, leading scientists in space research, among whom Eugene Levy of the USA Space Science Board[58], are wilfully left out of space policy negotiations though they had been involved in those decisions for decades. This situation brings to mind what is quoted on p. 158 of this chapter where Prof. Oppenheimer infers that leading scientists are called to hand over their discoveries to the military and then are requested to leave it at that. In other words: the time to sit together and find out about 'the basic facts, assumptions and objectives' has gone; the fact must be accepted that no longer international law, or space law for that matter, is effective to prevent an increasing militarization of space.

Books such as High Frontiers[59] make it sufficiently clear that the way to the demilitarization of space is, in fact, a very long one.

Another proposal worth mentioning here is the one by Gorove[60] who discussed the possibility that arms control measures do not necessarily have to be all-encompassing but may relate to certain types of activity, such as research and development. They may cover materials suitable for weapons production, or they may cover certain types of weapons such as nuclear, chemical, biological and other weapons of mass destruction, as well as directed energy, particle beam and anti-satellite weapons irrespective of whether they are part of so-called dedicated systems or not or whether they are at present still undeveloped.

It would, indeed, be excellent if this path, set out already by Oppenheimer, be followed in such a way that the types of research leading to the further development of weaponry in any form and to be used in outer space, should come to a standstill. Though such a standstill might be judged by many to be irrealistic or even impossible due to economic difficulties if not due to difficulties related to the nature of science itself, a precedent is available in the form of the DNA recombinant investigations which, a few years ago, were postponed or even stopped for ethical reasons in some countries in Western Europe.

If a complete ban of the above type of space research be impossible - which it obviously will be - the proposal by Gorove to create specific arms control measures for specific results of scientific research certainly deserves a wide follow-up, in legal as well as in space political circles.

In view of the possibility that the 1967 Outer Space Treaty may be provided with an additional protocol or even be open for reformulation (see the proposals by Italy[61], in section 4.2 of this chapter), the above proposal by Gorove should certainly be taken into account.

It is also interesting to note what space lawyers' opinions are in regard to the establishment of an international satellite monitoring agency. From the discussion on this subject during the 1982 session of the International Institute of Space Law[62] it became clear that neither the USA nor the USSR support the French ISMA proposal, and are even very much against it, on the arguments of the costs of such a system for the USA and the impairment of security on the part of the USSR.
But, according to the French space lawyer De Saint-Lager (CNES)[62] those arguments are not convincing because they ignore the principles of economy and the retention of the same level of security. Dr. de Saint-Lager suggested, as a way out of the opposing views of the USA and the USSR, the regionalization of the ISMA-project, such because it is not only the USA and the USSR which are involved in demilitarization.

In the above we voiced only a few out of many space lawyers' opinions, by way of examples. The discussions on demilitarization in space legal circles are mainly concentrated on the discussion of Article IV of the 1967 Outer Space Treaty which is, as said before in this chapter, of a rather ambiguous nature. Outside this strictly legal environment it is the international balance of power, changes in which serve as the background for the formulation of rules of space law, which, on a global scope, is being tried to safeguard.

In resuming the foregoing we conclude that the matter of the prevention of an arms race in outer space, though not of a recent date, is receiving new impetus parallel to the increasing militarization of outer space.

Our general description of the main space systems used in outer space or under development for military purposes sufficiently indicates that the development and use of such systems is at present such that it would very well be possible that - if the precious balance of power becomes unbalanced - life on Earth is at stake. The question, then, is whether disarmament as it is strived for is sufficient both in structure and in outline. There is no doubt that real concern exists worldwide, both outside and inside official organizations. With a view to the international character of the matter of demilitarization of outer space the greater part of the concern took and still is taking shape in bi- and multi-lateral talks and treaties, as well as in a number of international bodies.

A sad event in this respect is that though many treaties in existence unequivocally prohibit the use of outer space for military purposes, the signatory parties - especially the major space powers - to those treaties do not abide by the treaty texts, but, instead, often accelerate the refinement and development of military space systems, and even design new techniques such as laser beams especially for the purpose of heightening the quality and quantity of their national defense systems.

Nevertheless, recent treaty proposals such as the ones by the USSR of 1981 and 1983, as well as the French proposal for the establishment of an international satellite monitoring agency, are to be seen as positive landmarks in the struggle for the prevention of an arms race in outer space.

The task of space law in this respect is of a modest but important nature. Within the United Nations, an international body with global scope, many ideas and suggestions have been put forward as to the maintenance of peace and especially so in its Legal Sub-Committee where as soon as spaceflight started, space legal rules were formulated. Critical remarks could be heard as to the effectiveness of these rules in relation to international space policy, but the fact remains that their normative value may have contributed to the clarification of the limits set to space legal rules by international space policy. The roads of international space policy are, in themselves, not differing from the ones in the early forties of this century. Space law tries to contribute to, but did not lead to the demilitarization of outer space.

Space lawyers as well as all others can only *strive* for peace; in our opinion lawyers should contribute to it by formulating more unequivocal rules as well as by closer co-operation with disarmament experts. If all goodwill expressed all around the globe concerning the maintenance of peace could be materialized in clear-cut rights and obligations of States, peace would have a greater chance to prevail in future.

1. Sänger, E., 1958: *Raumfahrt - technische Uberwinding des Krieges* p. 85 ff; Rowohlt Hamburg/FRG
2. *Science*, vol. 219, 18.3.83, p. 1300
3. *New Scientist*, 19.8.82, p. 466
4. *Science*, vol. 217, 10.9.82, p. 1011
5. *Aviation Week and Space Technology (AW&ST)*, 24.1.83, p. 28
6. *Physics Today*, September 1982, p. 51
7. *New Scientist*, 11.11.82, p. 350/351
8. *AW&ST* 14.3.83, p. 110
9. *New Scientist* (note 7), p. 150; Proceedings IISL Paris, 1982
10. *SIPRI Yearbook* 1982, p. 299 ff
11. *New Scientist*, 2.9.82, p. 602
12. *Journal of the British Interplanetary Society*, vol. 35, 1982, pp. 86-92
13. *AW&ST*, 18.10.82, p. 15
14. extracted from: Magno, P., 1982: *Military space programmes*, p. 11, published in the *Proceedings of IAF*, pp. 127-130; see also *New Scientist*, 11.11.82, p. 346, and *SIPRI Yearbook* 1982, p. 310-311
15. *New Scientist*, 2.9.82, p. 602
16. see note 14
17. *New Scientist*, 2.9.82, p. 602
18. *ibidem*
19. *AW&ST*, 12.4.82, p. 19
20. *AW&ST*, 20.9.82, p. 15
21. *AW&ST*, 12.4.82, p. 16
22. *AW&ST*, 12.4.82, p. 16
23. *ibidem*
24. *ibidem*, p. 17
25. *AW&ST*, 18.7.83, p. 18
26. *Science*, vol. 215, 12.3.82, p. 1372 ff
27. UN Document A/36/192, 20.8.81 and A/AC.206/14, of August 6, 1981
28. *SIPRI Yearbook* 1982, p. 302 ff
29. UN Document A/AC.206/14, 6.8.81
30. *New Scientist*, 11.11.82, and *Science*, vol. 217, 23.7.82
31. they bear the names 'Declaration of Legal Principles Governing Activities of States in the Exploration and Use of Outer Space', and 'International Co-operation in the Peaceful Uses of Outer Space', respectively
32. for the complete text of the three Resolutions, see:
    Reijnen, 1981: *Utilization of Outer Space and International Law*;
    Elsevier Scientific Publishing Company, Amsterdam/Oxford/New York, pp. 151-162
33. in: Staff Report prepared for the Use of the Committee on Aeronautical and Space Sciences of the United States Senate, December 30, 1976
34. *SIPRI Yearbook* 1982, p. 440
35. Reijnen, G.C.M., 1981: *Utilization of outer space and international law*, Elsevier Scientific Publishing Company, Amsterdam/Oxford/New York
36. Brownlie, I. 1977: *Principles of Public International Law*, p. 607 ff., Clarendon Press Oxford
37. official title: Treaty on Principles Governing the Activities of States in the Exploration and Use of Outer Space, including the Moon and other celestial bodies
38. Reijnen, *op. cit.*, p. 46
39. from: *Statements on Outer Space at the first Committee of the United Nations General Assembly*, 36th regular session of the General Assembly, 1981, PV 7, p. 36/37
40. UN Committee on Disarmament Document CD/9, March 26, 1979
41. UN Document A/36/192, of August 20, 1981 (Annex VI to this chapter)
42. SIPRI Yearbook 1982, p. 443/444
43. Almond, H.H., 1982: 'The French proposal for an International Satellite Monitoring Agency'; published in: Proceedings 25th Colloquium on the Law of Outer Space, September/October 1982, Paris/France, pp. 171-185
44. see note 43
45. from a statement by the representative of Chile at the First Committee Meetings on Outer Space, 36th regular session of the UN General Assembly, 1981
46. UN Document A/AC.105/C.2/SR.387, of April 4, 1983

184 47. UN Document A/AC.105/320, of April 13, 1983
48. UN Document A/AC.105/PV.249, June 28, 1983, p. 36
49. Same document as mentioned in note 48, pp. 63-65
50. 1982 Report of the Committee on Disarmament to the UN General Assembly; 37th Session, Document no. 27/A/37/27, with supplement (of 128 pages)
51. Webster's New Collegiate Dictionary G & C Merriam Co., Springfield/Mass. USA
52. Gorove, S, 1977: Studies in space law; Sijthoff Leyde p. 90
53. Article I of the Outer Space Treaty reads as follows:
'The exploration and use of outer space, including the moon and other celestial bodies, shall be carried out for the benefit and in the interests of all countries, irrespective of their degree of economic or scientific development, and shall be the province of all mankind. Outer space, including the moon and other celestial bodies, shall be free for exploration and use by all States without discrimination of any kind, on a basis of equality and in accordance with international law, and there shall be free access to all areas of celestial bodies. There shall be freedom of scientific investigation in outer space, including the moon and other celestial bodies, and States shall facilitate and encourage international co-operation in such investigation'. (Quoted from the Staff Report prepared for the Use of the Committee on Aeronautical and Space Sciences of the United States Senate, December 30, 1976)
54. Szabó, J.: 'Killer satellites and space law to-day', in: Proceedings of the 25th Colloquium on the Law of Outer Space, September/October 1982, Paris/France, pp. 151-153
55. Article II of the Outer Space Treaty reads:
'Outer space, including the moon and other celestial bodies, is not subject to national appropriation by claim of sovereignty, by means of use or occupation, or by any other means' (source: the same as mentioned under quotation 53, hereabove)
56. UN Document A/Conf.39/27, adopted May 22, 1969 and entered into force in February 1980
57. Galloway, E., 1982: *Expanding Article IV of the 1967 Space Treaty: a proposal*; in: *Proceedings, 25th Colloquium on the Law of Outer Space*, September/October 1982, Paris/France, pp. 151-153
58. *Physics Today*, September 1982, p. 51
59. *'High Frontier - a new national strategy'* by Lt. Gen. D.O. Graham. H.F. is a private, non-profit organization, established in 1981 in the USA
60. Gorove, S., 1982: in: *Proceedings 25th Colloquium on the Law of Outer Space*; p. 96
61. Already in 1968 Italy requested the inclusion in the agenda of the twentythird session of the UN General Assembly of an item dealing with the necessity of amending Article IV of the 1967 Space Treaty. In an explanatory memorandum Italy brought the attention of the world community to a number of what she considered as loopholes in this Treaty, in particular to a/ the absence of any prohibition of the stationing of nuclear weapons or other kinds of weapons of mass destruction in orbit around the Moon or other celestial bodies, b/ the absence of any prohibition concerning nuclear weapons or other kinds of weapons of mass destruction in any kind of semi-orbits, c/ the absence of any prohibition against the inclusion of nuclear weapons or other kinds of weapons of mass destruction into spacecraft moving towards deep space. An improved text, on the basis of the above, was then suggested, to be discussed by the Committee on Disarmament. An amendment of Article IV of the 1967 Space Treaty did not materialize, however
62. *Proceedings of the 25th Colloquium on the Law of Outer Space*, September/October, 1982, Paris/France, p. 186.

From: SPACEFLIGHT; Vol. 26, No. 4, April 1984, p. 191

SATELLITE DIGEST-172

Robert D. Christy
Continued from the March issue

A monthly listing of satellite and spacecraft launches compiled from open sources.

The heading to each launch gives the name of the satellite, its international designation and its number in the NORAD catalogue. Launch times are given in Universal Time and are accurate to about five minutes except where marked with an asterisk, where the time is to the nearest minute as announced by the launching agency.

COSMOS 1507 1983-110A, 14450

Launched: 0830, 29 Oct 1983 from Tyuratam by F-1.
Spacecraft data: Not available but probably several tonnes mass.
Mission: Electronic reconnaissance covering shipping movements.
Orbit: 433 x 442 km, 93.35 min, 65.06 deg, maintained by low thrust motor.

COSMOS 1508 1983-111A, 14483

Launched: 1230, 11 Nov 1983 from Plesetsk by C-1.
Spacecraft data: Not available but may be similar to the navigation satellites.
Mission: Possibly ionospheric research.
Orbit: 397 x 1964 km, 109.05 min, 82.93 deg.

COSMOS 1509 1983-112A, 14490

Launched: 1215, 17 Nov 1983 from Plesetsk by A-2.
Spacecraft data: Possibly based on the Vostok manned spacecraft with spherical re-entry module, instrument unit and cylindrical, supplementary payload at the forward end. Length about 6 m, diameter (max) 2.4 m, and mass around 6000 kg.
Mission: Military photo-reconnaissance, recovered after 14 days.
Orbit: 225 x 290 km, 89.70 min, 72.86 deg.

MOLNIYA 1(59) 1983-114A, 14516

Launched: 1646, 18 Nov 1983 from Plesetsk by A-2-e.
Spacecraft data: Cylindrical body housing instrumentation and the payload surmounted by a conical motor section; power is provided by a 'windmill' of six solar panels, overall length 3.4 m, diameter 1.6 m and mass around 1800 kg.
Mission: Communications satellite to help operate long distance telephone and telegraph communications, and broadcasting of Central TV to Orbita receiving stations in the Soviet far north, the Soviet far east and central Asia.
Orbit: Injected from a low parking orbit into an elliptical one of 442 x 39145 km, 702.32 min, 62.81 deg, later raised to 464 x 39894 km, 717.85 min, 62.82 deg to ensure daily ground track repeats.

COSMOS 1510 1983-115A, 14521

Launched: 1234, 24 Nov 1983 from Plesetsk by C-1.
Spacecraft data: Not available but may be similar to the navigation satellites.
Mission: Possibly geodetic.
Orbit: 1479 x 1524 km, 116.04 min, 73.62 deg.

ANNEX II

From: COSPAR INFORMATION BULLETIN No. 99, April 1984, pp. 93, 95

5. SURVEY OF SATELLITES AND SPACE PROBES

5.1. LIST OF SATELLITES AND SPACE PROBES

26 AUGUST-29 DECEMBER 1983

National Name / COSPAR Designation	Country of Origin	Launch Date / Ligetime or Descent Date	Available Information	Initial Orbital Elements			
				Apogee (km)	Perigee (km)	Incl. (deg.)	Period (min.)
Progress 18[1] 1983-106A	USSR	20 October 16 November	Automatic cargo-spacecraft, carried fuel and other loads aboard	347	329	51.63	91.22
Cosmos 1505 1983-107A	USSR	21 October 4 November	Carried scientific instruments, radio system for precise measurement of orbital elements, and radio telemetry system	415	358	72.88	92.30
Cosmos 1506 1983-108A	USSR	26 October 1200 years	Carries scientific instruments, radio system for precise measurement of orbital elements, and radio telemetry system	1015	953	82.93	104.80
10th Meteor	USSR	28 October	Carries scientific meteorological instruments and service	890	754	81.17	101.36

Cosmos 1507 1983-110A	USSR	29 October 30 years	Carries scientific instruments, radio system for precise measurement of orbital elements, and radio telemetry system	443	435	65.06	93.34
Cosmos 1508[2] 1983-111A	USSR	11 November 30 years	Carries scientific instruments, radio system for precise measurement of orbital elements, and radio telemetry system	1966	400	82.93	109.07
Cosmos 1509 1983-112A	USSR	17 November 1 December	Carried scientific instruments, radio system for precise measurement of orbital elements, and radio telemetry system	292	227	72.86	89.71
No Name 1983-113A	USA	18 November 80 years		883	816	98.74	101.42
59th Molniya 1 1983-114A	USSR	23 November 17¼	Carries instruments for transmitting TV programmes and multichannel radio communication, and service systems	39145	442	62.81	702.23
Cosmos 1510 1983-115A	USSR	24 November 10000 years	Carries scientific instruments, radio system for precise measurement of orbital elements, and radio telemetry system	1526	1481	73.62	116.03
STS-9 (Columbia) 1983-116A	USA	28 November 8 December	On board were US Astronauts J. Young, B. Shaw, O. Garriott R. Parker, B. Lichtenberg and the first ESA Astronaut, U. Merbold of the FRG. The European-built Spacelab on board Columbia contained 38 different sets of experiment hardware, representing seven major science disciplines. These were NASA and ESA sponsored experiments	252	239	57.02	89.39

(1) Progress 18 docked with Soyuz T9-Salyut 7 (second airlock on 22 October and undocked on 13 November 1983.
(2) 2500th successful space launch.

Treaty Between the United States of America and the Union of Soviet Socialist Republics on the Limitation of Anti-Ballistic Missile Systems

ENTERED INTO FORCE: 3 October 1972

The United States of America and the Union of Soviet Republics, hereinafter referred to as the Parties,

Proceeding from the premise that nuclear war would have devastating consequenses for all mankind,

Considering that effective measures to limit anti-ballistic missile systems would be a substantial factor in curbing the race in strategic offensive arms and would lead to a decrease in the risk of outbreak of war involving nuclear weapons,

Proceeding from the premise that the limitation of anti-ballistic missile systems, as well as certain agreed measures with respect to the limitation of strategic offensive arms, would contribute to the creation of more favorable conditions for further negotiations on limiting strategic arms,

Mindful of their obligations under Article VI of the Treaty on the Non-Proliferation of Nuclear Weapons,

Declaring their intention to achieve at the earliest possible date the cessation of the nuclear arms race and to take effective measures towards reductions in strategic arms, nuclear disarmament, and general and complete disarmament,

Desiring to contribute to the relaxation of international tension and the strengthening of trust between States,

Have agreed as follows:

Article I

1.   Each party undertakes to limit anti-ballistic missile (ABM) systems and to adopt other measures in accordance with the provisions of this Treaty.

2.   Each Party undertakes not to deploy ABM systems for a defense of the territory of its country and not to provide a base for such a defense, and not to deploy ABM systems for defense of an individual region except as provided for in Article III of this Treaty.

Article II

1.   For the purpose of this Treaty an ABM system is a system to counter strategic ballistic missiles or their elements in flight trajectory, current-

ly consisting of:

     (a)   ABM interceptor missiles, which are interceptor missiles constructed and deployed for an ABM role, or of a type tested in an ABM mode;

     (b)   ABM launchers, which are launchers constructed and deployed for launching ABM interceptor missiles; and

     (c)   ABM radars, which are radars constructed and deployed for an ABM role, or of a type tested in an ABM mode.

    2.   The ABM system components listed in paragraph 1 of this Article include those which are:

     (a)   operational;

     (b)   under construction;

     (c)   undergoing testing;

     (d)   undergoing overhaul, repair or conversion; or

     (e)   mothballed.

Article III

Each Party undertakes not to deploy ABM systems or their components except that:

     (a)   within one ABM system deployment area having a radius of one hundred and fifty kilometers and centered on the Party's national capital, a Party may deploy: (1) no more than one hundred ABM launchers and no more than one hundred ABM interceptor missiles at launch sites, and (2) ABM radars within no more than six ABM radar complexes, the area of each complex being circular and having a diameter of no more than three kilometers; and

     (b)   within one ABM system deployment area having a radius of one hundred and fifty kilometers and containing ICBM silo launchers, a Party may deploy: (1) no more than one hundred ABM launchers and no more than one hundred ABM interceptor missiles at launch sites, (2) two large phased-array ABM radars comparable in potential to corresponding ABM radars operational or under construction on the date of signature of the Treaty in an ABM system deployment area containing ICBM silo launchers, and (3) no more than eighteen ABM radars each having a potential less than the potential of the smaller of the above-mentioned two large phased-array ABM radars.

Article IV

The limitations provided for in Article III shall not apply to ABM systems or their components used for development or testing, and located within current or additionally agreed test ranges. Each Party may have no more than a total of fifteen ABM launchers at test ranges.

Article V

1. Each Party undertakes not to develop, test, or deploy ABM systems or components which are sea-based, air-based, space-based, or mobile land-based.

2. Each Party undertakes not to develop, test, or deploy ABM launchers for launching more than one ABM interceptor missile at a time from each launcher, not to modify deployed launchers to provide them with such a capability, not to develop, test, or deploy automatic or semi-automatic or other similar systems for rapid reload of ABM launchers.

Article VI

To enhance assurance of the effectiveness of the limitations on ABM systems and their components provided by the Treaty, each Party undertakes:

(a)   not to give missiles, launchers, or radars, other than ABM interceptor missiles, ABM launchers, or ABM radars, capabilities to counter strategic ballistic missiles or their elements in flight trajectory, and not to test them in an ABM mode; and

(b)   not to deploy in the future radars for early warning of strategic ballistic missile attack except at locations along the periphery of its national territory and oriented outward.

Article VII

Subject to the provisions of this Treaty, modernization and replacement of ABM systems or their components may be carried out.

Article VIII

ABM systems or their components in excess of the numbers or outside the areas specified in this Treaty, as well as ABM systems or their components prohibited by this Treaty, shall be destroyed or dismantled under agreed procedures within the shortest possible agreed period of time.

Article IX

To assure the viability and effectiveness of this Treaty, each Party undertakes not to transfer to other States, and not to deploy outside its national territory, ABM systems or their components limited by this Treaty.

Article X

Each Party undertakes not to assume any international obligations which would conflict with this Treaty.

The Parties undertake to continue active negotiations for limitations on strategic offensive arms.

Article XII

1.   For the purpose of providing assurance of compliance with the provisions of this Treaty, each Party shall use national technical means of verification at its disposal in a manner consistent with generally recognized principles of international law.

2.   Each Party undertakes not to interfere with the national technical means of verification of the other Party operating in accordance with paragraph 1 of this Article.

3.   Each Party undertakes not to use deliberate concealment measures which impede verification by national technical means of compliance with the provisions of this Treaty. This obligation shall not require changes in current construction, assembly, conversion, or overhaul practices.

Article XIII

1.   To promote the objectives and implementation of the provisions of this Treaty, the Parties shall establish promptly a Standing Consultative Commission, within the framework of which they will:

(a)   consider questions concerning compliance with the obligations assumed and related situations which may be considered ambiguous;

(b)   provide on a voluntary basis such information as either Party considers necessary to assure confidence in compliance with the obligations assumed;

(c)   consider questions involving unintended interference with national technical means of verification;

(d)   consider possible changes in the strategic situation which have a bearing on the provisions of this Treaty;

(e)   agree upon procedures and dates for destruction or dismantling of ABM systems or their components in cases provided for by the provisions of this Treaty;

(f)   consider, as appropriate, possible proposals for further increasing the viability of this Treaty; including proposals for amendments in accordance with the provisions of this Treaty;

(g)   consider, as appropriate, proposals for further measures aimed at limiting strategic arms.

2.   The Parties through consultation shall establish, and may amend as appropriate, Regulations for the Standing Consultative Commission governing procedures, composition and other relevant matters.

1.   Each Party may propose amendments to this Treaty. Agreed amendments shall enter into force in accordance with the procedures governing the entry into force of this Treaty.
2.   Five years after entry into force of this Treaty, and at five-year intervals thereafter, the Parties shall together conduct a review of this Treaty.

Article XV

1.   This Treaty shall be of unlimited duration.
2.   Each Party shall, in exercising its national sovereignty, have the right to withdraw from this Treaty if it decides that extraordinary events related to the subject matter of this Treaty have jeopardized its supreme interest. It shall give notice of its decision to the other Party six months prior to withdrawal from the Treaty. Such notice shall include a statement of the extraordinary events the notifying Party regards as having jeopardized its supreme interests.

Article XVI

1.   This Treaty shall be subject to ratification in accordance with the constitutional procedures of each Party. The Treaty shall enter into force on the day of the exchange of instruments of ratification.
2.   This Treaty shall be registered pursuant to Article 102 of the Charter of the United Nations.
DONE at Moscow on May 26, 1972, in two copies, each in the English and Russian languages, both texts being equally authentic.

For the United States of America   *For the Union of Soviet Socialist Republics*

President of the United States of   General Secretary of the Central
America   Committee of the CPSU

Agreed Statements, Common Understandings, and Unilateral Statements Regarding the Treaty Between the United States of America and the Union of Soviet Socialist Republics on the Limitation of Anti-Ballistic Missiles

1. Agreed Statements

The document set forth below was agreed upon and initialed by the Heads of the Delegations on May 26, 1972 (letter designations added);

AGREED STATEMENTS REGARDING THE TREATY BETWEEN THE UNITED STATES OF AMERICA AND THE UNION OF SOVIET SOCIALIST REPUBLICS ON THE LIMITATION OF ANTI-BALLISTIC MISSILE SYSTEMS

The Parties understand that, in addition to the ABM radars which may be deployed in accordance with subparagraph (a) of Article III of the Treaty, those non-phased-array ABM radars operational on the date of signature of the Treaty within the ABM system deployment area for defense of the national capital may be retained.

(B)

The Parties understand that the potential (the product of mean emitted power in watts and antenna area in square meters) of the smaller of the two large phased-array ABM radars referred to in subparagraph (b) of Article III of the Treaty is considered for purposes of the Treaty to be three million.

(C)

The Parties understand that the centre of the ABM system deployment area centered on the national capital and the centre of the ABM system deployment area containing ICBM silo launchers for each Party shall be separated by no less than thirteen hundred kilometers.

(D)

In order to insure fulfillment of the obligation not to deploy ABM systems and their components except as provided in Article III of the Treaty, the Parties agree that in the event ABM systems based on other physical principles and including components capable of substituting for ABM interceptor missiles, ABM launchers, or ABM radars are created in the future, specific limitations on such systems and their components would be subject to discussion in accordance with Article XIII and agreement in accordance with Article XIV of the Treaty.

(E)

The Parties understand that Article V of the Treaty includes obligations not to develop, test or deploy ABM interceptor missiles for the delivery by each ABM interceptor missile of more than one independently guided warhead.

(F)

The Parties agree not to deploy phased-array radars having a potential (the product of mean emitted power in watts and antenna area in square me-

194 ters) exceeding three million, except as provided for in Articles III, IV and VI of the Treaty, or except for the purposes of tracking objects in outer space or for use as national technical means of verification.

(G)

The Parties understand that Article IX of the Treaty includes the obligation of the US and the USSR not to provide to other States technical descriptions or blue prints specially worked out for the construction of ABM systems and their components limited by the Treaty.

2. Common Understandings

Common understanding of the Parties on the following matters was reached during the negotiations:

A. Location of ICBM Defenses

The U.S. Delegation made the following statement on May 26, 1972:

Article III of the ABM Treaty provides for each side one ABM system deployment area centered on its national capital and one ABM system deployment area containing ICBM silo launchers. The two sides have registered agreement on the following statement: "The Parties understand that the center of the ABM system deployment area centered on the national capital and the center of the ABM system deployment area containing ICBM silo launchers for each Party shall be separated by no less than thirteen hundred kilometers." In this connection, the U.S. side notes that its ABM system deployment area for defense of ICBM silo launchers, located west of the Mississippi River, will be centered in the Grand Forks ICBM silo launcher deployment area. (See Agreed Statement (C).)

B. ABM Test Ranges

The U.S. Delegation made the following statement on April 26, 1972:

Article IV of the ABM Treaty provides that "the limitations provided for in Article III shall not apply to ABM systems or their components used for development or testing, and located within current or additionally agreed test ranges." We believe it would be useful to assure that there is no misunderstanding as to current ABM test ranges. It is our understanding that ABM test ranges encompass the area within which ABM components are located for test purposes. The current U.S. ABM test ranges are at White Sands, New Mexico, and at Kwajalein Atoll, and the current Soviet ABM test range is near Sary Shagan in Kazakhstan. We consider that non-phased array radars of types used for range safety or instrumentation purposes may be located outside of ABM test ranges. We interpret the reference in Article IV to "additionally agreed test ranges" to mean that ABM components will not be located at any other test ranges without prior agreement between our Governments that there will be such additional ABM test ranges.

On May 5, 1972, the Soviet Delegation stated that there was a common understanding on what ABM test ranges were, that the use of the types of non-ABM radars for range safety or instrumentation was not limited under the Treaty, that the reference in Article IV to "additionally agreed" test ranges was sufficiently clear, and that national means permitted identifying current test ranges.

C. Mobile ABM Systems

On January 29, 1972, the U.S. Delegation made the following statement:

Article V (1) of the Joint Draft Text of the ABM Treaty includes an undertaking not to develop, test, or deploy mobile land-based ABM systems and their components. On May 5, 1971, the U.S. side indicated that, in its view, a prohibition on deployment of mobile ABM systems and components would rule out the deployment of ABM launchers and radars which were not permanent fixed types. At that time, we asked for the Soviet view of this interpretation. Does the Soviet side agree with the U.S. side's interpretation put forward on May 5, 1971?

On April 13, 1972, the Soviet Delegation said there is a general common understanding on this matter.

D. Standing Consultative Commission

Ambassador Smith made the following statement on May 22, 1972:

The United States proposes that the sides agree that, with regard to initial implementation of the ABM Treaty's Article XIII on the Standing Consultative Commission (SCC) and of the consultation Articles to the Interim Agreement on offensive arms and the Accidents Agreement*, agreement establishing the SCC will be worked out early in the follow-on SALT negotiations; until that is completed, the following arrangements will prevail: when SALT is in session, any consultation desired by either side under these Articles can be carried out by the two SALT Delegations; when SALT is not in session, ad hoc arrangements for any desired consultations under these Articles may be made through diplomatic channels.

---

* See Article 7 of Agreement to Reduce the Risk of Outbreak of Nuclear War Between the United States of America and the Union of Soviet Socialist Republics, signed Sept. 30, 1971.

Minister Semenov replied that, on an ad referendum basis, he could agree that the U.S. statement corresponded to the Soviet understanding.

E. Standstill

On May 6, 1972, Minister Semenov made the following statement:

In an effort to accommodate the wishes of the U.S. side, the Soviet Delegation is prepared to proceed on the basis that the two sides will in fact observe the obligations of both the Interim Agreement and the ABM Treaty beginning from the date of signature of these two documents.

In reply, the U.S. Delegation made the following statement on May 20, 1972:

The U.S. agrees in principle with the Soviet statement made on May 6 concerning observance of obligations beginning from date of signature but we would like to make clear our understanding that this means that, pending rectification and acceptance, neither side would take any action prohibited by the agreements after they had entered into force. This understanding would continue to apply in the absence of notification by either signatory of its intention not to proceed with ratification or approval.

The Soviet Delegation indicated agreement with the U.S. statement.

3. Unilateral Statements

The following noteworthy unilateral statements were made during the negotiations by the United States Delegation:

A. Withdrawal from the ABM Treaty

On May 9, 1972, Ambassador Smith made the following statement:

The U.S. Delegation has stressed the importance the U.S. Government attaches to achieving agreement on more complete limitations on strategic offensive arms, following agreement on an ABM Treaty and on an Interim Agreement on certain measures with respect to the limitation of strategic offensive arms. The U.S. Delegation believes that an objective of the follow-on negotiations should be to constrain and reduce on a long-term basis threats to the survivability of our respective strategic retaliatory forces. The USSR Delegation has also indicated that the objectives of SALT would remain unfulfilled without the achievement of an agreement providing for more complete limitations on strategic offensive arms. Both sides recognize that the initial agreements would be steps toward the achievement of more complete limitations on strategic arms. If an agreement providing for more complete strategic offensive arms limitations were not achieved within five years, U.S. supreme interests could be jeopardized. Should that occur, it would constitute a basis for withdrawal from the ABM Treaty. The U.S. does not wish to see such a situation occur, nor do we believe that the USSR does. It is because we wish to prevent such a situation that we emphasize the importance the U.S. Government attaches to achievements of more complete limitations on strategic offensive arms. The U.S. Executive will inform the Congress, in connection with Congressional consideration of the ABM Treaty and the Interim Agreement, of this statement of the U.S. position.

B. Tested in ABM Mode

On April 7, 1972, the U.S. Delegation made the following statement:

Article II of the Joint Text Draft uses the term "tested in an ABM mode", in defining ABM components, and Article VI includes certain obligations concerning such testing. We believe that the sides should have a common understanding of this phrase. First, we would note that the testing provisions of the ABM Treaty are intended to apply to testing which occurs after the date of signature of the Treaty, and not to any testing which may have occurred in the past. Next, we would amplify the remarks we have made on this subject during the previous Helsinki phase by setting forth the objectives which govern the U.S. view on the subject, namely, while prohibiting testing of non-ABM components for ABM purposes: not to prevent testing of ABM components, and not to prevent testing of non-ABM components for non-ABM purposes. To clarify our interpretation of "tested in an ABM mode," we note that we would consider a launcher, missile or radar to be "tested in an ABM mode" if, for example, any of the following events occur: (1) a launcher is used to launch an ABM interceptor missile, (2) an interceptor missile is flight tested against a target vehicle which has a flight trajectory with characteristics of a strategic ballistic missile flight trajectory, or is flight tested in conjunction with the test of an ABM interceptor missile or an ABM radar at the same test range, or is flight tested to an altitude inconsistent with the interception of targets against which air defenses are deployed, (3) a radar makes measurements on a cooperative target vehicle of the kind referred to in item (2) above during the reentry portion of its trajectory or makes measurements in conjunction with the test of an ABM interceptor missile or an ABM radar at the same test range. Radars used for purposes such as range safety or instrumentation would be exempt from application of these criteria.

C. No-Transfer Article of ABM Treaty

On April 18, 1972, the U.S. Delegation made the following statement:

In regard to this Article (IX), I have a brief and I believe self-explanatory statement to make. The U.S. side wishes to make clear that the provisions of this Article do not set a precedent for whatever provision may be considered for a Treaty on Limiting Strategic Offensive Arms. The question of transfer of strategic offensive arms is a far more complex issue, which may require a different solution.

D. No Increase in Defense of Early Warning Radars

On July 28, 1970, the U.S. Delegation made the following statement:

Since Hen House radars (Soviet ballistic missile early warning radars) can detect and track ballistic missile warheads at great distances, they have a significant ABM potential. Accordingly, the U.S. would regard any increase in the defenses of such radars by surface-to-air missiles as inconsistent with an agreement.

Interim Agreement Between the United States of America and the Union of Soviet Socialist Republics on Certain Measures With Respect to the Limitation of Strategic Offensive Arms

ENTERED INTO FORCE: 3 October 1972

The United States of America and the Union of Soviet Socialist Republics, hereinafter referred to as the Parties,

Convinced that the Treaty on the Limitations of Anti-Ballistic Missile Systems and this Interim Agreement on Certain Measures with Respect to the Limitation of Strategic Offensive Arms will contribute to the creation of more favorable conditons for active negotiations on limiting strategic arms as well as to the relaxation of international tension and the strengthening of trust between States,

Taking into account the relationship between strategic offensive and defensive arms,

Mindful of their obligations under Article VI of the Treaty on the Non-Proliferation of Nuclear Weapons,

Have agreed as follows:

Article I

The Parties undertake not to start construction of additional fixed land-based intercontinental ballistic missile (ICBM) launchers after July 1, 1972.

Article II

The Parties undertake not to convert land-based launchers for light

ICBMs, or for ICBMs of older types deployed prior to 1964, into land-based
launchers for heavy ICBMs of types deployed after that time.

Article III

The Parties undertake to limit submarine-launched ballistic missile (SLBM) launchers and modern ballistic missile submarines to the numbers operational and under construction on the date of signature of this Interim Agreement, and in addition to launchers and submarines constructed under procedures established by the Parties as replacements for an equal number of ICBM launchers of older types deployed prior to 1964 or for launchers on older submarines.

Article IV

Subject to the provisions of this Interim Agreement, modernization and replacement of strategic offensive ballistic missiles and launchers covered by this Interim Agreement may be undertaken.

Article V

1. For the purpose of providing assurance of compliance with the provisions of this Interim Agreement, each Party shall use national technical means of verification at its disposal in a manner consistent with generally recognized principles of international law.

2. Each party undertakes not to interfere with the national technical means of verification of the other Party operating in accordance with paragraph 1 of this Article.

3. Each Party undertakes not to use deliberate concealment measures which impede verification by national technical means of compliance with the provisions of this Interim Agreement. This obligation shall not require changes in current construction, assembly, conversion, or overhaul practices.

Article VI

To promote the objectives and implementation of the provisions of this Interim Agreement, the Parties shall use the Standing Consultative Commission established under Article XIII of the Treaty on the Limitation of Anti-Ballistic Missile Systems in accordance with the provisions of that Article.

Article VII

The Parties undertake to continue active negotiations for limitations on strategic offensive arms. The obligations provided for in this Interim Agreement shall not prejudice the scope or terms of the limitations on strategic offensive arms which may be worked out in the course of further negotiations.

Article VIII

1. This Interim Agreement shall enter into force upon exchange of written notices of acceptance by each Party, which exchange shall take place simultaneously with the exchange of instruments of ratification of the Treaty on the Limitation of Anti-Ballistic Missile Systems.

2. This Interim Agreement shall remain in force for a period of five years unless replaced earlier by an agreement on more complete measures limiting strategic offensive arms. It is the objective of the Parties to conduct active follow-on negotiatons with the aim of concluding such an agreement as soon as possible.

3. Each Party shall, in exercising its national sovereignty, have the right to withdraw from this Interim Agreement if it decides that extraordinary events related to the subject matter of this Interim Agreement have jeopardized its supreme interests. It shall give notice of its decision to the other Party six months prior to withdrawal from this Interim Agreement. Such notice shall include a statement of the extraordinary events the notifying Party regards as having jeopardized its supreme interests.

DONE at Moscow on May 26, 1972, in two copies, each in the English and Russian languages, both texts being equally authenic.

For the United States of America

President of the United States of America

For the Union of Soviet Socialist Republics

General Secretary of the Central Committee of the CPSU

Protocol to the Interim Agreement Between the United States of America and the Union of Soviet Socialist Republics on Certain Measures With Respect to the Limitation of Strategic Offensive Arms

The United States of America and the Union of Soviet Socialist Republics, hereinafter referred to as the Parties,

Having agreed on certain limitations relating to submarine-launched ballistic missile launchers and modern ballistic missile submarines, and to replacement procedures, in the Interim Agreement,

Have agreed as follows:

The Parties understand that, under Article III of the Interim Agreement, for the period during which that Agreement remains in force:

The U.S. may have no more than 710 ballistic missile launchers on submarines (SLBMs) and no more than 44 modern ballistic missile submarines.

The Soviet Union may have no more than 950 ballistic missile launchers on
submarines and no more than 62 modern ballistic missile submarines.

Additional ballistic missile launchers on submarines up to the above-mentioned levels, in the U.S.-over 656 ballistic missile launchers on nuclear-powered submarines, and in the U.S.S.R.-over 740 ballistic missile launchers on nuclear-powered submarines, operational and under construction, may become operational as replacements for equal numbers of ballistic missile launchers of older types deployed prior to 1964 or of ballistic missile launchers on older submarines.

The deployment of modern SLBMs on any submarine, regardless of type, will be counted against the total level of SLBMs permitted for the U.S. and the U.S.S.R.

This Protocol shall be considered an integral part of the Interim Agreement.

DONE at Moscow this 26th day of May, 1972

For the United States of
America

President of the United
States of America

For the Union of Soviet Socialist
Republics

General Secretary of the Central
Committee of the CPSU

Agreed Statements, Common Understandings, and Unilateral Statements Regarding the Interim Agreement Between the United States of America and the Union of Soviet Socialist Republics on Certain Measures With Respect to the Limitation of Strategic Offensive Arms

1. Agreed Statements

The document set forth below was agreed upon and initialed by the Heads of the Delegations on May 26, 1972 (letter designations added):

AGREED STATEMENTS REGARDING THE INTERIM AGREEMENT BETWEEN THE UNITED STATES OF AMERICA AND THE UNION OF SOVIET SOCIALIST REPUBLICS ON CERTAIN MEASURES WITH RESPECT TO THE LIMITATION OF STRATEGIC OFFENSIVE ARMS

(A)

The Parties understand that land-based ICBM launchers referred to in the Interim Agreement are understood to be launchers for strategic ballistic missiles capable of ranges in excess of the shortest distance between the northeastern border of the continental U.S. and the northwestern border of the continental U.S.S.R.

(B)

The Parties understand that fixed land-based ICBM launchers under active construction as of the date of signature of the Interim Agreement may be completed.

(C)

The Parties understand that in the process of modernization and replacement the dimensions of land-based ICBM silo launchers will not be significantly increased.

(D)

The Parties understand that during the period of the Interim Agreement there shall be no significant increase in the number of ICBM or SLBM test and training launchers, or in the number of such launchers for modern land-based heavy ICBMs. The Parties further understand that construction or conversion of ICBM launchers at test ranges shall be undertaken only for purposes of testing and training.

(E)

The Parties understand that dismantling or destruction of ICBM launchers of older types deployed prior to 1964 and ballistic missile launchers on older submarines being replaced by new SLBM launchers on modern submarines will be initiated at the time of the beginning of sea trials of a replacement submarine, and will be completed in the shortest possible agreed period of time. Such dismantling or destruction, and timely notification thereof, will be accomplished under procedures to be agreed in the Standing Consultative Commission.

2. Common Understandings

Common understanding of the Parties on the following matters was reached during the negotiations:

A. Increase in ICBM Silo Dimensions

Ambassador Smith made the following statement on May 26, 1972:

The Parties agree that the term "significantly increased" means that an increase will not be greater than 10-15 percent of the present dimensions of land-based ICBM silo launchers.

Minister Semenov replied that this statement corresponded to the Soviet
understanding.

B. Standing Consultative Commission

Ambassador Smith made the following statement on May 22, 1972:

The United States proposes that the sides agree that, with regard to initial implementation of the ABM Treaty's Article XII on the Standing Consultative Commission (SCC) and of the consultations Articles to the Interim Agreement on offensive arms and the Accidents Agreement*, agreement establishing the SCC will be worked out early in the follow-on SALT negotiations; until that is completed the following arrangements will prevail: when SALT is in session, any consultation desired by either side under these Articles can be carried out by the two SALT Delegations; when SALT is not in session, *ad hoc* arrangements for any desired consultations under these Articles may be made through diplomatic channels.

Ministers Semonov replied that, on an *ad referendum* basis, he could agree that the U.S. statement corresponded to the Soviet understanding.

C. Standstill

On May 6, 1972, Minister Semenov made the following statement:

In an effort to accommodate the wishes of the U.S. side, the Soviet Delegation is prepared to proceed on the basis that the two sides will in fact observe the obligations of both the Interim Agreement and the ABM Treaty beginning from the date of signature of these two documents.

In reply, the U.S. Delegation made the following statement on May 20, 1972:

The U.S. agrees in principle with the Soviet statement made on May 6 concerning observance of obligations beginning from date of signature but we would like to make clear our understanding that this means that, pending ratification and acceptance, neither side would take any action prohibited by the agreements after they had entered into force. This understanding would continue to apply in the absence of notification by either signatory of its intention not to proceed with ratification or approval.

The Soviet Delegation indicated agreement with the U.S. statement.

---

* See Article 7 of Agreement to Reduce the Risk of Outbreak of Nuclear War Between the United States of America and the Union of Soviet Socialist Republics, signed Sept. 30, 1971.

(a) The following noteworthy unilateral statements were made during the negotiations by the United States Delegation:

A. Withdrawal from the ABM Treaty

On May 9, 1972, Ambassador Smith made the following statement:

The U.S. Delegation has stressed the importance the U.S. Government attaches to achieving agreement on more complete limitations on strategic offensive arms, following agreement on an ABM Treaty and on an Interim Agreement on certain measures with respect to the limitation of strategic offensive arms. The U.S. Delegation believes that an objective of the follow-on negotiations should be to constrain and reduce on a long-term basis threats to the survivability of our respective strategic retaliatory forces. The USSR Delegation has also indicated that the objectives of SALT would remain unfulfilled without the achievement of an agreement providing for more complete limitations on strategic offensive arms. Both sides recognize that the initial agreements would be steps toward the achievement of more complete limitations on strategic arms. If an agreement providing for more complete strategic offensive arms limitations were not achieved within five years, U.S. supreme interests could be jeopardized. Should that occur, it would constitute a basis for withdrawal from the ABM Treaty. The U.S. does not wish to see such a situation occur, nor do we believe that the USSR does. It is because we wish to prevent such a situation that we emphasize the importance the U.S. Government attaches to achievement of more complete limitations on strategic offensive arms. The U.S. Executive will inform the Congress, in connection with Congressional consideration of the ABM Treaty and the Interim Agreement, of this statement of the U.S. position.

B. Land-Mobile ICBM Launchers

The U.S. Delegation made the following statement on May 20, 1972:

In connection with the important subject of land-mobile ICBM launchers, in the interest of concluding the Interim Agreement the U.S. Delegation now withdraws its proposal that Article I or an agreed statement explicitly prohibit the deployment of mobile land-based ICBM launchers. I have been instructed to inform you that, while agreeing to defer the question of limitation of operational land-mobile ICBM launchers to the subsequent negotiations on more complete limitations on strategic offensive arms, the U.S. would consider the deployment of operational land-mobile ICBM launchers during the period of the Interim Agreement as inconsistent with the objectives of that Agreement.

The U.S. Delegation made the following statement on May 20, 1972:

I wish to emphasize the importance that the United States attaches to the provisions of Article V, including in particular their application to fitting out or berthing submarines.

D. "Heavy" ICBM's

The U.S. Delegation made the following statement on May 26, 1972:

The U.S. Delegation regrets that the Soviet Delegation has not been willing to agree on a common definition of a heavy missile. Under these circumstances, the U.S. Delegation believes it necessary to state the following: The United States would consider any ICBM having a volume significantly greater than that of the largest light ICBM now operational on either side to be a heavy ICBM. The U.S. proceeds on the premise that the Soviet side will give due account to this consideration.

(b) The following noteworthy unilateral statement was made by the Delegation of the U.S.S.R. and is shown here with the U.S. reply:

On May 17, 1972, Minister Semenov made the following unilateral "Statement of the Soviet Side":

Taking into account that modern ballistic submarines are presently in the possession of not only the U.S., but also of its NATO allies, the Soviet Union agrees that for the period of effectiveness of the Interim 'Freeze' Agreement the U.S. and its NATO allies have up to 50 such submarines with a total of up to 800 ballistic missile launchers thereon (including 41 U.S. submarines with 656 ballistic missile launchers). However, if during the period of effectiveness of the Agreement U.S. allies in NATO should increase the number of their modern submarines to exceed the numbers of submarines they would have operational or under construction on the date of signature of the Agreement, the Soviet Union will have the right to a corresponding increase in the number of its submarines. In the opinion of the Soviet side, the solution of the question of modern ballistic missile submarines provided for in the Interim Agreement only partially compensates for the strategic imbalance in the deployment of the nuclear-powered missile submarines of the USSR and the U.S. Therefore, the Soviet side believes that this whole question, and above all the question of liquidating the American missile submarine bases outside the U.S., will be appropriately resolved in the course of follow-on negotiations.

On May 24, Ambassador Smith made the following reply to Minister Semenov:

206   The United States side has studied the "statement made by the Soviet side" of May 17 concerning compensation for submarine basing and SLBM submarines belonging to third countries. The United States does not accept the validity of the considerations in that statement.

On May 26, Minister Semenov repeated the unilateral statement made on May 17. Ambassador Smith also repeated the U.S. rejection on May 26.

ANNEX IV

AA 330
SA (83) 32

North Atlantic Assembly
29th annual session
he Hague, 2-7 October 1983.

RESOLUTION 145

on Ballistic Missile Defence (1)

The Assembly,

Recalling its 1982 Resolution on Arms Control in Outer Space, which stressed the need for verifiable agreements governing weapons in space;

Noting the disagreement about the feasibility and desirability of ballistic missile defence systems;

Concerned that the Soviet Union has already tested anti-satellite weapons and has a large-scale ballistic missile defence research programme underway;

Aware that the United States is also investigating anti-satellite techniques and ballistic missile defence technologies;

Convinced that the Atlantic Alliance should not fall behind in these areas of research in order to negotiate from a position of strength and - if necessary - to match future Soviet deployment of ballistic missile defence systems:

URGES member governments of the North Atlantic Alliance:

1. to continue to determine as accurately as possible the nature and scale of Soviet ballistic missile defence programmes in order to ensure that there

(1) Presented by the Scientific and Technical Committee

will be no profound disparity in Soviet and United States' ballistic missile defence capabilities;

2. to continue, with the Soviet Union, to observe arms control agreements governing deployment of ballistic missile defence systems, and to seek to improve upon such agreements under appropriate conditions;

3. to seek vigorously a verifiable arms control agreement with the Soviet Union governing anti-satellite weapons;

4. to take all possible steps to avoid an arms race in weapons for use in space and to forgo deployment of such systems if the Soviet Union formally agrees to a parallel commitment;

5. to assess carefully the degree of protection that different prospective ballistic missile defence systems would afford the Alliance as a whole, to take account of these aspects should deployment of such systems be unavoidable under the terms of ballistic missile defence agreements, and to consider carefully ways of ensuring joint participation in the research and development necessary for the creation of ballistic missile defences.

ANNEX V

UNITED NATIONS
GENERAL ASSEMBLY

Distr.
GENERAL

A/38/19 4*
23 August 1983
ENGLISH
ORIGINAL: RUSSIAN

Thirty-eighth session

REQUEST FOR THE INCLUSION OF A SUPPLEMENTARY ITEM
IN THE AGENDA OF THE THIRTY-EIGHTH SESSION

CONCLUSION OF A TREATY ON THE PROHIBITION
OF THE USE OF FORCE IN OUTER SPACE
AND FROM SPACE AGAINST THE EARTH

Letter dated 19 August 1983 from the First Vice-Chairman of the
Council of Ministers of the Union of Soviet Socialist Republics,

* Reissued for technical reasons.

Minister for Foreign Affairs of the USSR, to the Secretary-General.

The Soviet Union requests the inclusion in the agenda of the thirty-eighth session of the General Assembly of an item entitled "Conclusion of a treaty on the prohibition of the use of force in outer space and from space against the Earth".

In proposing this item, the Soviet Union is seeking to avoid the militarization of outer space. Of particular danger in this respect are the plans to create and deploy various space-weapons systems capable of destroying targets both in space and on the Earth.

The Soviet Union considers it most imperative to have a reliable means of counteracting these plans to make space a source of mortal danger to all mankind, by taking urgent and effective measures to prevent the arms race from spreading to outer space, which it has not yet penetrated.

To this end, in 1981 at the United Nations the Soviet Union submitted a proposal concerning the conclusion of a treaty on the prohibition of the stationing of weapons of any kind in outer space. That proposal was approved by the General Assembly. However, for well-known reasons, the drafting of that treaty has not yet actually begun.

But time is running out, and now the Soviet Union is proposing that a further step should be taken forthwith in the form of an agreement on the general prohibition of the use of force both in outer space and from space against the Earth. It is submitting the relevant draft treaty for consideration at the current session.

The most important feature of the draft treaty is the combining of the political-legal obligations of States not to allow the use of force in their relations with each other in space and from space with measures of a material nature aimed at banning the militarization of outer space.

More precisely, the Soviet Union is advocating a complete ban on the testing and deployment in space of any space-based weapon for the destruction of objects on the Earth, in the atmosphere and in outer space.

It is also proposing a radical solution to the question of anti-satellite weapons: the unconditional pledge of States not to create new anti-satellite systems and to destroy any anti-satellite systems that they may already have.

The parties to the treaty would also undertake to refrain in every way from destroying, damaging, disturbing the normal functioning or changing the flight trajectory of space objects of other States.

In addition, the treaty would ban the testing and use for military, including anti-satellite, purposes of manned spacecraft, which should be used solely

Action on the series of far-reaching measures proposed by the Soviet Union would be a major and truly tangible contribution towards the attainment of the goal approved earlier by the United Nations, namely, ensuring that space is used exclusively for peaceful purposes.

I request you to consider this letter as an explanatory memorandum under the rules of procedure of the General Assembly and to circulate it, together with the enclosed draft treaty, as an official document of the General Assembly.

A. GROMYKO
First Vice-Chairman
of the Council of Ministers of the USSR,
Minister for Foreign Affairs of the USSR.

ANNEX

TREATY ON THE PROHIBITION OF THE USE OF FORCE
IN OUTER SPACE AND FROM SPACE AGAINST THE EARTH

The States Parties to this Treaty,

Guided by the principle whereby Members of the United Nations shall refrain in their international relations from the threat or use of force in any manner inconsistent with the purposes of the United Nations,

Seeking to avert an arms race in outer space and thus to lessen the danger to mankind of the threat of nuclear war,

Desiring to contribute towards attainment of the goal whereby the exploration and utilization of outer space, including the Moon and other celestial bodies, would be carried out exclusively for peaceful purposes,

Have agreed on the following:

Article 1

It is prohibited to resort to the use or threat of force in outer space and the atmosphere and on the Earth through the utilization, as instruments of destruction, of space objects in orbit around the Earth, on celestial bodies or stationed in space in any other manner.

It is further prohibited to resort to the use or threat of force against space objects in orbit around the Earth, on celestial bodies or stationed in outer space in any other manner.

In accordance with the provisions of article 1, States Parties to this Treaty undertake:

1.   Not to test or deploy by placing in orbit around the Earth or stationing on celestial bodies or in any other manner any space-based weapons for the destruction of objects on the Earth, in the atmosphere or in outer space.

2.   Not to utilize space objects in orbit around the Earth, on celestial bodies or stationed in outer space in any other manner as means to destroy any targets on the Earth, in the atmosphere or in outer space.

3.   Not to destroy, damage, disturb the normal functioning or change the flight trajectory of space objects of other States.

4.   Not to test or create new anti-satellite systems and to destroy any anti-satellite systems that they may already have.

5.   Not to test or use manned spacecraft for military, including anti-satellite, purposes.

Article 3

The State Parties to this Treaty agree not to assist, encourage or induce any State, group of States, international organization or natural or legal person to engage in activities prohibited by this Treaty.

Article 4

1.   For the purpose of providing assurance of compliance with the provisions of this Treaty, each State Party shall use the national technical means of verification at its disposal in a manner consistent with generally recognized principles of international law.

2.   Each State Party undertakes not to interfere with the national technical means of verification of other States Parties operating in accordance with paragraph 1 of this article.

Article 5

1.   The States Parties to this Treaty undertake to consult and co-operate with each other in solving any problems that may arise in connection with the objectives of the Treaty or its implementation.

2.   Consultations and co-operation as provided in paragraph 1 of this article may also be undertaken by having recourse to appropriate international procedures within the United Nations and in accordance with its Charter. Such recourse may include utilization of the services of the Consultative Committee of States Parties to the Treaty.

3.   The Consultative Committee of States Parties to the Treaty shall be convened by the depositary within one month after the receipt of a request from any State Party to this Treaty. Any State Party may nominate a representative to serve on the Committee.

Article 6

Each State Party to this Treaty undertakes to adopt such internal measures as it may deem necessary to fulfil its constitutional requirements in order to prohibit or prevent the carrying out of any activity contrary to the provisions of this Treaty in any place whatever under its jurisdiction or control.

Article 7

Nothing in this Treaty shall affect the rights and obligations of States under the Charter of the United Nations.

Article 8

Any dispute which may arise in connection with the implementation of this Treaty shall be settled exclusively by peaceful means through recourse to the procedures provided for in the Charter of the United Nations.

Article 9

This Treaty shall be of unlimited duration.

Article 10

1.   This Treaty shall be open to all States for signature at United Nations Headquarters in New York. Any State which does not sign this treaty before its entry into force in accordance with paragraph 3 of this article may accede to it at any time.

2.   This Treaty shall be subject to ratification by signatory States. Instruments of ratification and accession shall be deposited with the Secretary-General of the United Nations.

3.   This Treaty shall enter into force between the States which have deposited instruments of ratification upon the deposit with the Secretary-General of the United Nations of the fifth instrument of ratification, provided that such instruments have been deposited by the Union of Soviet Socialist Republics and the United States of America.

4.   For States whose instruments of ratification or accession are deposited after the entry into force of this Treaty, it shall enter into force on the date of the deposit of their instruments of ratification or accession.

5.   The Secretary-General of the United Nations shall promptly inform

212 all signatory and acceding States of the date of each signature, the date of deposit of each instrument of ratifiaction or accession, the date of entry into force of this Treaty as well as other notices.

Article 11

This Treaty, of which the Arabic, Chinese, English, French, Russian and Spanish texts are equally authentic, shall be deposited with the Secretary-General of the United Nations, who shall send duly certified copies thereof to the Governments of the signatory and acceding States.

ANNEX VI

UNITED NATIONS
GENERAL
ASSEMBLY

Distr.
GENERAL

A/36/192*

20 August 1981
ENGLISH
ORIGINAL: RUSSIAN

Thirty-sixth session

REQUEST FOR THE INCLUSION OF A SUPPLEMENTARY ITEM IN THE AGENDA OF THE THIRTY-SIXTH SESSION

CONCLUSION OF A TREATY ON THE PROHIBITION OF THE STATIONING OF WEAPONS OF ANY KIND IN OUTER SPACE

Letter dated 10 August 1981 from the Minister for Foreign Affairs of the Union of Soviet Socialist Republics addressed to the Secretary-General

The Soviet Union requests the inclusion in the agenda of the thirty sixth session of the General Assembly of an item entitled "Conclusion of a treaty on the prohibition of the stationing of weapons of any kind in outer space".

In 1982, mankind will observe the twenty-fifth anniversary of the beginning of the conquest of space, which is one of the greatest achievements of science and technology in the twentieth century. The use of outer space is already producing considerable benefit to mankind today in such areas as communications, study of the earth's natural resources, meteorology, navigation

* Reissued for technical reasons

and many other areas. It may be said that people are beginning to make space "habitable".

At the very beginning of the space age, as early as 1958, the Soviet Union made a proposal in the United Nations envisaging the banning of the use of outer space for military purposes. Over all the years which followed, it invariably stated and continues to state that space should be a sphere of exclusively peaceful co-operation. And it is gratifying to note that much has been done in this regard.

1963 saw the conclusion of the international Treaty banning nuclear weapon tests in the atmosphere, in outer space and under water. The 1967 Treaty on Principles Governing the Activities of States in the Exploration and Use of Outer Space including the Moon and Other Celestial Bodies, provides for the use of the moon and other celestial bodies exclusively for peaceful purposes and also prohibits the placing in orbit around the earth or stationing in outer space in any other manner any objects carrying nuclear weapons or other kinds of weapons of mass destruction. The 1979 Agreement Governing the Activities of States on the Moon and Other Celestial Bodies develops and spells out the obligations of States to ensure the exclusively peaceful use of the moon and other celestial bodies within the solar system.

However, all these international instruments do not exclude the possibility of the stationing in outer space of those kinds of weapons which are not covered by the definition of weapons of mass destruction. Consequently, the danger of the militarization of outer space still exists and has recently been increasing.

The Soviet Union considers that this is inadmissible. It believes that outer space should always remain unsullied and free from any weapons and should not become a new arena for the arms race or a source of aggravating relations between States. In the opinion of the Soviet Union, the attainment of these goals would be promoted by the conclusion of an international treaty on the prohibition of the stationing of weapons of any kind in outer space.

The draft treaty on this subject proposed by us is enclosed with this letter.

I should be grateful if you would consider this letter as an explanatory memorandum in accordance with the rules of procedure of the General Assembly and circulate it and the draft treaty as official documents of the General Assembly.

(Signed) A. GROMYKO
Minister for Foreign Affairs of the USSR

A/36/192
English
Annex

Draft treaty on the prohibition of the stationing
of weapons of any kind in outer space

The States Parties to this treaty,

Guided by the goals of strengthening peace and international security

Proceeding on the basis of their obligations under the Charter of the United Nations to refrain from the threat or use of force in any manner inconsistent with the Purposes of the United Nations,

Desiring not to allow outer space to become an arena for the arms race and a source of aggravating relations between States,

Have agreed on the following:

ARTICLE 1

1.   States Parties undertake not to place in orbit around the earth objects carrying weapons of any kind, install such weapons on celestial bodies, or station such weapons in outer space in any other manner, including on reusable manned space vehicles of an existing type or of other types which States Parties may develop in the future.

2.   Each State Party to this treaty undertakes not to assist, encourage or induce any State, group of States or international organization to engage in activities contrary to the provisions of paragraph 1 of this article.

ARTICLE 2

States Parties shall use space objects in strict accordance with international law, including the Charter of the United Nations, in the interest of maintaining international peace and security and promoting international co-operation and mutual understanding.

ARTICLE 3

Each State Party undertakes not to destroy, damage, disturb the normal functioning or change the flight trajectory of space objects of other States Parties, if such objects were placed in orbit in strict accordance with article 1, paragraph 1, of this treaty.

1.   For the purpose of providing assurance of compliance with the provisions of this treaty, each State Party shall use the national technical means of verification at its disposal in a manner consistent with generally recognized principles of international law.

2.   Each State Party undertakes not to interfere with the national technical means of verification of other States Parties operating in accordance with paragraph 1 of this article.

3.   In order to promote the objectives and provisions of this treaty, the States Parties shall, when necessary, consult each other, make inquiries and provide information in connexion with such inquiries.

ARTICLE 5

1.   Any State Party to this treaty may propose amendments to this treaty. The best of any proposed amendment shall be submitted to the depositary who shall promptly circulate it to all States Parties.

2.   The amendment shall enter into force for each State Party to this Treaty which has accepted it, upon the deposit with the depositary of instruments of acceptance by the majority of States Parties. Thereafter, the amendment shall enter into force for each remaining State Party on the date of deposit of its instrument of acceptance.

ARTICLE 6

This treaty shall be of unlimited duration.

ARTICLE 7

Each State Party shall in exercising its national sovereignty have the right to withdraw from this treaty if it decides that extraordinary events related to the subject matter of this treaty have jeopardized its supreme interests. It shall give notice to the Secretary-General of the United Nations of the decision adopted six months before withdrawing from the treaty. Such notice shall include a statement of the extraordinary events which the notifying State Party regards as having jeopardized its supreme interests.

ARTICLE 8

1.   This treaty shall be open to all States for signature at United Nations Headquarters in New York. Any State which does not sign this treaty before its

216 entry into force in accordance with paragraph 3 of this article may accede to it at any time.

2. This treaty shall be subject to ratification by signatory States. Instruments of ratification accession shall be deposited with the Secretary-General of the United Nations.

3. This treaty shall enter into force between the States which have deposited instruments of ratification upon the deposit with the Secretary-General of the United Nations of the fifth instrument of ratification.

4. For States whose instruments of ratification or accession are deposited after the entry into force of this treaty, it shall enter into force on the date of the deposit of their instruments of ratification or accession.

5. The Secretary-General of the United Nations shall promptly inform all signatory and acceding States of the date of each signature, the date of deposit of each instrument of ratification and accession, the date of entry into force of this treaty as well as other notices.

ARTICLE 9

This treaty, of which the Arabic, Chinese, English, French, Russian and Spanish texts are equally authentic, shall be deposited with the Secretary-General of the United Nations, who shall send duly certified copies thereof to the Governments of the signatory and acceding States.

ANNEX VII

UNITED
NATIONS
G-eneral Assembly

Dist.
GENERAL

A/37/669
6 December 1982

ORIGINAL: ENGLISH

Thirty-seventh session
Agenda item 57

CONCLUSION OF A TREATY ON THE PROHIBITION OF THE STATIONING OF WEAPONS OF ANY KIND IN OUTER SPACE

Report of the First Committee

Rapporteur: Mr. Luvsangiin ERDENECHULUUN (Mongolia)

1.   The item entitled "Conclusion of a treaty on the prohibition of the stationing of weapons of any kind in outer space: report of the Committee on Disarmament" was included in the provisional agenda of the thirty-seventh session in accordance with General Assembly resolution 36/99 of 9 December 1981.

2.   At its 4th plenary meeting, on 24 September 1982, the General Assembly, on the recommendation of the General Committee, decided to include the item in its agenda and to allocate it to the First Committee.

3.   At its 2nd meeting, on 29 September, the First Committee decided to hold a combined general debate on the items allocated to it relating to disarmament, namely items 39 to 57, 133 and 136. The general debate on these items and on items 138 and 139, which were allocated to the First Committee by the General Assembly at its 24th plenary meeting, on 8 October 1982, took place at the 3rd to 28th meetings, from 18 October to 5 November (see A/C.1/37/PV.3-28).

4.   In connection with item 57, the First Committee had before it the following documents:

(a)   Report of the Committee on Disarmament; 1/

b)   Letter dated 19 October 1982 from the Permanent Representative of Italy to the United Nations addressed to the Secretary-General, transmitting the texts of the resolutions adopted by the 69th Inter-Parliamentary Conference, held in Rome from 12 to 23 September 1982 (A/37/578).

II. CONSIDERATION OF PROPOSALS

A. Draft resolution A/C.1/37/L.8

5.   On 27 October, Bulgaria, the German Democratic Republic, Mongolia and the Ukrainian Soviet Socialist Republic submitted a draft resolution (A/C.1/37/L.8), which was later also sponsored by the Byelorussian Soviet Socialist Republic, Cuba, Czechoslovakia, Hungary and Viet Nam. The draft resolution, which was introduced by the representative of Mongolia at the 38th meeting, on 19 November, read as follows:

"The General Assembly,

"Guided by the objectives of strengthening peace and international security,

---

1/ Official Records of the General Assembly, Thirty-seventh Session, Supplement No. 27 (A/37/27 and Corr.1).

82-35233 0618d (E)

"Expressing the general interest of all mankind in the further exploration and use of outer space for peaceful purposes for the benefit of all States and in the interests of developing friendly relations and mutual understanding among them,

"Recognizing the danger threatening mankind in the event of outer space becoming an arena for the arms race,

"Endeavouring to keep outer space from becoming an arena for the arms race and a source of tension in relations among States,

"Taking into account the draft Treaty on the prohibition of the stationing of weapons of any kind in outer space, submitted to the General Assembly by the Soviet Union, and also the views and considerations put forward in the course of the discussion of this question at the thirty-seventh session,

"Referring to its resolution 36/99 of 15 January 1982 on the conclusion of a treaty on the prohibition of the stationing of weapons of any kind in outer space,

"Noting the discussion at the session of the Committee on Disarmament held in 1982 on the question of the agenda item entitled 'Prevention of an arms race in outer space',

"Recalling that the States parties to the Treaty on Principles Governing the Activities of States in the Exploration and Use of Outer Space, including the Moon and Other Celestial Bodies, 2/ undertook in article III to carry out activities in the exploration and use of outer space, including the Moon and other celestial bodies, in accordance with international law, including the Charter of the United Nations, in the interests of maintaining peace and security and developing international co-operation and mutual understanding,

"Recalling paragraph 80 of the Final Document of the Tenth Special Session of the General Assembly, 3/ in which it is stated that in order to prevent an arms race in outer space, further measures should be taken and appropriate international negotiations held in accordance with the spirit of the Treaty on Principles Governing the Activities of States in the Exploration and Use of Outer Space, including the Moon and Other Celestial Bodies,

"Stressing the need to prevent an arms race in outer space,

"Recognizing the threat that would be represented by the stationing in outer space of weapons of any kind, including anti-satellite systems, which would exert a destabilizing influence on international peace and security,

"Convinced of the need for further measures to keep outer space from being converted into an area of military confrontation contrary to the spirit of the 1967 Treaty on outer space, 2/

2/ Resolution 2222 (XXI), annex.
3/ Resolution S-10/2.

"Considering it imperative for the international community to give attention to concrete measures for the prevention of an arms race in outer space and, in this context, to the question of anti-satellite systems in the Committee on Disarmament,

"1.   Requests the Committee on Disarmament to activate work on the preparation of an international agreement, including the establishment of an ad hoc working group, to begin discussions of substance, with a view to the adoption of effective measures to prevent the spread of an arms race in outer space;

"2.   Calls upon the Union of Soviet Socialist Republics and the United States of America to renew bilateral talks on the question of anti-satellite systems;

"3.   Decides to include in the provisional agenda of its thirty-eighth session an item entitled "Conclusion of a treaty on the prohibition of the stationing of weapons of any kind in outer space."

6.   At the 43rd meeting, on 24 November, the representative of Mongolia indicated that the sponsors would not press draft resolution A/C.1/37/L.8 to a vote, as its main elements and ideas had been reflected in draft resolution A/C.1/37/L.64/Rev.1.

B.   Draft resolution A/C.1/37/L.64 and Rev.1

7.   On 18 November, Algeria, Argentina, Bangladesh, Brazil, Cuba, Egypt, India, Indonesia, Mexico, Morocco, Nigeria, Peru, Sri Lanka, the Sudan, Viet Nam and Yugoslavia submitted a draft resolution entitled "Prevention of an arms race in outer space" (A/C.1/37/L.64), which was later also sponsored by Colombia, the Congo, Ecuador, Ghana, Maldives, Romania, Singapore and Venezuela. The draft resolution was introduced by the representative of Sri Lanka at the 38th meeting, on 19 November.

8.   On 23 November, Algeria, Argentina, Bangladesh, Brazil, Colombia, the Congo, Cuba, Ecuador, Egypt, Ghana, India, Indonesia, Liberia, Maldives, Mexico, Morocco, Nigeria, Peru, Romania, Singapore, Sri Lanka, the Sudan, Venezuela, Viet Nam and Yugoslavia submitted a revised text of the draft resolution (A/C.1/37/L.64/Rev.1), which was later also sponsored by Benin, Bulgaria, the Byelorussian Soviet Socialist Republic, Czechoslovakia, the German Democratic Republic, Hungary, Ireland, Mongolia, Sweden and the Ukrainian Soviet Socialist Republic, and in which the following changes had been introduced:

220   (a)   The third preambular paragraph, which read:

"Reaffirming that exploration and use of outer space, including the Moon and other celestial bodies, shall be exclusively for peaceful purposes and shall be carried out for the benefit and in the interest of all countries, irrespective of their degree of economic or scientific development, and shall be the province of all mankind,"

was replaced by the following:

"Reaffirming that exploration and use of outer space, including the Moon and other celestial bodies, shall be carried out for the benefit and in the interest of all countries, irrespective of their degree of economic or scientific development, and shall be the province of all mankind",

(b) A new preambular paragraph, which read:

"Reaffirming further the will of all States that exploration and use of outer space, including the Moon and other celestial bodies, shall be exclusively for peaceful purposes,"

was added after the third preambular paragraph:

(c) Operative paragraph 1, which read:

"Reaffirms that outer space shall be used exclusively for peaceful purposes and shall not become an arena for an arms race;"

was replaced by the following:

"Reaffirms the will of all States that outer space shall be used exclusively for peaceful purposes and that it shall not become an arena for an arms race;".

.   At its 45th meeting, on 26 November, the Committee adopted draft resolution A/C.1/37/L.64/Rev.1 by a recorded vote of 118 to 1, with 8 abstentions (see para. 10). The voting was as follows: 4/

In favour: Afghanistan, Algeria, Angola, Argentina, Austria, Bahamas, Bahrain, Bangladesh, Benin, Bhutan, Bolivia, Brazil, Bulgaria, Burma, Burundi, Byelorussian Soviet Socialist Republic, Central African Republic, Chad, Chile, China, Colombia, Congo, Cuba, Cyprus, Czechoslovakia, Democratic Yemen, Denmark, Djibouti, Dominican Republic, Ecuador, Egypt, Ethiopia, Fiji, Finland, France, Gabon, German Democratic Republic, Germany, Federal Republic of, Ghana, Greece, Guatemala,

4/ The delegation of the Niger subsequently indicated that it had intended to vote in favour of the draft resolution.

Guinea, Guyana, Hungary, Iceland, India, Indonesia, Iran (Islamic Republic of), Iraq, Ireland, Italy, Ivory Coast, Jamaica, Japan, Jordan, Kenya, Kuwait, Lao People's Democratic Republic, Lebanon, Liberia, Libyan Arab Jamahiriya, Madagascar, Malawi, Malaysia, Mali, Malta, Mauritania, Mexico, Mongolia, Morocco, Mozambique, Nepal, New Zealand, Nicaragua, Nigeria, Norway, Oman, Pakistan, Panama, Papua New Guinea, Paraguay, Peru, Philippines, Poland, Portugal, Qatar, Romania, Rwanda, Sao Tome and Principe, Saudi Arabia, Senegal, Sierra Leone, Singapore, Somalia, Spain, Sri Lanka, Sudan, Suriname, Sweden, Syrian Arab Republic, Thailand, Togo, Trinidad and Tobago, Tunisia, Turkey, Uganda, Ukrainian Soviet Socialist Republic, Union of Soviet Socialist Republics, United Arab Emirates, United Republic of Cameroon, United Republic of Tanzania, Uruguay, Venezuela, Viet Nam, Yemen, Yugoslavia, Zaire, Zambia.

Against: United States of America.

Abstaining: Australia, Belgium, Canada, Israel, Luxembourg, Netherlands, Niger, United Kingdom of Great Britain and Northern Ireland.

III. RECOMMENDATION OF THE FIRST COMMITTEE

10.   The First Committee recommends to the General Assembly the adoption of the following draft resolution:

Prevention of an arms race in outer space

The General Assembly,

Inspired by the great prospects opening up before mankind as a result of a man's entry into outer space twenty-five years ago,

Recognizing the common interest of all mankind in the exploration and use of outer space for peaceful purposes,

Reaffirming that exploration and use of outer space, including the Moon and other celestial bodies, shall be carried out for the benefit and in the interest of all countries, irrespective of their degree of economic or scientific development, and shall be the province of all mankind,

Reaffirming further the will of all States that exploration and use of outer space, including the Moon and other celestial bodies, shall be exclusively for peaceful purposes,

Recalling that the States parties to the Treaty on Principles Governing the Activities of States in the Exploration and Use of Outer Space, including the Moon and Other Celestial Bodies, 5/ undertook in article III to carry on activities in the exploration and use of outer space, including the Moon and other celestial bodies, in accordance with international law and the Charter of the United Nations, in the interest of maintaining international peace and security and promoting international co-operation and understanding,

Reaffirming, in particular, article IV of the said Treaty which stipulates that States parties to the Treaty undertake not to place in orbit around the earth any objects carrying nuclear weapons or any other kind of weapons of mass destruction, to install such weapons on celestial bodies, or to station such weapons in outer space in any other manner,

Reaffirming paragraph 80 of the Final Document of the Tenth Special Session of the General Assembly, 6/ in which it is stated that, in order to prevent an arms race in outer space, further measures should be taken and appropriate international negotiations held in accordance with the spirit of the Treaty,

Recalling its resolutions 36/97 of 9 December 1981 and 36/99 of 9 December 1981,

Gravely concerned at the danger posed to all mankind by an arms race in outer space,

Mindful of the widespread interest expressed by Member States in the course of the negotiations on and following the adoption of the above-mentioned Treaty to ensure that the exploration and use of outer space should be for peaceful purposes, and taking note of proposals submitted to the General Assembly at its tenth special session devoted to disarmament, and at its regular sessions and to the Committee on Disarmament,

Noting the grave concern expressed by the Second United Nations Conference on the Exploration and Peaceful Uses of Outer Space over the extension of an arms race into outer space and the recommendations made to the competent organs of the United Nations, in particular the General Assembly, and also to the Committee on Disarmament,

Convinced that further measures are needed for the prevention of an arms race in outer space,

Recognizing that, in the context of multilateral negotiations for preventing an arms race in outer space, the resumption of bilateral negotiations between the Union of Soviet Socialist Republics and the United States of America can play a positive role,

5/ Resolution 2222 (XXI), annex.

6/ Resolution S-10/2.

Noting that in the course of its session in 1982 the Committee on Disarmament considered this subject both at its formal and informal meetings as well as through informal consultations,

Aware of the various proposals submitted by Member States to the Committee on Disarmament, particularly concerning the establishment of a working group on outer space as well as the draft mandate,

Noting, in particular, the express wishes of the overwhelming majority of members of the Committee on Disarmament for the establishment, without delay, of a working group on outer space,

1.   Reaffirms the will of all States that outer space shall be used exclusively for peaceful purposes and that it shall not become an arena for an arms race,

2.   Declares that any use other than for exclusively peaceful purposes of outer space runs counter to the agreed objective of general and complete disarmament under effective international control;

3.   Emphasizes that further effective measures to prevent an arms race in outer space should be adopted by the international community;

4.   Calls upon all States, in particular those with major space capabilities, to contribute actively to the objective of peaceful uses of outer space and to take immediate measures to prevent an arms race in outer space;

5.   Requests the Committee on Disarmament to consider as a matter of priority the question of preventing an arms race in outer space;

6.   Further requests the Committee on Disarmament to establish an ad hoc working group on the subject at the beginning of its session in 1983 with a view to undertaking negotiations for the conclusion of an agreement or agreements, as appropriate, to prevent an arms race in outer space in all its aspects;

7.   Requests the Committee on Disarmament to report on its consideration of this subject to the General Assembly at its thirty-eighth session;

8.   Requests the Secretary-General to transmit to the Committee on Disarmament all documents relating to the consideration of this subject by the General Assembly at its thirty-seventh session;

9.   Decides to include in the provisional agenda of its thirty-eighth session an item entitled "Prevention of an arms race in outer space".

7/ Official Records of the General Assembly, Thirty-seventh Session, Supplement No. 27 (A/37/27 and Corr.1)

MEMORANDUM FROM THE FRENCH GOVERNMENT CONCERNING AN INTERNATIONAL SATELLITE MONITORING AGENCY.

1.   In its memorandum submitted on 24 February 1978 to the Preparatory Committee for the Special Session of the General Assembly Devoted to Disarmament, France proposes the establishment of a satellite monitoring agency.

2.   In view of the work that is to be done during this session, France wishes to describe its proposal in greater detail with a view to enabling other States to make their observations and comments.

3.   The progress space technology has made in the field of earth observation satellites constitutes a new development in international life.

4.   These satellites, particularly those of a military type, have already attained a very high level of precision in their observation capability, and further progress will undoubtedly be made in that technology. At present the information secured by means of such satellites is collected by two countries which have the greatest experience in space technology and are in a position to make observations of the surface of the earth at such places and for such observation periods as they choose. The satellites available to those two countries, moreover, play an important role in the verification of their bilateral disarmament agreements.

5.   France considers that, within the framework of current disarmament efforts, this new monitoring method should be placed at the service of the international community.

6.   The information gathered by observation satellites is such that a new approach and new methods for monitoring disarmament agreements and for helping to strengthen international confidence and security can be envisaged. Many resolutions of the United Nations have stressed how essential it is that disarmament agreements should be subject to rigorous and efficacious international monitoring. Accordingly, the use of observation satellites as a means of conducting such monitoring should enable some of these difficulties to be overcome and thereby lead to progress towards disarmament.

7.   Apart from monitoring questions, the information gathered by observation satellites could provide the essential elements for settling disputes between States by making it possible, on conditions to be determined later, for the facts giving rise to such disputes to be more satisfactorily assessed.

8.   To that end, a satellite monitoring agency would become an essential ad-

junct to disarmament agreements and to measures to increase international confidence and security by providing interested parties with information that they were entitled to demand.

9.   France hereby submits the main elements of its proposal for a satellite monitoring agency under the following headings:

Guiding principles

Functions

Statute

Technical resources

Financing

Settlement of disputes.

1.   Guiding principles of the work of the Agency

10.   The purpose of the international satellite monitoring Agency shall be to the advance disarmament efforts and the strengthening of international security and confidence.

11.   The Agency shall act in accordance with the purposes and principles of the United Nations Charter, in conformity with the policy followed by the United Nations with regard to disarmament and in conformity with all agreements under international law concluded in pursuance of that policy.

12.   The Agency shall be responsible for collecting, processing and disseminating information secured by means of earth observation satellites. It shall have available to it the technical resources necessary for the accomplishment of its task. Those resources shall be expanded gradually in accordance with the provisions of its statute.

13.   The Agency shall in performing its functions respect the sovereign rights of States, bearing in mind the provisions of its statute and those of agreements concluded between it and any State or group of States in accordance with the provisions of that statute.

2.   Functions of the Agency

14.   The functions of the Agency shall include:

participation in monitoring the implementation of international disarmament and security agreements;

participation in the investigation of a specific situation.

(a) Monitoring the implementation of international disarmament and security agreements

15. Arrangements for the participation of the Agency in these agreements would differ, depending on whether they are agreements already in force or agreements yet to be concluded.

16. In the case of agreements already in force, the Agency would constitute a new instrument for ensuring greater effectiveness in monitoring them. More-' over, when provision had already been made in such agreements for national monitoring measures, the Agency's measures would be of the same category.

17. As regards the procedure, an inventory of existing agreements would be made with a view to determining, according to the nature of the armaments covered and the commitments entered into, to what extent monitoring by observation satellite would be applicable to them. If it were found to be applicable, the Agency would propose that its services should be made available to the parties to the agreement. Those that its services should be made available to the parties to the agreement. Those parties, if they unanimously accepted that offer, would jointly specify the link to be established between the agreement in question and the Agency's monitoring work.

18. Similarly, in the case of future disarmament and security agreements, the Agency would constitute an essential adjunct to their monitoring of agreements in any case in which the information gathered by the Agency could be used effectively for the purposes of such monitoring.

19. To that end, standard clauses of agreements would be prepared by the Agency and submitted to States desiring to conclude disarmament agreements with others.

20. At the time, provision might be made for regional international organizations with functions in the sphere of security to solicit the Agency's services.

(b) Investigation of a specific situation

21. A State could report to the Agency when it had good reason to believe that an agreement to which it was a party was being infringed by another State or when the conduct of that other State jeopardized its security. The Agency, in order to proceed to an investigation, should then obtain the consent of the State to be investigated.

22. The Security Council might also take action by invoking Article 34 of the United Nations Charter which authorizes it to "investigate any dispute or any situation which might lead to international friction or give rise to a dispute".

23.   On account both of its purpose, which is to advance disarmament efforts, and of its essential universality, the Agency should be part of the United Nations system.

24.   To that end, France proposes that the Agency should be established as a specialized agency of the United Nations.

25.   The characteristics of the specialized agencies are ideally situated to the specific role of the Agency and to the need to endow it with substantial financial and technical resources, which will be of a new type.

26.   Details of the statute proposed by France for the Agency will be the subject of further proposals. For the moment, however, the following general outline is proposed:

> Membership of the Agency would be open to any State Member of the United Nations or member of a specialized agency;

> The decision-making and deliberative bodies of the Agency would include at least a plenary organ and a restricted organ having balanced representation of all regions of the world;

> The Agency would have the personnel required for the accomplishment of its task. The personnel would include, in particular, qualified technical personnel to process and analyse the data collected by observation satellites.

4.   Technical resources

27.   The complexity of observation satellite installations and the costliness of space applications (ground segment and space segment) suggest that gradual expansion of the technical resources of the Agency would be advisable. The growth of the Agency's resources could, in any event, proceed concurrently with the expansion of the functions assigned to it.

28.   Consequently, when it started to operate, the Agency, since it would have no satellite of its own, would need to be able to rely on the data collected by the observation satellites of those States which possess them. Procedures for transmitting such data to the Agency could be worked out in agreement with those States.

29.   Nevertheless, in order to ensure that the Agency had a sufficient degree of autonomy, it should, when it went into operation, itself have the technical capacity to interpret the data so transmitted. To that end it should have its own processing centre.

30. Accordingly, France proposes that the expansion of the technical resources of the Agency should take place in three successive stages:

> Stage 1:   the Agency would have a centre for processing data supplied by those States having observation satellites;

> Stage 2:   the Agency would establish data-receiving stations which would be directly linked to those States' satellites;

> Stage 3:   the Agency itself would have the observation satellites required for the performance of its task.

31.   The sequence of these stages would be determined by the statute of the Agency, taking account in particular of the gradual expansion of its competence.

32.   Moreover, the statute of the Agency should state that the information collected or received was to be used for no purpose other than the performance of the Agency's tasks.

5.   Financing

33.   The magnitude of the technical resources that should be available to the Agency requires that a variety of sources of financing be used, such as:

> Mandatory payments, provided for by budgetary rules comparable to those of the United Nations;

> Voluntary payments, among which account might be taken of the technical resources made available to the Agency by those States having observation satellites;

> Funds paid in return for services provided by the Agency, particularly if States used its services to monitor a disarmament or security agreement concluded by them.

6.   Settlement of disputes

34.   In the event of disputes arising either between States or between States and the Agency, machinery for the settlement of disputes should be provided. In view of the specificity of the Agency's functions, France proposes that such disputes, if not settled by other peaceful means, should be submitted to arbitration. To that end, an arbitration committee would be established, and arrangements for its composition and operation would be incorporated in the statute of the Agency.

35.   To that end France will submit a draft clause on machinery for the settlement of disputes.

36.   In submitting these proposals on a satellite monitoring agency to the States participating in the special session of the General Assembly devoted to disarmament, France hopes that they can be examined in the course of the deliberations of the session.

37.   Since, however, it is well aware of the scope of this proposal and the questions raised by it, France proposes that a committee of experts be established to consider the conditons in which a satellite monitoring agency might be established.

38.   That committee would be composed of a limited number of experts, in order to ensure its satisfactory functioning, account being taken of equitable geographical distribution. The committee could be instructed to report on its work to the thirty-fourth session of the General Assembly.

39.   To that end, France proposes that the terms of reference of the committee of experts to consider the proposal for an international monitoring agency should cover the following points:

(a)   The guiding principles of the work of the Agency;

(b)   Its functions, *i.e.*:

(i)   Participation in monitoring the implementation of international disarmament or security agreements whether already in force or to be concluded:

(ii)   Participation in the investigation of a specific situation (either at the request of one State, with the consent of the State to be inspected, or at the request of the Security Council),

(c)   Its institutions (its position within the United Nations system structures, rules for making decisions);

(d)   The technical resources available to the Agency and their gradual expansion;

(e)   The financing of the Agency at various stages of its activity;

(f)   Machinery for the settlement of disputes.

PARLIAMENTARY ASSEMBLY OF THE COUNCIL OF EUROPE

Thirty-fourth ordinary session

RECOMMENDATION 957 (1983)[1]

on the proposal for an international satellite monitoring agency

The Assembly,

1.   Having regard to its Resolutions 788 (1983) and 789 (1983) on the European space programme and the 2nd United Nations Space Conference (Vienna, August 1982);

2.   Recalling the terms of its Resolution 747 (1981) on prospects for human needs and the earth's resources;

3.   Reaffirming its view, expressed in paragraph 19 of this resolution, that these prospects, which are at present cause for alarm, could be dramatically improved by even a small reduction in arms expenditure and the re-direction of resources to specific urgent needs of the developing countries-as, for example, improvements in their communications infrastructures;

4.   Considering that for many countries high levels of arms expenditure are caused by uncertainty in the international environment, affecting in particular their relations with neighbouring countries;

5.   Believing that this uncertainty could be reduced by the operations of an international satellite monitoring agency, the data and information from which could be made freely and publicly available- see Resolution 789 (1983) and the report of the Committee on Science and Technology on the 2nd United Nations Space Conference (Doc. 4998);

6.   Considering that an international satellite monitoring agency, by thus making for reductions in arms expenditure in many countries, could cause resources to be released for improving social and economic conditions throughout the world;

7.   Believing that Europe has now achieved a sufficient level of capability in space technology to take a credible political initiative towards the setting-up of such an agency - see Resolution 788 (1983) and the report of the Committee on Science and Technology on the European space programme (Doc. 4995);

1. *Assembly debate* on 24 January 1983 (21st Sitting) (see Doc. 4998, report of the Committee on Science and Technology).
Text adopted by the Assembly on 24 January 1983 (21st Sitting).

8.   Having regard to the fact that the benefits of the European space capability accrue to all states members of the Council of Europe (whether or not they are members or associates of the European Space Agency);

9.   Believing, therefore, that the member states of the Council of Europe share accordingly an equal responsibility for working towards the realisation of the potential of space technology for contributing to a more stable international political environment and more balanced world development,

10.   Recommends that the Committee of Ministers, on the occasion of their forthcoming exchange of views on United Nations matters with the participation of experts, review the state of action on the proposal for the setting-up of an international satellite monitoring agency, and examine possibilities for renewed initiatives in this direction, either individually or collectively or in association with non-European industrialized or developing countries having a space capability.

ASSEMBLÉE PARLEMENTAIRE DU CONSEIL DE L'EUROPE

Trente-quatrième session ordinaire

RECOMMENDATION 957 (1983)[1]

relative à la proposition de créer une agence
internationale de satellites de contrôle

L'Assemblée,

1.   Compte tenu de ses Résolutions 788 (1983) et 789 (1983), relatives au programme spatial européen et à la 2e Conférence spatiale des Nations Unies (Vienne, août 1982);

2.   Rappelant les termes de sa Résolution 747 (1981), relative aux perspectives mondiales - besoins de l'humanité et ressources de la planète;

3.   Réaffirmant, conformément aux vues exprimées au paragraphe 19 de cette résolution, que ces perspectives, actuellement préoccupantes, pourraient être considérablement améliorées par même une faible réduction des dépenses d'armement et par une réaffectation des crédits ainsi dégagés en vue de satisfaire certains besoins urgents précis des pays en voie de développement, telle, par exemple, l'amélioration de leurs infrastructures de communication;

1. *Discussion par l'Assemblée* le 24 janvier 1983 (21e séance) (voir Doc. 4998, rapport de la commission de la science et de la technologie).
Texte adopté par l'Assemblée le 24 janvier 1983 1983 (21e séance).

4. Considérant que, pour un grand nombre de pays, l'importance des dépenses d'armement est due à l'incertitude qui règne sur la scène internationale et qui influe notamment sur leurs relations avec les pays voisins;

5. Persuadée que les activités d'une agence internationale de satellites de contrôle, dont les observations pourraient être rendues librement et publiquement disponibles, permettraient de réduire cette incertitude - voir à ce sujet la Résolution 789 (1983) et le rapport de la commission de la science et de la technologie sur la 2e Conférence spatiale des Nations Unies (Doc. 4998);

6. Considérant qu'une agence internationale de satellites de contrôle, en favorisant ainsi la réduction des dépenses d'armement dans un grand nombre de pays, pourrait rendre disponibles des ressources permettant d'améliorer les conditions de vie socio-économiques dans le monde entier;

7. Constatant que l'Europe a désormais atteint dans le domaine de la technologie spatiale une capacité suffisante pour prendre une initiative politique crédible en vue de la création d'une telle agence - voir la Résolution 788 (1983) et le rapport de la commission de la science et de la technologie sur l'avenir du programme spatial européen (Doc. 4995);

8. Eu égard au fait que tous les Etats membres du Conseil de l'Europe (qu'ils soient ou non membres ou membres associés de l'Agence spatiale européenne) tirent profit de cette capacité technologique;

9. Estimant, par conséquent, que tous les Etats membres du Conseil de l'Europe se doivent de contribuer à la réalisation du potentiel de la technologie spatiale de nature à instaurer un environnement politique international plus stable et un développement mondial plus équilibré,

10. Recommande au Comité des Ministres, à l'occasion de son prochain échange de vues sur les questions relatives aux Nations Unies auquel participeront les experts, de faire le point des suites données à la proposition de créer une agence internationale de satellites de contrôle, et d'examiner la possibilité de prendre à nouveau des initiatives dans ce sens, soit individuellement, soit collectivement, soit en association avec des pays non européens industrialisés ou en voie de développement possédant déjà ou en voie de développement possédant déjà une capacité spatiale.

UNITED NATIONS
GENERAL ASSEMBLY

Distr.
GENERAL

Thirty-seventh session
Agenda item 57

A/RES/37/83
18 January 1983

RESOLUTION ADOPTED BY THE GENERAL ASSEMBLY

(on the report of the First Committee (A/37/669))

37/83. Prevention of an arms race in outer space

The General Assembly,

Inspired by the great prospects opening up before mankind as a result of man's entry into outer space twenty-five years ago,

Recognizing the common interest of all mankind in the exploration and use of outer space for peaceful purposes,

Reaffirming that the exploration and use of outer space, including the Moon and other celestial bodies, shall be carried out for the benefit and in the interest of all countries, irrespective of their degree of economic or scientific development, and shall be the province of all mankind,

Reaffirming further the will of all States that the exploration and use of outer space, including the Moon and other celestial bodies, shall be exclusively for peaceful purposes,

Recalling that the States Parties to the Treaty on Principles Governing the Activities of States in the Exploration and Use of Outer Space, including the Moon and Other Celestial Bodies, 1/ undertook in article III to carry on activities in the exploration and use of outer space, including the Moon and other celestial bodies, in accordance with international law and the Charter of the United Nations, in the interest of maintaining international peace and security and promoting international co-operation and understanding,

Reaffirming, in particular, article IV of the said Treaty which stipulates that States Parties to the Treaty undertake not to place in orbit around the earth any objects carrying nuclear weapons or any other kind of weapons of mass destruction, to install such weapons on celestial bodies, or to station such weapons in outer space in any other manner,

---

1/ Resolution 2222 (XXI), annex.

Reaffirming paragraph 80 of the Final Document of the Tenth Special Session of the General Assembly, 2/ in which it is stated that, in order to prevent an arms race in outer space, further measures should be taken and appropriate international negotiations held in accordance with the spirit of the Treaty,

Recalling its resolutions 36/97 C and 36/99 of 9 December 1981,

Gravely concerned at the danger posed to all mankind by an arms race in outer space,

Mindful of the widespread interest expressed by Member States in the course of the negotiations on and following the adoption of the above-mentioned Treaty in ensuring that the exploration and use of outer space should be for peaceful purposes, and taking note of proposals submitted to the General Assembly at its tenth special session, devoted to disarmament, and at its regular sessions and to the Committee on Disarmament,

Noting the grave concern expressed by the Second United Nations Conference on the Exploration and Peaceful Uses of Outer Space over the extension of an arms race into outer space 3/ and the recommendations made to the competent organs of the United Nations, in particular the General Assembly, and also to the Committee on Disarmament,

Convinced that further measures are needed for the prevention of an arms race in outer space,

Recognizing that, in the context of multilateral negotiations for preventing an arms race in outer space, the resumption of bilateral negotiations between the Union of Soviet Socialist Republics and the United States of America can play a positive role,

Taking note of the report of the Committee on Disarmament, 4/

Noting that in the course of its session in 1982 the Committee on Disarmament considered this subject both at its formal and informal meetings as well as through informal consultations,

Aware of the various proposals submitted by Member States to the Committee on Disarmament, particularly concerning the establishment of a working group on outer space and its draft mandate,

---

2/ Resolution S-10/2

3/ See Report of the Second United Nations Conference on the Exploration and Peaceful Uses of Outer Space, Vienna, 9-21 August 1982 (A/CONF.101/10 and Corr.1 and 2).

4/ Official Records of the General Assembly, Thirty-seventh Session, Supplement No. 27 (A/37/27 and Corr.1).

Noting, in particular, the express wishes of the overwhelming majority of members of the Committee on Disarmament for the establishment, without delay, of a working group on outer space,

1.   Reaffirms the will of all States that outer space shall be used exclusively for peaceful purposes and that it shall not become an arena for an arms race;

2.   Declares that any use of outer space other than for exclusively peaceful purposes runs counter to the agreed objective of general and complete disarmament under effective international control;

3.   Emphasizes that further effective measures to prevent an arms race in outer space should be adopted by the international community;

4.   Calls upon all States, in particular those with major space capabilities, to contribute actively to the objective of the peaceful use of outer space and to take immediate measures to prevent an arms race in outer space;

5.   Requests the Committee on Disarmament to consider as a matter of priority the question of preventing an arms race in outer space;

6.   Further requests the Committee on Disarmament to establish an ad hoc working group on the subject at the beginning of its session in 1983, with a view to undertaking negotiations for the conclusion of an agreement or agreements, as appropriate, to prevent an arms race in all its aspects in outer space;

7.   Requests the Committee on Disarmament to report on its consideration of this subject to the General Assembly at its thirty-eighth session;

8.   Requests the Secretary-General to transmit to the Committee on Disarmament all documents relating to the consideration of this subject by the General Assembly at its thirty-seventh session;

9.   Decides to include in the provisional agenda of its thirty-eighth session an item entitled "Prevention of an arms race in outer space".

98th plenary meeting
9 December 1982

UNITED NATIONS
GENERAL ASSEMBLY

Distr.
GENERAL

A/RES/37/99
20 January 1983

Thirty-seventh session
Agenda item 55

RESOLUTIONS ADOPTED BY THE GENERAL ASSEMBLY

(on the report of the First Committee (A/37/667))

37/99. General and complete disarmament

A

Non-stationing of nuclear weapons on the territories of States where there are no such weapons at present

The General Assembly,

Conscious that a nuclear war would have devastating consequences for the whole of mankind,

Recalling its resolution 33/91 F of 16 December 1978, which contains an appeal to all nuclear-weapon States to refrain from stationing nuclear weapons on the territories of States where there are no such weapons at present and to all non-nuclear-weapon States that do not have nuclear weapons on their territories to refrain from any steps that would directly or indirectly result in the stationing of such weapons on their territories,

Recalling further its resolutions 35/156 C of 12 December 1980 and 36/97 E of 9 December 1981, in which it requested the Committee on Disarmament to proceed without delay to talks with a view to elaborating an international agreement on the non-stationing of nuclear weapons on the territories of States where there are no such weapons at present,

Noting with regret that the appeals by the General Assembly remain unheeded,

Considering that the non-stationing of nuclear weapons on the territories of States where there are no such weapons at present would constitute a step towards the larger objective of the subsequent complete withdrawal of nuclear weapons from the territories of other States, thus contributing to the prevention of the spread of nuclear weapons and leading eventually to the total elimination of nuclear weapons,

Bearing in mind the clearly expressed intention of many States to prevent the stationing of nuclear weapons on their territories,

Deeply alarmed by plans and practical steps leading to a build-up of nuclear-weapon arsenals on the territories of other States,

1.   Requests once again the Committee on Disarmament to proceed without delay to talks with a view to elaborating an international agreement on the non-stationing of nuclear weapons on the territories of States where there are no such weapons at present;

2.   Calls upon all nuclear-weapon States not to station nuclear weapons on the territories of States where there are no such weapons at present and to refrain from further action involving the stationing of nuclear weapons on the territories of other States;

3.   Calls upon all nuclear-weapon States to freeze qualitatively nuclear weapons on the territories of other States;

4.   Requests the Secretary-General to transmit to the Committee on Disarmament all documents relating to the discussion of this question by the General Assembly at its thirty-seventh session;

5.   Requests the Committee on Disarmament to submit a report on the question to the General Assembly at its thirty-eighth session;

6.   Decides to include in the provisional agenda of its thirty-eighth session the item entitled "Non-stationing of nuclear weapons on the territories of States where there are no such weapons at present: report of the Committee on Disarmament".

101st plenary meeting
13 December 1982

B

Report of the Independent Commission on Disarmament and Security Issues

The General Assembly,

Concerned over the alarming state of the arms race and the risks it causes to the survival of humanity,

Recognizing the central role of the United Nations in reducing tension, in safeguarding and promoting confidence between States and in furthering common security and the cause of disarmament,

238   Having noted the report of the Independent Commission on Disarmament and Security Issues entitled "Common security", 1/ submitted to the General Assembly at its twelfth special session, the second special session devoted to disarmament,

Convinced that the Commission has made an important contribution to the discussion and deliberation on disarmament and security issues and that its recommendations and proposals, embodied in its programme of action, should be further considered within the United Nations system,

Noting that the recommendations in the report were addressed to Governments and to the United Nations and its organs,

Convinced of the importance of ensuring an effective follow-up to the report in the United Nations system and in other relevant contexts,

1.   Requests the Secretary-General to transmit the report of the Independent Commission on Disarmament and Security Issues to the Disarmament Commission;

2.   Further requests the Disarmament Commission to consider those recommendations and proposals in the report that relate to disarmament and arms limitation and to suggest, in a report to the General Assembly, how best to ensure an effective follow-up thereto within the United Nations system or otherwise;

3.   Decides to include in the agenda of its thirty-eighth session an item entitled "Independent Commission on Disarmament and Security Issues: report of the Disarmament Commission".

101st plenary meeting
13 December 1982

C

Prohibition of the development, production,
stockpiling and use of radiological weapons

The General Assembly,

Recalling the resolution of the Commission for Conventional Armaments of 12 August 1948, which defined weapons of mass destruction to include atomic explosive weapons, radioactive material weapons, lethal chemical and biological weapons and any weapons developed in the future which

1/ See A/S-12/AC.1/PV.4, p.18

have characteristics comparable in destructive effect to those of the atomic bomb or the other weapons mentioned above,

Recalling its resolution 2602 C (XXIV) of 16 December 1969,

Recalling paragraph 76 of the Final Document of the Tenth Special Session of the General Assembly 2/ in which it is stated that a convention should be concluded prohibiting the development, production, stockpiling and use of radiological weapons,

Reaffirming its resolution 36/97 B of 9 December 1981 on the conclusion of such a convention,

Convinced that such a convention would serve to spare mankind the potential dangers of the use of radiological weapons and thereby contribute to strengthening peace and averting the threat of war,

Noting that negotiations on the conclusion of an international convention prohibiting the development, production, stockpiling and use of radiological weapons have been conducted in the Committee on Disarmament,

Taking note of those parts of the reports of the Committee on Disarmament to the General Assembly at its twelfth special session and its thirty-seventh session that deal with those negotiations, including the report of the Ad Hoc Working Group on Radiological Weapons, 3/

Recognizing that notwithstanding the progress achieved in those negotiations, divergent views continue to exist in connection with various aspects,

Taking into consideration that the peaceful applications of nuclear energy involve the establishment of a large number of nuclear installations with a high concentration of radioactive materials, and bearing in mind that the destruction of such nuclear facilities by military attacks could have disastrous consequences,

Noting with satisfaction the wide recognition of the need to reach agreement on the comprehensive prohibition of radiological weapons,

1. Requests the Committee on Disarmament to continue negotiations with a view to an early conclusion of the elaboration of a treaty prohibiting the development, production, stockpiling and use of radiological weapons, in order that it may be submitted to the General Assembly at its thirty-eighth session;

2/ Resolution S-10/2.

3/ Official Records of the General Assembly, Twelfth Special Session, Supplement No. 2 (A/S-12/2), paras. 67-75 and ibid., Thirty-seventh Session, Supplement No. 27 (A/37/27 and Corr.1), paras. 76-89.

2.   Further requests the Committee on Disarmament to continue its search for a solution to the question of prohibition of military attacks on nuclear facilities, including the scope of such prohibiton, taking into account all proposals submitted to it to this end;

3.   Takes note of the recommendation of the Ad Hoc Working Group on Radiological Weapons, in the report adopted by the Committee on Disarmament, to establish at the beginning of its session to be held in 1983, an ad hoc working group, to continue negotiations on the prohibition of radiological weapons; 4/

4.   Requests the Secretary-General to transmit to the Committee on Disarmament all documents relating to the discussion by the General Assembly at its thirty-seventh session of the prohibition of the development, production, stockpiling and use of radiological weapons;

5.   Decides to include in the provisional agenda of its thirty-eighth session the item entitled "Prohibition of the development, production, stockpiling and use of radiological weapons".

101st plenary meeting
13 December 1982

D

Prevention of an arms race in outer space
and prohibition of anti-satellite systems

The General Assembly

Inspired by the great prospects opening up before mankind as a result of man's entry into outer space,

Believing that any activity in outer space should be for peaceful purposes and carried on for the benefit of all peoples, irrespective of the degree of their economic and scientific development,

Recalling that the States parties to the Treaty on Principles Governing the Activities of States in the Exploration and Use of Outer Space, including the Moon and Other Celestial Bodies, 5/ have undertaken, in article III, to carry on activities in the exploration and use of outer space, including the Moon and other celestial bodies, in accordance with international law and the

4/ See Official Records of the General Assembly, Thirty-seventh Session, Supplement No. 27 (A/37/27 and Corr.1), para. 83.

5/ Resolution 2222 (XXI), annex.

Charter of the United Nations, in the interests of maintaining international peace and security and promoting international co-operation and understanding,

Reaffirming, in particular, article IV of the above-mentioned Treaty, which stipulates that States parties to the Treaty undertake not to place in orbit around the earth any objects carrying nuclear weapons or any other kinds of weapons of mass destruction, install such weapons on celestial bodies or station such weapons in outer space in any other manner,

Reaffirming also paragraph 80 of the Final Document of the Tenth Special Session of the General Assembly, 2/ which states that, in order to prevent an arms race in outer space, further measures should be taken and appropriate international negotiations held in accordance with the spirit of the Treaty,

Aware of the need to prevent an arms race in outer space and in particular of the threat posed by anti-satellite systems and their destabilizing effects on international peace and security,

Recalling its resolutions 36/97 C and 36/99 of 9 December 1981,

Noting the grave concern expressed by the Second United Nations Conference on the Exploration and Peaceful Uses of Outer Space 6/ over the possible extension of an arms race into outer space, and the recommendations made to the competent organs of the United Nations, in particular the General Assembly, and also to the Committee on Disarmament,

Noting also that, in the course of its session in 1982, the Committee on Disarmament considered this subject both at its formal and informal meetings, as well as through informal consultations,

Taking note of the part of the report of the Committee on Disarmament relating to the item entitled "Prevention of an arms race in outer space", 7/

1.   Reaffirms that further effective measures to prevent an arms race in outer space should be adopted by the international community;

2.   Notes with appreciation the contribution made by Member States to the discussion of the item in the Committee on Disarmament and in the General Assembly;

3.   Requests the Committee on Disarmament to continue substantive consideration of:

6/ See Report of the Second United Nations Conference on the Exploration and Peaceful Uses of Outer Space, Vienna, 9-21 August 1982 (A/CONF.101/10 and Corr.1 and 2).

7/ Official Records of the General Assembly, Thirty-seventh Session, Supplement No. 27 (A/37/27 and Corr.1), paras. 97-106.

(a)   The question of negotiating effective and verifiable agreements aimed at preventing an arms race in outer space, taking into account all existing and future proposals designed to meet this objective;

(b)   As a matter of priority, the question of negotiating an effective and verifiable agreement to prohibit anti-satellite systems as an important step towards the fulfilment of the objectives set out in sub-paragraph (a) above;

4.   Expresses the hope that the Committee on Disarmament will take the appropriate steps, such as the possible establishment of a working group, in order to promote the objectives set forth in paragraphs 1 and 3 above;

5.   Requests the Committee on Disarmament to report on the consideration given to this subject to the General Assembly at its thirty-eight session;

6.   Decides to include in the provisional agenda of its thirty-eighth session the item entitled "Prevention of an arms race in outer space and prohibition of anti-satellite systems".

101st plenary meeting
13 December 1982

E

Prohibition of the production of fissionable
material for weapons purposes

The General Assembly,

Recalling its resolutions 33/91 H of 16 December 1978, 34/87 D of 11 December 1979, 35/156 H of 12 December 1980 and 36/97 G of 9 December 1981, in which it requested the Committee on Disarmament, at an appropriate stage of the implementation of the Programme of Action set forth in section III of the Final Document of the Tenth Special Session of the General Assembly, 2/ and of its work on the item entitled "Nuclear weapons in all aspects", to consider urgently the question of adequately verified cessation and prohibition of the production of fissionable material for nuclear weapons and other nuclear explosive devices and to keep the Assembly informed of the progress of that consideration,

Noting that the agenda of the Committee on Disarmament for 1982 included the item entitled "Nuclear weapons in all aspects" and that the Committee's programme of work for both parts of its session held in 1982 contained the item entitled "Cessation of the nuclear arms race and nuclear disarmament",

Recalling the proposals and statements made in the Committee on Disarmament on those items,

Considering that the cessation of production of fissionable material for weapons purposes and the progressive conversion and transfer of stocks to peaceful uses would be a significant step towards halting and reversing the nuclear arms race,

Considering that the prohibition of the production of fissionable material for nuclear weapons and other explosive devices also would be an important measure in facilitating the prevention of the proliferation of nuclear weapons and explosive devices,

Requests the Committee on Disarmament, at an appropriate stage of its work on the item entitled "Nuclear weapons in all aspects", to pursue its consideration of the question of adequately verified cessation and prohibition of the production of fissionable material for nuclear weapons and other nuclear explosive devices and to keep the General Assembly informed of the progress of that consideration.

101st plenary meeting
13 December 1982

F

Review and supplement of the comprehensive study on the question of nuclear-weapon-free zones in all its aspects

The General Assembly,

Conscious of the need to make every effort towards achieving a cessation of the nuclear arms race, nuclear disarmament and general and complete disarmament under strict and effective international control,

Recognizing, in pursuance of these ends, the urgent need to prevent the proliferation of nuclear weapons in the world,

Affirming that the establishment of nuclear-weapon-free zones is a contribution to disarmament,

Recalling its resolution 3572 (XXX) of 11 December 1975 on the comprehensive study of the question of nuclear-weapon-free zones in all its aspects,

Recalling the views, observations and suggestions made on it by Governments, and by the International Atomic Energy Agency and other international organizations concerned, and the report of the Secretary-General containing them, 8/

8/ Official Records of the General Assembly, Thirtieth Session, Supplement No. 27A (A/10027/Add.1).

Considering that questions related to the establishment of nuclear-weapon-free zones in various parts of the world have been addressed in a number of recent studies undertaken by the United Nations in the field of disarmament,

Considering further that the experience of the Treaty for the Prohibiton of Nuclear Weapons in Latin America (Treaty of Tlatelolco) 9/ would be of great value for the other regions of the world,

Recognizing that these developments should be recorded in a new complementary study of this subject,

1. Decides that a study should be undertaken to review and supplement the comprehensive study of the question of nuclear-weapon-free zones in all its aspects in the light of information and experience accumulated since 1975;

2. Requests the Secretary-General, with the assistance of an ad hoc group of qualified governmental experts, to carry out the study and to submit it to the General Assembly at its thirty-ninth session, bearing in mind the savings that may be made within existing budgetary appropriations;

3. Calls upon interested Governments and international organizations concerned to extend such assistance as may be required from time to time for the carrying out of the study;

4. Decides to include in the provisional agenda of its thirty-ninth session an item entitled "Study of the question of nuclear-weapon-free zones in all its aspects".

101st plenary meeting
13 December 1982

G

Measures to provide objective information on
military capabilities

The General Assembly,

Deeply concerned about the continuing escalation of the arms race, in particular the nuclear arms race, its extremely harmful effects on world peace and security and the deplorable waste of human and material resources for military purposes,

Recalling the Final Document of the Tenth Special Session of the General Assembly, 2/ which states, inter alia, that, in order to facilitate the process of

9/ United Nations, Treaty Series, vol. 634, No. 9068, p. 326

disarmament, it is necessary to take measures and to pursue policies to strengthen international peace and security and to build confidence among States, in accordance with the purposes and principles of the Charter of the United Nations,

Bearing in mind that the Final Document also states that diarmament, relaxation of international tensions, respect for the right of self-determination and national independence, the peaceful settlement of disputes in accordance with the Charter of the United Nations and the strengthening of international peace and security are diretly related to each other, that progress in any of these spheres has a beneficial effect on all of them and that, in turn, failure in one sphere has negative effects on others,

Recalling also paragraph 105 of the Final Document, in which Member States are encouraged to ensure a better flow of information with regard to the various aspects of disarmament, to avoid dissemination of false and tendentious information concerning armament and to concentrate on the danger of escalation of the arms race and on the need for general and complete disarmament under effective international control,

Noting that misperceptions of the military capabilities and the intentions of potential adversaries, which could be caused, inter alia, by lack of objective information, could induce States to undertake armaments programmes leading to the acceleration of the arms race, in particular the nuclear arms race, and to heightened international tensions,

Aware that objective information on military capabilities, in particular among nuclear-weapon States and other military significant States, could contribute to the building of confidence among States and to the conclusion of concrete disarmament agreements and, thereby, help to halt and reverse the arms race,

1.   Calls upon all States, in particular nuclear-weapon States and other military significant States, to consider additional measures to facilitate the provision of objective information on, and objective assessments of, military capabilities;

2.   Invites all States to communicate to the Secretary-General their views and proposals concerning such measures;

3.   Requests the Secretary-General to submit to the General Assembly at its thirty-eighth session a report containing, first, the replies of Member States called for under paragraph 2 above, and, secondly, on the basis of these replies, a preliminary analysis of the possible role of the United Nations in the context of measures to facilitate the provision of objective information on, and objective assessments of, military capabilities.

101st plenary meeting
13 December 1982

Review Conference of the Parties to the Treaty on the Prohibition of the Emplacement of Nuclear Weapons and Other Weapons of Mass Destruction on the Sea-Bed and the Ocean Floor and in the Subsoil Thereof

The General Assembly,

Recalling its resolution 2660 (XXV) of 7 December 1970, in which it commended the Treaty on the Prohibition of the Emplacement of Nuclear Weapons and Other Weapons of Mass Destruction on the Sea-Bed and the Ocean Floor and in the Subsoil Thereof, 10/

Noting the provisions of article VII of that Treaty concerning the holding of review conferences,

Bearing in mind that, in its Final Declaration, 11/ the First Review Conference of the Parties to the Treaty on the Prohibition of the Emplacement of Nuclear Weapons and Other Weapons of Mass Destruction on the Sea-Bed and the Ocean Floor and in the Subsoil Thereof, held at Geneva from 20 June to 1 July 1977, decided that a further review conference should be held at Geneva in 1982, unless a majority of States parties indicated to the depositaries that they wished such a conference to be postponed, in which case it should be convened not later than 1984,

Recalling its resolution 32/87 A of 12 December 1977, in which it made an assessment of the outcome of the first Review Conference,

Bearing in mind all the relevant paragraphs of the Final Document of the Tenth Special Session of the General Assembly, 2/ the first special session devoted to disarmament,

1.   Notes that, following appropriate consultations, a preparatory committee for the second Review Conference of the Parties to the Treaty on the Prohibition of the Emplacement of Nuclear Weapons and Other Weapons of Mass Destruction on the Sea-bed and the Ocean Floor and in the Subsoil Thereof is to be established prior to holding a further review conference in 1983;

2.   Requests the Secretary-General to render the necessary assistance and to provide such services, including summary records, as may be required for the Review Conference and its preparation;

10/ Resolution 2660 (XXV), annex.

11/ See A/C.1/32/4.

3.   Recalls its expressed hope for the widest possible adherence to the
Treaty.

101st plenary meeting
13 December 1982

I

Review Conference of the Parties to the Convention on the Prohibition of Military or Any Other Hostile Use of Environmental
Modification Techniques

The General Assembly,

Recalling its resolution 31/72 of 10 December 1976, in which it referred
the Convention on the Prohibition of Military or Any Other Hostile Use of
Environmental Modification Techniques 12/ to all States for their consideration, signature and ratification and expressed the hope for the widest possible
adherence to the Convention,

Noting that paragraph 1 of article VIII of the Convention provides that:
that:

"Five Years after the entry into force of this Convention, a conference of
the States Parties to the Convention shall be convened by the Depositary at
Geneva, Switzerland. The conference shall review the operation of the Convention with a view to ensuring that its purposes and provisions are being realized, and shall in particular examine the effectiveness of the provisions of paragraph 1 of article I in eliminating the dangers of military or any other hostile use
of environmental modification techniques",

Bearing in mind that the Convention will have been in force for five years
on 5 October 1983,

1.   Notes that the Secretary-General, as Depositary of the Convention,
intends to convene the Review Conference of the Parties to the Convention on
the Prohibition of Military or Any Other Hostile Use of Environmental Modification Techniques called for in paragraph 1 of article VIII of the Convention
at the earliest practicable time after 5 October 1983 and that, to that end, he
will hold consultations with the Parties to the Convention with regard to questions relating to the Conference and its preparation, including the establishment of a preparatory committee for the Conference;

2.   Requests the Secretary-General to render the necessary assistance
and to provide such services, including summary records, as may be required
for the Review Conference and its preparation;

12/ Resolution 31/72, annex.

3.   Also notes that arrangements for meeting the costs of the Review Conference and its preparation are to be made by the Conference.

101st plenary meeting
13 December 1982.

J

Military research and development

The General Assembly,

Mindful of the important task of the United Nations to evaluate the state of the arms race, in particular the nuclear arms race, and to deliberate all relevant issues of disarmament,

Recalling the provisions of paragraph 39 of the Final Document of the Tenth Special Session of the General Assembly, 2/ the first special session devoted to disarmament, according to which qualitative and quantitative disarmament measures are both important for halting the arms race and efforts to that end must include negotiations on the limitation and cessation of the qualitative improvement of armaments, especially weapons of mass destruction and the development of new means of warfare, so that ultimately scientific and technological achievements may be used solely for peaceful purposes,

Recalling further, that according to paragraph 103 of the Final Document, the United Nations Centre for Disarmament should intensify its activities in the presentation of information concerning the armaments race and disarmament,

Noting the impact of military research and development on the arms race, in particular in relation to major weapons systems such as nuclear weapons and other weapons of mass destruction,

Concerned that, at present, a large proportion of all scientists and technicians in the world are involved in military programmes,

Noting also that in the arms race, particularly as regards nuclear weapons and other weapons of mass destruction, there is an increasing emphasis on the qualitative aspects,

Recognizing that research and development in certain fields may contribute to disarmament and have conflict-preventing effects,

Aware of the fundamental importance of research and development for peaceful purposes, and of the inalienable right of all States to develop, also in co-operation with other States, their research and development for such purposes,

Convinced of the need to focus attention on the military use of research and development and to prepare the ground for further substantial consideration of this matter,

Recalling the suggestions on military research and development submitted to the General Assembly at its twelfth special session, the second special session devoted to disarmament,

Convinced also that increased information on military research and development could contribute to promoting confidence between States and enhance the possibility of reaching agreements on arms limitation and disarmament,

Convinced further that a study on the military application of research and development would make a valuable contribution to increasing available knowledge on military research and development in all States, particularly research and development by the major military Powers, and to the dissemination of factual information on these issues, as well as the analysis thereof,

1. Requests the Secretary-General, with the assistance of qualified governmental experts, bearing in mind the savings that might be made from the existing budgetary appropriations, to carry out a comprehensive study on the scope, role and direction of the military use of research and development, the mechanisms involved, its role in the overall arms race, in particular the nuclear arms race, and its impact on arms limitation and disarmament, particularly in relation to major weapons systems, such as nuclear weapons and other weapons of mass destruction, with a view to preventing a qualitative arms race and to ensuring that scientific and technological achievements may ultimately be used solely for peaceful purposes;

2. Invites all States to submit to the Secretary-General not later than 15 April 1983 their views on the subject of the study and to co-operate with the Secretary-General so that the objectives of the study may be achieved;

3. Requests the Secretary-General to report on this subject to the General Assembly at its thirty-ninth session.

101st plenary meeting
13 December 1982

K

Institutional arrangements relating to the process of disarmament

The General Assembly,

Recalling its resolution 31/90 of 14 December 1976, by which it decided to keep the strengthening of the role of the United Nations in the field of disarmament under continued review,

Recalling also its resolution 34/87 E of 11 December 1979, in which it, inter alia:

(a)   Reaffirmed that the United Nations had a central role and primary responsibility in the field of disarmament,

(b)   Noted that the growing disarmament agenda and the complexity of the issues involved, as well as the more active participation of a large number of Member States, created increasing demands on United Nations management of disarmament affairs for purposes such as the promotion, substantive preparation, implementation and control of the process of disarmament,

Reaffirming the importance of the Committee on Disarmament as the single multilateral disarmament negotiating forum, in conformity with paragraph 120 of the Final Document of the Tenth Special Session of the General Assembly, 2/ the first special session devoted to disarmament,

Recognizing the growing importance attached to disarmament questions since the tenth special session, as evidenced by the increasing work-load placed on the Centre for Disarmament of the Secretariat and on the Committee on Disarmament,

Bearing in mind the close relationship between matters concerning International security and disarmament and the interest in close co-operation between the units in the Secretariat dealing with them,

Noting the proposals submitted to the General Assembly at its twelfth special session, the second special session devoted to disarmament, with a view to taking certain action to strengthen the United Nations disarmament machinery,

Noting also that the twelfth special session placed increasing duties on the Centre for Disarmament in requesting it to provide the central guidance in co-ordinating the World Disarmament Campaign activities within the United Nations system,

Having considered the relevant parts of section II F of the report of the Committee on Disarmament, 13/

Reaffirming paragraph 28 of the Final Document of the Tenth Special Session of the General Assembly,

Noting that it was not possible to complete the first review of the membership of the Committee on Disarmament during the twelfth special session of the General Assembly in conformity with paragraph 120 of the Final Document of the Tenth Special Session and with Assembly resolution 36/97 J of 9 December 1981,

Noting also that the consultations in the Committee on Disarmament on the basis of paragraphs 55 and 62 of the Concluding Document of the Twelfth Special Session of the General Assembly 14/ have not been completed,

Requests the Committee on Disarmament to report to the General Assembly at its thirty-eighth session on the review of the membership of the Committee, taking into account paragraph 120 of the Final Document of the Tenth Special Session and paragraphs 55 and 62 of the Concluding Document of the Twelfth Special Session;

II

Bearing in mind the suggestion that the single multilateral disarmament negotiating forum should have the designation of a conference,

Reaffirming the validity of the provisions contained in paragraph 120 of the Final Document of the Tenth Special Session of the General Assembly,

Commends to the Committee on Disarmament that it considers designating itself as a conference without prejudice to paragraph 120 of the Final Document;

III

Recalling paragraph 124 of the Final Document of the Tenth Special Session of the General Assembly,

Requests the Secretary-General to revive the Advisory Board on Disarmament Studies in line with his note of 26 October 1982 15/ and to entrust it

---

13/ Official Records of the General Assembly, Thirty-seventh Session, Supplement No. 27 (A/37/27 and Corr.1).

14/ A/S-12/32.

15/ A/37/550.

252 with the functions listed therein, taking into account the provisions of section IV of the present resolution and further relevant decisions of the General Assembly in this regard;

IV

Aware of the need of the international community to be provided with more diversified and complete data on problems relating to international security, the armaments race and disarmament so as to facilitate progress, through negotiations towards greater security for all States,

Convinced that negotiations on disarmament and continuing efforts to secure greater security at a lower level of armaments would benefit from objective and factual studies and analyses,

Reaffirming the importance of ensuring that disarmament studies should be conducted in accordance with the criteria of scientific independence,

Conscious that sustained research and study activity by the United Nations in the field of disarmament would promote informed participation by all States in disarmament efforts,

Stressing the need to undertake more in-depth, forward-looking and long-term research on disarmament within the United Nations,

Recalling its resolution 34/83 M of 11 December 1979,

1.   Expresses its gratitude to the Board of Trustees of the United Nations Institute for Training and Research for its contribution to the establishment and development of the United Nations Institute for Disarmament Research;

2.   Notes with satisfaction the activities carried out by the United Nations for Disarmament Research since its establishment;

3.   Decides that:

(a)   The United Nations Institute for Disarmament Research shall:

(i)   Function as an autonomous institution working in close relationship with the Department for Disarmament Affairs; 16/

(ii)   Be organized in a manner to ensure participation on an equitable political and geographical basis;

(iii)   Continue to undertake independent research on disarmament and related security issues;

16/ See section V of the present resolution.

(iv)   Duly take into account the recommendations of the General Assembly;

(b)   The Secretary-General's Advisory Board on Disarmament Studies shall function as the Board of Trustees of the Institute;

(c)   The headquarters of the Institute shall be at Geneva;

(d)   Activities of the Institute shall be funded by voluntary contributions from States and public and private organizations;

4.   Invites Governments to consider making contributions to the United Nations Institute for Disarmament Research;

5.   Requests the Secretary-General to give administrative and other support to the United Nations Institute for Disarmament Research;

6.   Requests the Board of Trustees to draft the statute of the United Nations Institute for Disarmament Research on the basis of the Institute's present mandate, to be submitted to the General Assembly at its thirty-eighth session;

7.   Invites the Director of the United Nations Institute for Disarmament Research to report to the General Assembly at its thirty-eighth session on the implementation of the present resolution and the activities carried out by the Institute;

V

1.   Requests the Secretary-General to transform the Centre for Disarmament of the Secretariat appropriately strengthened with the existing overall resources of the United Nations, into a Department for Disarmament Affairs headed by an Under-Secretary-General, which will be so organized as to reflect fully the principle of equitable geographical distribution;

2.   Requests the Secretary-General to report to the General Assembly at its thirty-eighth session on the practical implementation of the present resolution.

101st plenary meeting
13 December 1982

From: *Aviation Week and Space Technology*, February 7, 1984, pp. 20, 21.

Fiscal 1984 Aerospace Budgets

USAF Funding Development Mission

Washington- The Air Force will play a key role in developing both strategic nuclear force and tactical command, control, communications and intelligence systems for the Defense Dept., spending $ 1.5 billion in Fiscal 1984.
Funding of $ 3.6 billion for intelligence and communications research and development in the new Pentagon budget request emphasizes strategic communications for nuclear weapons employment. The Air Force command, control and communications plan includes:
— Development of mobile ground terminals and deployment for processing Defense Support Program early warning spacecraft information, upgrading the survivability of satellites and connecting processing facilities.
— Development of integrated operational nuclear detonation detection system sensors for near real-time detection and location of nuclear detonations. The new budget includes approximately $ 1 million in this area.
— Provisions for redundant communications connectivity for warning systems to command centers to assure timely delivery of survival orders to airborne forces and communications assets.
The USAF research, development, test and evaluation funding in Fiscal 1984 is $ 13.6 billion, with five-year defense plan funding in this area of $ 14.1 billion in Fiscal 1985, $ 12.6 billion in Fiscal 1986, $ 10.8 billion in Fiscal 1987 and $ 12.2 billion in Fiscal 1988.
The Air Force Fiscal 1984 request also contains $ 971.1 million for both procurement and research and development funding for satellite systems and to support space operations through the space shuttle and boosters. The programs are:
— General Electric Air Force Satellite Communications System - $ 219.3 million, including $ 30.7 million for procurement.
— RCA Defense Meteorological Satellite Program - $ 60.6 million, including $ 33.9 million for procurement.
— General Electric Defense Satellite Communications System - £158 million, including $ 117 million in procurement.
— General Dynamics NavStar Global Positioning System - $ 341.6 million, including $ 238.6 million for procurement and $ 7.3 for military construction.
— Boeing inertial upper stage space launch support - $ 174.9 million, including $ 140.2 million in procurement.
— Martin Marietta Titan 3 boosters - $ 15.7 million, all in research and development.
A number of other USAF research and development programs relate to space activities and to command, control and communications programs. They are:
— MilStar satellite system for nuclear force survivability - $ 149.9 million in

development for the spacecraft, mission control element and extremely high-frequency terminal programs. The first launch for this constellation of satellites is in 1987. Planned funding in Fiscal 1985 is $ 260.8 million, $ 208.9 million in Fiscal 1986, $ 164.6 million in Fiscal 1987 and $ 47 million in Fiscal 1988.

— Satellite control facility - $ 72.4 million, with a large portion of funding allocated for data systems modernization - a major network upgrade to replace computers at remote tracking sites and at Sunnyvale, Calif., with an integrated centralized system.

— Consolidated space operations center - $ 72.6 million for a satellite control segment and shuttle control segment. TRW has been awarded a contract for system integration services. Funding in other fiscal years includes $ 73.9 million, $ 90.8 million, &79.4 million and $ 44.8 million in Fiscal 1985 through 1988, respectively.

The Air Force is asking Congress for $ 36.7 million, $ 29.7 million, $ 30.1 million, $ 27.2 million and $ 48.7 million to develop the Forest Green system in Fiscal 1984 through Fiscal 1988, respectively. The program would provide advanced radiation detectors integrated into the Defense Support Program to increase detection range for deep space nuclear detonations. Forest Green also would provide integration of hydroacoustic data from subsurface nuclear detonations and development of airborne nuclear radiation detection sensors.

USAF also is seeking $ 132.2 million in Fiscal 1984 for the minimum essential emergency communications network. Included are a higher power 100-kw. airborne transmitter for Boeing EC-135 aircraft, an improved trailing wire transmitting antenna, an improved receive antenna system and a miniature receive terminal system for bombers.

The service is asking for $ 20.9 million in the new budget for improvements to the Boeing E-4B national emergency airborne command post aircraft. The improvements planned include nuclear effects hardening, increased endurance, greater floor space, greater payload capability and survivable communications.

Block 2 changes for the E-4B fleet also are planned, and funding would provide for a multiple super-high-frequency channel for antijam communications to single-channel transponders on Defense Satellite Communications System and Satellite Data Systems spacecraft.

Other Air Force research and development funding sought in Fiscal 1984 includes:

— North American Aerospace Defense Command combined operations center - $ 49.4 million.

— Worldwide military command and control system automatic data processing - $ 16.1 million.

— Strategic Air Command communications - $ 15.2 million.

— Surveillance radar sites - $ 5.7 million.

— Distant early warning radar stations - $ 31.2 million.

— Over-the-horizon radar - $ 99.1 million.

— Ballistic missile early warning system - $ 10.8 million.

— Spacetrack surveillance using ground-based electro-optical deep space surveillance sensors - $ 5.6 million. The system is designed to assist the USAF antisatellite program through a global network of five sites to detect, track and identify spacecraft to altitudes of more than 22,000 naut. mi. Construction of a facility and refurbishment of the sensor at Diego Garcia is scheduled in Fiscal 1984. A charge-coupled device sensor also will be added.

Defense support program research and development funds in Fiscal 1984 are $ 48.6 million to continue designing replacement satellites for space shuttle compatibility and improved missile warning and attack assessment. The Fiscal 1984 request would continue integration of satellites on various launch vehicle configurations, including the shuttle. It also would start ground station hardware and software design for survivability improvements included on spacecraft.

USAF is seeking $ 180.8 million in the new budget for defense research sciences. Funding for geophysics is $ 40.6 million; for materials technology, $ 47.6 million; $ 61.1 million for aerospace propulsion; $ 70.1 million for avionics, and $ 22.54 million for training and simulation technology. Other development includes:
— Rocket propulsion - $ 35.2 million.
— Advanced weapons - $ 45.7 million.
— Conventional munitions - $ 40.8 million.
— Command, control and communications technology - $ 69.2 million.
— Advanced airborne radar development - $ 4.1 million.
— Aircraft propulsion subsystems integration - $ 27 million.
— Advanced aircraft avionics - $ 25.2 million.
— Flight vehicle technology - $ 15 million.
— Reconnaissance sensors and processing technology - $ 7.7 million.
— Aerospace structures and materials - $ 22.7 million.
— Advances turbine engine gas generator - $ 26.9 million.
— Advanced tactical fighter - $ 37.3 million.
— Advanced fighter technology integration - $ 19.4 million.
— Advanced strategic missile systems - $ 97.5 million.
— Advanced concepts - $ 292.4 million.
— Advanced technology cruise missile - $ 17.8 million.
— Space test program - $ 71 million.
— Advanced military spaceflight capability - $ 2.7 million.
— Advanced warning system - $ 30.8 million.
— Space surveillance technology - $ 22.5 million.
— Advanced space communications - $ 39.9 million.
— Satellite systems survivability - $ 34 million.
— Advanced radiation technology - $ 82.5 million.
— Very-high-speed integrated circuits - $ 125.1 million.
— Space laser program - $ 36 million.
— Conventional weapons technology - $ 32 million.
— Special programs - $ 129.9 million.
— Aircraft engine component improvement program - $ 142 million.
— Next-generation trainer - $ 123.4 million.
— Advanced medium-range air-to-air missile - $ 188.6 million.
— Space defense system - $ 205.6 million.